Another
100
SCOTSMAN
WALKS

Robin Howie

Jan,

Thank you for your kind assistance
at 'Muchty Station.

Robin Howie   July 2016

MKRY
PUBLISHING

Published in 2016 by MKRY Publishing

ISBN Paperback: 978-0-9931698-2-3
Ebook: 978-0-9931698-3-0

First published in The Scotsman newspaper.

A CIP catalogue copy of this book can be found in the British Library.

Maps © Ashworth Maps and Interpretation Ltd 2016.
Contains Ordnance Survey data © Crown copyright and database right 2016.

Cover photograph of Robin Howie by J Wyllie.
All photographs are by the Author except where attributed.

Published with the help of Indie Authors World

ACKNOWLEDGEMENTS

I wrote a weekly walking column in The Scotsman for 15 years, during which time I was blessed by the number of friends who continue to share with me the love of just getting out and about.

My grateful thanks go to Margaret, who understands my need to be outdoors, and to the mostly eccentric group who, almost regardless of weather, have accompanied me – the main 'culprits' being Jim (Jimbo) Wyllie, Rhona Fraser, John Blackwood and the nameless Mountain Maid and Hare.

Thanks also to Julia Lister who edited the book and found all the changes that the passage of time can bring to favoured refreshment spots. I am also obliged to my proof-readers; any errors or omissions are of course solely my responsibility.

Another 100 Scotsman walks is my second book, consisting of walks first published in *The Scotsman*, and my considerable thanks go to Indie Authors World (the trading name of the Indie Authors Scotland partnership of Sinclair and Kim Macleod, in Bishopbriggs), for leading me through this new-for-me venture. I am indebted to Mick Ashworth of Ashworth Maps for the beautiful maps that appear at the start of each section,

The first *100 Scotsman Walks* was published in 2001 by Whittles Publishing Ltd, Dunbeath, Caithness, KW6 6EG, Scotland (www. whittlespublishing.com, ISBN 978-184995-031-2). My thanks go to Keith Whittles for his faith in that publication.

DISCLAIMER

The author has made every effort to ensure that the information contained in Another 100 Scotsman Walks has been brought up to date. However, there is always constant change – to paths and forestation and especially to places of refreshment – and the author can accept no responsibility for errors, however caused. Nevertheless, the author would welcome information on any discrepancies and / or comments from readers.

CONTENTS

INTRODUCTION

For over 15 years, Robin Howie's popular walking column appeared in The Scotsman every Saturday. Very well known in Scottish hill-walking circles, his first book, 100 Scotsman Walks, published by Whittles Publishing Ltd and still in print, covered those first ten years. His second book, Another 100 Scotsman Walks, with many colour photographs, covers the most recent five years. It is a collection of mostly shorter walks covering much of Scotland that will appeal to a wide range of walkers, including children and those less active.

Each walk, indicated by a location map, includes a Fact File identifying the relevant Ordnance Survey map for the walk, along with the walk's distance, height, terrain, starting point, walking time and the all-important refreshment spot.

Completed all or some of the Munros, Corbetts, Donalds, Grahams or Marilyns? Wanting something easier and new? 'Doing the Howies' should be bags of fun!

Borders & Galloway

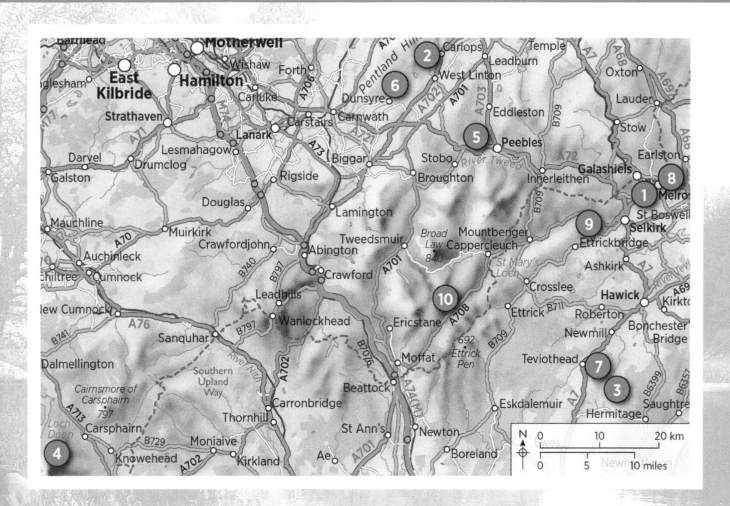

1 - Abbotsford

2 - Carlops

3 - Calcleuch Head

4 - Corserine

5 - Hamiton Hill

6 - Pentland Way

7 - Teviothead

8 - The Borders Railway

9 - The Duchess Drive, Bowhill

10 - White Coomb

1 - An Abbotsford circular walk

Many a walk can utilise the green credentials of the Borders Railway (half-hourly six days a week, hourly on Sundays); in this instance, starting from the Tweedbank terminus, mid-way between Galashiels and Melrose. Having studied the booklet *Paths around Abbotsford* (contact Scottish Borders Council, telephone 0300-100-1800), I devised a circular anti-clockwise route passing by Abbotsford, Cauldshiels Loch and Rhymer's Glen. The walk follows part of the signposted 68-mile Borders Abbeys Way (BAW) that links the four ruined abbeys at Melrose, Kelso, Jedburgh and Dryburgh.

I explored the walk in late October, experiencing a truly Keats autumn day of mists and mellow fruitfulness, with the early morning low mist only hinting at distant views. Indeed, on the minor road walk to Cauldshiels Loch, the sudden emergence of passing walkers made the stroll all the more atmospheric. The mist-enshrouded tranquil loch was hidden until but a few yards distant yet, within minutes, the sun broke through and the cloudy curtain started to rise. Reputed to be bottomless, the loch is allegedly home to a water kelpie but, as the extent of the tranquil loch gradually became clear, it was a swan that serenely emerged from the mist. What a day to remember!

From the station, turn sharp right and follow the path that goes alongside the railway line, heading back for ¼ mile to the Redbrick Viaduct across the Tweed. Turn left, signposted Public Path; by now you are on the BAW. At a path junction, slant right to reach the lovely mixed-woodland banks of the river from where there are good views back to the viaduct.

Cauldshiels Loch

FACT FILE	
Map	OS map 73, Peebles, Galashiels & Selkirk
Distance	7 miles
Height	150m
Terrain	waymarked paths and minor roads
Start point	Tweedbank railway station
Time	3 hours
Nearest town	Melrose
Refreshment spot	Abbotsford Visitor Centre restaurant

An underpass avoids crossing the A6091 after which a broad track leads to the Abbotsford Visitor Centre – and the restaurant. Cross the B6360, from where the minor tarmac road rises southwards to Cauldshiels Loch; a twisting though BAW-signposted approach, albeit at a sharp turn right, the BAW-signposted telegraph pole may not be immediately obvious. Nearing the loch, turn left, leaving the road for a forestry track which gently rises past a felled area. At a lorry turning area, slant left through a gate and down a lovely path to the loch.

Time to leave the BAW. Turn left by the Melrose Paths sign and traverse the glorious north bank path where I met mother and daughter, Julie and Kate, also with cameras to hand. At the east end of the loch, turn left by a gate, signposted Melrose Paths, and follow a drystane dyke. Now into open country, Bowden Moor, ahead lie the Eildon Hills. For seven years, Thomas the Rhymer lived with the Queen of the Fairies deep within the hollow hills – but that is another story.

At a wooden sign, Melrose via Rhymer's Glen, turn left to enter Mars Lee Wood. The top section is of tall conifers which give an immediate mysteriously dark (though signposted) entry to a broad track. With the Huntly Burn on the right, it is a secluded curving descent – but where

A swan emerging from the mist on Cauldshiels Loch

is Thomas? Only one runner, John McGillivray, passed me by.

Reach a road and turn right (no signs) and descend past the long-stay car park of the Borders General Hospital and so to the A6091, the Melrose bypass. Use the subway to reach the north side, a point where the bridge of the old Melrose railway can be identified. Turn left up Ley Road and follow the line of the old track bed parallel to the A6091. Continue to a minor road, cross over and enter Darnick Community Woodland of lovely grassy paths.

At the north end of the wood, cross with care the old Melrose road and follow the pavement by the road to Gattonside. Just before the bridge over the Tweed, turn left, signposted Tweedbank station ½ mile, and return to the terminus by the old tarmac track bed.

2 - A Carlops circular walk by the Bore Stane and Cauldstane Slap

FACT FILE

Map	OS map 65, Falkirk & Linlithgow
Distance	12 miles
Height	300m
Terrain	paths and tracks of varying standard
Start point	car park, southern end of Carlops
Time	5 to 6 hours
Nearest village	Carlops
Refreshment spot	Allan Ramsay Hotel, Carlops

One walk in a Midlothian Walking Festival brochure caught my attention. The Pentlands to Carlops Circular is a remote ramble past the Bore Stane and the Cauldstane Slap – a route which admittedly does more than stray into the Borders. Two of the walk leaders, John Pope and Arthur Mackenzie, kindly agreed to join myself, Alan and the Mountain Hare at Carlops. (There is a regular, almost hourly, MacEwans bus service to Carlops.) We met by the Carlops Rock, allegedly used as a test for

witches (carlines). If they flew they were witches; if they died they weren't.

Go to the north end of the village, turn left where signposted, pass a lovely waterfall, skirt Patie's Mill, and so to a small grassy valley. A rough and possibly muddy path continues by the east bank of the burn, fast flowing on our day, which is later crossed by a narrow metal footbridge with a sign on the far bank (Balerno by North Esk Reservoir).

The Carlops Rock

The path joins the Carlops/North Esk Reservoir track (a more direct but less attractive option from the village). Follow this all the way to the west side of the reservoir, which was built in 1850 to give a constant supply of water to the numerous paper mills in Penicuik. The last mill closed in 2004 and the reservoir is now a wildlife

The small bird hide at Dulverton

sanctuary. The small Dulverton bird hide was erected by Friends of the Pentlands (**www.pentlandfriends.org.uk**).

Continue north-west; the track, signposted Buteland, is muddy at first then grassier. Once past a gate, and where the track fades away to an old quarry, the path goes right, crossing a three-planked footbridge over the Henshaw Burn, then gently ascends through heathery moorland to the Bore Stane, the three-mile midpoint between Carlops and Buteland. Unremarkable except for its name, a small stony outcrop marks the high point of this old through route. Speculate about that name whilst appreciating the conical peaks of Scald Law and the Kips to the north-east.

Head westwards on the north side of a dyke, following a track at first, then a muddy and rough path to 561m East Cairn Hill, a steady heathery ascent rewarded by good views to the Forth. The actual highest point, by 6m, is the bump on the east side, traversed in reaching the prominent cairn, an ancient burial mound, now with a central recess, ideal for shelter.

It is then a roughish south-west approach by fence posts and over an often-boggy area to the much-signposted Cauldstane Slap, the high point of an old drove road also known as the Thieves Road. Turning

south, the path traverses heathery moorland then later joins a broader track that gives easier and faster walking to Baddinsgill Reservoir and the public road.

Continue south for ½ mile and turn left at a Tweed Trails signpost, Carlops via Stonypath. Descend to a long wooden bridge across the Lyne Water and follow the east bank – a meandering route and not the straight-line mapped path. From the large eastern sweep of the burn, climb grassy slopes and some stepped areas to reach the mapped path south of Baddinsgill House. Follow this major path of old that curves round Faw Mount.

Later, by now on a broad farm track, reach Stonypath Farm and, a few hundred yards beyond, look out for the green sign, Carlops 2 miles. Turn left on the Roman Road, an almost straight line of course, and now a broad track, such that Carlops is soon reached.

3 - Cauldcleuch Head

FACT FILE	
Map	OS map 79, Hawick & Eskdale
Distance	8 miles
Height	400m
Terrain	road and track to grassy slopes
Start point	parking spot, map ref 464052, on road leading to Skelfhill
Time	3 to 4 hours
Nearest town	Hawick
Refreshment spot	Brydon's Bakery Restaurant, 16 High Street, Hawick

Nothing whatsoever to do with the self-styled Donald, he of the surname Trump, Donalds are defined as Scottish hills south of the Highland boundary fault with a height of at least 610m/2000ft and with a drop of at least 30m/98.4ft. There are 118 Donalds, remarkably all with different names. Another list of hills, known as Grahams, are Scottish hills from 610m/2000ft to 761m/2499ft and with a drop of at least 150m all round. Then there are the Marilyns, hills of any height with a drop of at least 150m all round.

Would you believe it? The 619m/2031ft Cauldcleuch Head, nine miles SSW of Hawick, has sufficient height and drop to qualify as a Donald, Graham and Marilyn; a triple distinction at odds with its insignificant and, to be honest, rather dull summit area. The only remarkable aspect of Cauldcleuch Head is that it is the most isolated mainland Graham – at over 15 miles, the one furthest away from any other Graham. Indeed, the views from the summit are extensive: Hawick to the north, the vast expanse of the Eskdalemuir Forest smothering the area to the west, and, to the south, rolling moorland as far as the eye can see.

During a family and friends stay near Hawick in late October, celebrating Margaret's decade birthday party (year not specified!), I set off with Rhona and Jimbo for a short outing on a blustery day. That trip turned out to be longer and less satisfactory than expected.

Drive six miles south-west from Hawick on the A7 to where the road crosses the River Teviot. Pass a phone box, map ref 436079, and turn left on the charming minor tarmac road, signposted Skelfhill and Priesthaugh. From the road junction, map ref 464052, turn right towards the hamlet of Skelfhill. After some 200 yards, reach a signposted parking spot on the right-hand side, albeit the wooden sign is not very clear. This gives a starting height

Rhona, Jimbo and two dogs at Cauldcleuch

of 250m. This is sheep country and on our route there were cattle by the Skelfhill Burn so it is best to keep dogs at home.

The tarmac road curves round the Skelfhill farm buildings. A gravel track, later grassy, descends slightly into Skelfhill Hope (valley). Keep high at a junction, hence well above the Skelfhill Burn, on an easy stroll to just beyond the derelict cottage at Skelfhillhope. Keeping to the northern shoulder above the burn, climb south-east on grassy slopes to reach a fence line at the dip south of 534m Skelfhill Fell. Head south, then south-east, following the fence posts by the edge of the forest that covers the eastern slopes of Skelfhill Fell.

Make sure at two fence junctions to follow the correct route, finally south-west to the summit plateau of tussocky and wet terrain. A 608m, mapped spot height on the east side could be confusing on a misty day. On our blustery day, the hill lived up to its cold name. The 619m high point, just a junction of fences, lacks the grandeur of the shapelier 532m Skelfhill Pen after which the area is named. (Its small plateau, like a shelf, from the Old English, *scylf*, leads to the prominent peak at the southern end.)

The ascent will take less than two hours. Our ascent was much longer! We had followed the Priesthaugh Burn track into the forest from where a mapped path heads south to Swire Knowe. However, we could not find the path. I suspect it no longer exists. A clearing, not shown on the map, eventually gave exit from the forest, but only after a tedious traverse over rough and boggy ground – most definitely not recommended. It was then west up Windy Ridge.

4 - Corserine

Corserine, one of the (now) four Corbetts in rugged Galloway, has an 814m/2670ft summit trig point at the western end of a featureless mossy plateau; doubtless a reassuring sight on a poor day. From there, ridges spiral in all directions (the southern ridge being known as the Rhinns of Kells), with the cross-running or transverse ridges explaining the hill's name – *corse* is a common Scots version of cross. Despite having already climbed Corserine twelve times, Rhona was very keen to accompany me on my second visit.

From Polharrow Bridge on the A713, three miles NNW of St John's Town of Dalry, a minor road follows the south bank of the Polharrow Burn (incidentally the name of a well-known Scottish country dance). At the road end car park, map ref 552863, the hub of four estate 'roads', the Forrest Lodge track displays a large figurehead. This was once borne by a passenger liner, the first *Black Watch*, which entered service for Fred Olsen Cruise Lines between Newcastle and Oslo early in 1939, only to have a short but interesting life.

From the figurehead, walk west on Birger Natvig Road towards Fore Bush, then follow the track through the forest to a junction, map ref 534868. The main track, signposted Loch Harrow, goes straight on; a route taken by a party of four, climbing Corserine via Polmaddy Gairy (we met again at the summit).

However, the old route, by the south side of Loch Harrow, continues west on Burger Natvig Road. The track soon goes through a clearing giving views to North Gairy Top, our ascent route, with Corserine hidden behind. My 2006 map shows the track terminating at map ref 526865 (it does in fact now continue), after crossing a burn. With a lorry turning point on the right and an old wooden sign, without wording, on the left, the route leads straight up the hill through a broad forest ride.

FACT FILE	
Map	OS map 77, Dalmellington & New Galloway
Distance	9 miles
Height	700m
Terrain	track and forest path to mossy plateau
Start point	car park, map ref 552863, end of Polharrow Burn Road
Time	5 to 6 hours
Nearest towns	New Galloway and St John's Town of Dalry
Refreshment spot	The Green Tree House, Chapel Street, Moniaive

Memorial to the brave shepherd boy, Ralph Forlow - R Fraser

The path, at first vague and somewhat overgrown, becomes grassy and more obvious. Albeit with a few variations to avoid fallen timber, it gives a straight, attractive climb to reach the forest edge and on to a wooden post some 50 yards beyond the trees. Slant north-west over rough grassy terrain to reach a line of fence posts and a stile. Briefly follow the fence posts, then climb to North Gairy Top. This south-east ridge, giving excellent views, has a good path to the summit plateau, from where an all-terrain vehicle track leads to the trig point.

We returned by a different route, heading south to a col at 630m to join an old right of way, then more steeply ESE past a stand of trees to the *west* bank of the Hawse Burn. Follow a fence to reach a stile, then east to a wooden bridge, map ref 514852, across a small gorge, with a bench and marker posts on the far bank. Follow the east bank for a short distance to reach a large clearing, at the end of which is a memorial to the brave shepherd boy, Ralph Forlow, who died in the blizzard of 27th January 1954, aged 17 years.

Follow a stony track, mapped as a path, to reach a very new and unmapped smooth track on the left, with a sign for hillwalkers coming that way: "follow the coloured

Corserine summit trig point - R Fraser

markers for access over the burn and deer fence." The track heads north-east towards the hidden Loch Minnoch, then curves round the loch's north side to join Malcolm Mitchell Road. Turn right, descending parallel to the north bank of the Mid Burn. Turn north-east at the second junction for Burnhead, and so on the Professor Hans Heiberg Road to the car park to complete a circular walk.

Large figurehead, once borne by a passenger liner, the first "Black Watch"

5 - Hamilton Hill and White Meldon

FACT FILE	
Map	OS map 73, Peebles, Galashiels & Selkirk
Distance	8 miles
Height	500m
Terrain	paths, grassy slopes and sometimes muddy tracks
Start point	car park, south end of bridge over the Tweed, map ref 251402
Time	4 hours
Nearest town	Peebles
Refreshment spot	The Courthouse Restaurant, High Street, Peebles

Two days after a 9½-hour Glen Affric outing with Rhona (tackling 1181m/3875ft Mam Sodhail and its four outlying subsidiary Tops), it was a most welcome change to have a gentler stroll north-west of Peebles. The Mountain Hare showed me a circular walk over the more modest bumps of 371m Hamilton Hill, 427m White Meldon and 378m South Hill Head. Somewhat weary after those Mam Sodhail exertions, I must admit that we did not, on this occasion, climb to the top of White Meldon, included however in the following eight-mile walk.

Long founded before David II granted its charter as a royal burgh in 1367, the name Peebles is derived from the word *pebylls*, or tents, which were pitched by the first settlers. Start from the large free car park (with toilets) in Kingsmeadows Road at the south end of the bridge over the Tweed, map ref 251402. Follow the south bank tarmac path, heading west past a weir with mandatory herons to the Fotheringham footbridge, then cross to reach Hay Lodge Park on the north side. The graceful steel-truss bridge, opened in 1953 (then reopened in 2006 following

extensive adaptations), was gifted by J S Fotheringham, a former mayor of Johannesburg.

Continue west through the park to a line of trees, then north on a stepped path to a high wall, with a metal gate giving access to the A72. Cross the road with care to the opposite track, a right of way signposted The Meldons via Jedderfield and Upper Kidston, 3 miles. The broad gravelly track climbs gently, skirting then crossing Peebles golf course. Have due consideration for golfers, if only for your own safety!

Passing Jedderfield Farm, the track goes by a metal gate and curves its way by the edge of Jedderfield Plantation – a very muddy section on our visit, the ground having been churned up by cattle. Underfoot conditions improve on reaching another gate and stile, from where the track goes through the attractive wood. On exiting the trees, a grassy way gives an easy approach to the high communications mast and adjacent hut on a 357m bump, the south-west outlier of Hamilton Hill.

A most pleasant broad grassy ridge, giving superb open views of Corbett quality, then leads to the small cairn on Hamilton Hill. From there, descend north, then north-west, on grassy slopes to join a farm track circa map ref 232433 by the Kidston Burn. Follow this track south-west to a gate from where a grassy way by the edge of the field goes west to the farm road and so to Upper Kidston Farm. Just before the farm, turn right through a gate and follow the mapped path, in fact a rough track, to reach the dip between South Hill Head and White Meldon.

It is a short detour to the conical White Meldon. The name possibly comes from the Cumbric *maol din*, meaning bare hill-fort. White Meldon is indeed crowned by a substantial Iron-Age fort, described as "the largest native fort in the country." Four lines of defensive ramparts are discernible, plus a large stone burial cairn.

Return to the dip and so to South Hill Head, then head eastwards on a curving descent, making sure to reach a junction of dykes where there is a small awkward gate beneath some barbed wire. Descend to the northern bend of the mapped Roman Road, a grassy track where only vivid imagination can conjure up the thought of marching legionnaires. The 'road' skirts the southern flanks of the 357m hill and then climbs slightly to return to the plantation. On reaching Hay Lodge Park, choose whatever route appeals to return to the car park.

The Fotheringham footbridge

6 - The Pentland Way

The Pentlands run south-west from Edinburgh before fading away to the valley of the Clyde. The northern hills are the most visited and dramatic and provide spectacular views to the north; the south-west end is much less hilly, more remote and less visited.

The Pentland Way, a well-signposted 20-mile route from Dunsyre to Swanston, follows a variety of long-established tracks and paths. The Friends of the Pentlands, www.pentlandfriends.org.uk, who seek to promote the conservation, protection and enhancement of the Pentlands, have been responsible for several publications. The most recent, and highly recommended, is *The Pentland Way, a Walk with History*, by Bob Paterson, which brings to life much that may be invisible to casual walkers.

Given the lack of public transport and suitable parking (and alas nowadays no train), arguably Dunsyre is not the ideal start. Walkers could arrange to be dropped off at Dunsyre or alternatively start from Dolphinton which is on a bus route. Christine, the Mountain Maid and Hare and I facilitated our car-free linear stroll from Dunsyre to

FACT FILE	
Map	OS map 72, Upper Clyde Valley
Distance	8 miles
Height	150m
Terrain	minor road, path and track
Start point	Dolphinton
Time	3 to 4 hours
Nearest village	West Linton
Refreshment spot	Olde Toll Tea House, Main Street, West Linton

The pond at Ferniehaugh

West Linton by using the frequent Stagecoach bus service (phone Traveline 0871-200-2233) on the A702. Services 101 and 102 pass through West Linton and Dolphinton, albeit we then had a minor road walk to get to Dunsyre.

Alight at Dolphinton's southern bus stop by the road sign, 2¾ miles to Dunsyre. The quiet road passes by Blackmount Parish Church, rises round White Hill then gently descends to Dunsyre. Pass under the once bridge that carried the old railway line, then immediately turn right for the start of the Pentland Way by Dunsyre Mains (also signposted Public Footpath to Garvald 1¾ miles and West Linton 5½ miles).

On the right is The Halt, the old stationhouse, though now much altered and extended. Beside the track to Dunsyre House (the line of the track bed) is the still-obvious platform. The lady at The Halt showed us a picture of what used to be. Later on, a lengthy stretch of the grassy embankment is seen from the tarmac road. When the road turns left to Easton Farm, continue in a straight line, by now on a track.

When the track reaches a ford across the Medwin Water, follow the signposted path on the left to cross upstream by a footbridge. Pass by the public footpath to Crosswood via the Covenanter's Grave and, a few yards later, slant right as signposted and descend by a grassy path to the Medwin Water, spanned by a wooden bridge.

Follow the marked route by the north side of Garvald and note the sign for West Linton. Continue to Ferniehaugh, keeping straight ahead where the road splits, to reach the charming pond beautifully maintained by the owner at Ferniehaugh. Keep the pond on your right and continue in a straight line, then by track by the edge of a plantation. Traverse north-east across a moor, its bleakness relieved by the number of moorland birds and the remnants of pre-historic burial cairns.

The track reaches the high point at what is known as the Garral, an 18th century focal point for outlawed gatherings of Covenanters, and passes the source of the Garvald Burn, the Rumbling Well, unremarkable other than being part of Scotland's west/east watershed.

The way becomes a broad smooth track, descending past a small quarry on the left. Reach the West Water reservoir road and continue in a straight line, by now on a tarmac road which runs through West Linton golf course. Just beyond the club house is a T-junction. Leave the Way, turn right and descend for ½ mile to the A702 and the bus stop opposite the Gordon Arms Hotel.

7 - A Teviothead Circular Walk

Walking in the Land of the Reivers, by I W Landles and A G Brydon, describes 15 historical and enjoyable walks in typical Border countryside, with a pertinent reminder to follow the country code. Their aim – "to introduce you to the beauty of the Borderland whilst offering a glimpse into our reiving past" – is fully realised. Printed by Richardson & Son, Hawick, the book is highly recommended.

The Teviothead Circular Walk starts nine miles south of Hawick on the A7. Turn right for Falnash and Hislop and park with consideration once over the Teviot Bridge. Return to the A7 and walk south by the roadside verge to reach a minor road, signposted Carlenrig and Merrylaw. There is also a white sign, Teviothead Parish Church and Village Hall.

Nearing the church, but on the left, is the grave of Johnny Armstrong, one of the most notorious of the Border Reivers. Beyond the church it is a short climb, but once past Carlenrig the road levels off. Later, below on the left, the A7 is seen curving its way to Langholm and Carlisle.

The contrasting three-mile quiet country road traverses the ridge between the River Teviot and Limiecleuch Burn, with typical Borders rolling hillsides as the backdrop.

Teviothead parish church

Pass on the left the memorial to the motor cycle racing star Steve 'Hizzy' Hislop. Later on, the road slants down to the Teviot with a view ahead to the white house, Commonbrae.

After crossing the Teviot, go right through the Blackcleuch gate, but immediately turn left at the adjacent gate and follow a grassy track that goes diagonally to another gate and so to open hillside. On the left is a small burn with Commonbrae on the far bank. Higher up, that bank, mapped as wooded, is now clear fell. The track gently ascends to a gate, with a view south-east to the prominent communications mast on Comb Hill.

The track curves right towards 372m Rowantree Hill, then fades away. Traverse tussocky ground to reach a fence which is followed left to a new gate, the high point

FACT FILE	
Map	OS map 79, Hawick & Eskdale
Distance	9 miles
Height	450m
Terrain	quiet country road, grassy ridge and slopes
Start point	west side of bridge over the Teviot, map ref 407057
Time	4 to 5 hours
Nearest town	Hawick
Refreshment spot	Brydon's Bakery Restaurant, High Street, Hawick

Memorial to the motor cycle racing star Steve "Hizzy" Hislop

Ford across the Hazelhope Burn

of the rounded summit. Following fence then dyke, the sometimes tussocky Blackcleuch Rig gives a high-level walk, on what for me was a lovely spring day. On the way, pass an electrified fence (I did not stop to see if it was live).

When the dyke turns sharp left, head for the obvious circular sheep pen on the SSW side of Tanlaw Naze. Pass the pen and ascend the hill. Descending north-east, pass to the left of a high communication mast, then curve right to reach the broad gravely service track and follow that as it swings down the hillside to Falnash. There is a delightful ford across the Hazelhope Burn; dry feet can be maintained, however, by using a wooden footbridge a few yards upstream.

Follow the road to Birkiebrae, then take the track on the left and, once through a gate, follow a grassy track that slants up to an old slate quarry (now partly used as a rubbish dump). Head for the upper of two gates and follow the fence to the next gate, then cross another field, aiming for the north-west end of the wood beyond Parkhead.

Cross the small burn and go left by the dyke to a hunt gate. Turn right and go round the top end of the wood, then head east (left) for a hidden-at-first monument – a 50ft-high obelisk erected in 1874 and restored in 1999 to mark the bi-centenary of the Bard of Teviotdale, Henry Scott Riddell. A wooden door opens to reveal the interior, but there are no inside steps. Descend to a gate and towards Dryden Cottage, from where a track is followed by the banks of the Teviot to the parking area.

A 50ft high obelisk erected in 1874 to mark the bi-centenary of the Bard of Teviotdale, Henry Scott Riddell

8 - The Borders Railway

The long-debated Borders Railway from Waverley station to the 'current' terminus at Tweedbank (at 30 miles in length, the longest new domestic railway to be built in Britain for more than a century), was opened to passengers on 6th September 2015. Courtesy of the Mountain Maid and Hare celebrating a couple of biggish birthdays, Margaret and I were delighted to join other friends on a 1st class refreshments-provided excursion on the *Union of South Africa* steam train.

Waverley is the only station in the world named after a novel. Sir Walter Scott chose the name of a town in Surrey because it carried no connotations, yet that name is now ubiquitous. The 98-mile Edinburgh to Carlisle railway, completed in 1862, became known as the Waverley Line.

The highly controversial closure (the final passenger service was on 6th January 1969) left the Borders as the most extensive and populous area in Britain without a railway.

I describe the Tweedbank terminus (at the time of writing, little more than a platform and lacking a station building and toilets) as being 'current' because many still cling to the hope that one day the line to Hawick will be re-instated. A further extension to Carlisle seems unlikely.

But, for the moment, extending the line from Galashiels and across the Tweed by the Redbridge Viaduct to the new Tweedbank station (mid-way between Galashiels and Melrose) has been very successful despite some

Busy Tweedbank station

FACT FILE	
Map	OS map 73, Peebles, Galashiels & Selkirk
Distance	2 miles
Height	Negligible
Terrain	paths all the way
Start point	Abbey car and coach park, Melrose
Time	a gentle hour
Nearest towns	Melrose and Galashiels
Refreshment spot	Abbey Coffee Shop, Buccleuch Street, Melrose

teething problems. Indeed, 126,000 passenger journeys were made in the first month – the equivalent, if maintained, of 1.5 million a year, more than twice the forecast 650,000.

The cost has been trimmed back to £353m, partly by restricting the double-track to 9½ miles. Insufficient passing places may, initially at least, cause delays to the planned journey time of less than an hour, crucial if the line is to compete with the car.

The timing on our charter train was such that we had only two hours at Tweedbank, a time further reduced by the inclusive bus trip to Melrose. Nevertheless, Christine, Martin and I still had time for a gentle stroll by the Tweed back to the station.

An outing on the train and even with such a short walk would be ideal for a short family break, although I would suggest planning for a much longer stay in the Melrose area. The standard train service covering the seven stations between Waverley and Tweedbank is half-hourly six days a week, hourly on Sundays. Off peak day returns cost £11.20 at the time of writing.

From the Abbey car and coach park, turn left down Abbey Street, also signposted River Walk. Pass by Melrose Abbey where it is alleged the heart of Robert the Bruce lies beneath the high altar. Later turn left, leaving the tarmac road to follow the green sign, Borders Abbey Way. (The route also crosses the well-signed NCN Route 1 and the Southern Upland Way.)

Go along Chain Bridge Road and so to the impressive suspension bridge which gives access to Gattonside. Opened in 1826 and with major repairs in 1991, when the 'swing' was cancelled out, *take note that no more than eight people should be on the bridge at one time. Do cross and return!*

Head upstream on the south bank following the obvious path. It would be impossible to get lost. Pass by the Cauld, built to divert water by a lade to the Abbey Mill. Continue past the grounds of Waverley Castle Hotel built on Skirmish Hill, the skirmish being over the custody of the 14-year old King James V.

On approaching the Lowood road bridge spanning the river, stay on the south bank, turn left and cross the road as signposted, Tweedbank station ½ mile, and return by the old tarmac track bed to the terminus.

Union of South Africa steam train
Photo by G Current

9 - The Duchess's Drive, Bowhill

FACT FILE	
Map	OS map 73, Peebles, Galashiels & Selkirk
Distance	7 miles
Height	350m
Terrain	waymarked tracks and estate road
Start point	Bowhill House and Country Estate car park, map ref 425279
Time	3 hours
Nearest town	Selkirk
Refreshment spot	The Minstrel Tea Room, Bowhill House

A modest and new-to-me walk during the blustery and wet days of late May seemed like a good idea. The Mountain Hare, source of many a suggested walk, mentioned the Duchess's Drive at Bowhill, a pleasant mix of woodland and high moorland. Mapped as Duchess's (but with apostrophe variations seen elsewhere), the Drive is waymarked with small square signs, yellow arrows with a white background; also latterly with blue/white horse-shoe signs.

With a distance of seven miles and but 350m of ascent, it is ideal for a few hours between showers. There are excellent views all round from the high ground and I was lucky that the lowering cloud stayed well clear of 501m Fastheugh Hill and 450m Newark Hill.

Bowhill lies west of Selkirk by the junction of the A708 and the B7039 where the Yarrow Water is crossed by the General's Bridge. From there, a well-signposted tarmac estate road leads to the car park below which is Bowhill House, principle home of the Scotts of Buccleuch for two centuries. The House itself was closed on my day but the Country Estate is open April to September but closed Tuesdays outside of Easter holidays, July and August. There is an estate fee (at the time of writing, adults £4.50, children and concessions £3.50).

Turn left on the estate road from the car park, then immediately slant right on a track that leads to the wooded slopes of Pernassie Hill. The many, mapped side tracks may appear to be confusing but the way is well marked. Simply follow the yellow arrow signs on a well-graded easy ascent through the charming and partly open mixed woodland (freshly green from the recent rain on our day in May).

Pass by a stone seat, erected in memory of the 7th Duke of Buccleuch, on which is engraved a heart (used as part of the Douglas family crest), with the initials BQ and the dates 1864 and 1935. The family's full title is Buccleuch and Queensberry. Legend has it that Sir James Douglas, the Black Douglas, when bearing the heart of Robert the Bruce on crusade to the Holy land, fell mortally wounded. However, Bruce's heart in a silver casket was recovered and brought back to Melrose Abbey where it is buried.

Eventually reach the moorland giving good views south to the Ettrick Valley. Continue the gentle climb, turn right as signposted at a junction, pass by the watershed between the Craighope and Newark Burns and by a line of grouse butts to reach a gate. From there, a grassy path leads to the close-by Fastheugh Hill from where the Eildon Hills are easily spotted. Return to the track and, at the next junction, take the higher one round the northern side of the hill.

A gently sloping plateau overlooking the Yarrow Valley leads to Newark Hill, reached by a grassy track. The prominent cairn has seen better days but is still impressive. Return to the track.

Leaving the moorland behind, the track descends north to enter the coniferous Black Andrew Wood. Exit the wood and turn right on the estate road from where Broadmeadows Youth Hostel can be identified.

Keep left at a fork to go past Newark Castle, more commonly known as Newark Tower because of its architectural design and position on a knoll above the Yarrow Water. Attacked a number of times in the 16th century, in 1645 the Tower became a temporary prison after the Battle of Philiphaugh. One hundred prisoners were slaughtered in the courtyard. Cromwell's troops occupied the castle in 1650. The entrance door is padlocked.

Continue past the Old School House, then turn right onto the main drive for Bowhill House and so back to the car park.

10 - White Coomb and the Grey Mare's Tail

The National Trust for Scotland's Grey Mare's Tail Nature Reserve lies on the west side of the A708, nine miles north-east of Moffat. The name is thought to be descriptive of this, the fifth highest cascade in Britain, where the Tail Burn plunges 60m/200ft into a roaring linn or gorge. Robert Burns stayed nearby in 1789, by which time the Grey Mare's Tail and the dramatic scenery around the gorge had inspired geologists and naturalists and was already a tourist attraction. Tam o' Shanter, "weel mounted on his gray mare, Meg," was written a year later.

White Coomb, at 821m/2694ft, the highest hill in Dumfriesshire and a Corbett, overlooks the nature reserve. Both hill and waterfall are easily combined in a four-hour outing. On a previous visit I had climbed due north from Carrifran on a cold December day of first class visibility. This time, accompanied by the Mountain Lamb, there were neither extensive views from the summit nor any sight of the usual feral goats.

FACT FILE	
Map	Ordnance Survey map 79, Hawick & Eskdale
Distance	4 miles
Height	600m
Terrain	stepped path, burn crossing, then dyke-side path
Start point	Grey Mare's Tail car park off A708, map ref 186145
Time	3 hours
Nearest town	Moffat
Refreshment spot	Tibbie Shiels Inn, St Mary's Loch

Disappearing into the mist

From the well-signposted car park, map ref 186145, on the west side of the Tail Burn, cross by wooden bridge to the east bank path. (The path on the left side goes directly to the base of the waterfall.) The stone-stepped tourist path clings to the steep side of the gorge, high above the burn. On our day, the cloud level was down to 1000ft with the waterfall heard but not wholly seen. Especially on return, and if wet, take particular care. Fatalities have occurred here in the past.

The footpath continues to Loch Skeen, the highest large natural loch in the Southern Uplands, sitting at 1750ft above sea level, and home to the vendace, Britain's rarest freshwater fish which dates back to the Ice Age. However, once above the cascades, and where the path starts to level off into the hanging valley, look out for an old drystane dyke on the far bank. The Tail Burn now has to be crossed. It may be necessary to find a crossing spot higher up, even as far as the loch, and then traverse back to the dyke.

With a path on its right-hand side, the dyke heads westwards gently ascending. At a slight dip, pass briefly by fence posts marking the northern boundary of a wooded area, but with no sign of trees on our thick-mist day! On reaching the base of Rough Craigs, go further right of the dyke to find an eroded path that zigzags up the steeper ground then leads back to the dyke.

The gradient then eases on approaching the summit, at which point, the dyke suddenly turns WNW. Cross the dyke and head SSW for the short distance to the large cairn on the summit dome. *Coomb* is the old Scots place name for bosom. With thick clag reducing visibility to less than 100 yards, I took a compass bearing.

Most surprisingly on such a drizzly soaking day, I met a couple on top, Julia Jackson and Geoff Davies from Cumbria, fellow Munroists, who completed on Ben More, Mull, on 2nd May 2010. Remarkably, Geoff achieved this since becoming a Registered Blind Person. I should have asked him how he got up the In Pinn!

The Grey Mare`s Tail

Argyll & Bute

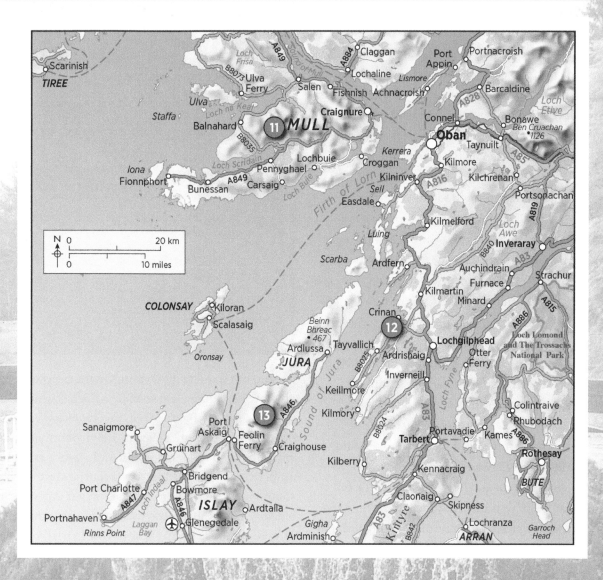

11 - Ben More -Mull

13 - Paps of Jura

12 - The Crinan Canal

11 - Ben More, Mull

Ben More, Mull (not to be confused with Ben More, Crianlarich, or Ben More Assynt) is the most popular choice of hill on which to complete a round of Munros. Perhaps it is the magnetic attraction of the only island Munro outwith Skye, or maybe it is because it takes a bit more organising to get there during the course of a round, but research undertaken by the maestro of Munro minutiae, Dave Hewitt, shows that something like 10% of all completions occur here – a truly astounding figure. Five hillwalkers completed on the one day in August 1995.

The journey to Mull requires a ferry service (or swimming, paddling etc for a very few) so there is a feeling of adventure in organising the expedition. A small ferry operates from Lochaline to Fishnish, more suitable for those travelling from the north, but the main ferry service is from Oban to Craignure, operated by Caledonian MacBrayne, with pre-booking for a car almost essential in the summer.

Ben More has the distinction of being a hill that is beautiful to look at from afar and whose summit is a wonderful viewpoint, especially on a late evening. Take note though that Mull gets over 100 inches of rain each year. Many travel the long way only to find that the weather forecast was better than actuality, as happened to Jimbo, John and me. We were a little bit too far west of the high pressure system and, while the bulk of the country sweltered in record-breaking March temperatures, we experienced a black and white day of

FACT FILE	
Map	OS map 48, Iona & Ben More
Distance	6 miles
Height	950m
Terrain	grassy slopes then zigzag path to stony summit
Start point	off the B8035 by Dhiseig, map ref 494359
Time	4-5 hours
Nearest town	Tobermory
Refreshment spot	Arlene's Coffee Shop, Craignure

no sun, but thankfully no rain. On the basis of "Well, we are now here," we were soon into thick clag at 2250ft.

More properly Beinn Mhor, this *big mountain*, while not of massive height at 966m/3169ft, dominates the sprawling and indented island and offers a choice of attractive ways to the top. My favourite start is from the south-east at Teanga Brideig, but on our day of strong blustery winds that route was quickly abandoned for the safer and easier way to the top. The 'tourist' route follows the Abhainn Dhiseig on its east bank then crosses to reach a well-formed zigzag path that easily leads to the small summit plateau.

Park on the grassy shore side of the B8035 at map ref 494359, east of the bridge over the Abhainn Dhiseig. By the track to Dhiseig is a Ben More Estate sign – Footpath to summit of Ben More, please keep dogs on lead. The Dhiseig track easily leads to the west side of the farm building; then, directed by a small metal arrow sign, continue on steadily rising grassy slopes by the side of the river's ravine. Later cross to the west bank. There are many crossing points but the most attractive spot is between two small waterfalls, circa map ref 507344.

The worn pathway now heads towards the not too obvious shallow and watery Coire nam Fuaran. At some

The Abhainn Dhiseig

500m, the grassy slopes are gradually left behind and an obvious, well-cairned and broad zigzag path eases the climb over steeper ground to the stony summit plateau. It is then a short walk to the shattered ruin of the once proud trig point amid the wide stone enclosure.

On arrival, it was one of those strange days where it was less windy than on the lower slopes. However, on our cold damp day of no views, we were not tempted to linger. One word of caution about a shared similarity with Skye: the compass is not accurate in the immediate vicinity of the top. Consequently, it is essential to know the first 100 yards of the return path along the plateau. Having said that, a curious thing happened when I was there in April 2004, for, unlike previous visits, I could detect no magnetic distortion. Demonstrating all this to John, this time there was a significant variation.

No view from the top

12 - The Crinan Canal

Described as Britain's most captivating short cut, the Crinan Canal is the nine-mile waterway that links the western sea with central Scotland – from Crinan to Ardrishaig – thus avoiding the oft-treacherous journey round the Mull of Kintyre. Look out for old puffers that once steamed through the canal – think of Para Handy, the crafty skipper of the *Vital Spark*. Passing through a scenic landscape, the canal bisects the ancient Kingdom of Dalriada.

Preserved as a working transport monument to this day, little has changed since its opening in 1801. Queen Victoria's sail on the canal in 1847 sparked a tourism boom and nowadays up to 3000 boats, mostly pleasure craft, pass through the canal each year and thousands of walkers and cyclists take advantage of the charming and interesting towpath.

There are 15 distinctive locks, numbered starting from Ardrishaig, seven bridges, and two lighthouses that guided sailors safely home. Then there is the 'automatic water waster' – a clever piece of engineering which maintains water levels in the canal.

The following walk covers the section from Crinan to Cairnbaan – and back. The overall walk, if done briskly, will only take three hours but, given the attraction of the locks, passing boats and the surrounding scenery, it would be surprising if you travelled that fast. Even on my damp day, it was a pleasure just to stroll along. Then

of course it is likely that you will be tempted to have a mid-walk break at the Cairnbaan Hotel. On a previous day in passing by, folk were sitting outside lapping up the sunshine.

Do take care when crossing locks or walking on the towpath and ensure dogs are kept under control. More information is available at the Canal Office, Pier Square,

FACT FILE	
Map	OS map 55, Lochgilphead & Loch Awe
Distance	9 miles
Height	negligible
Terrain	canal towpath
Start point	Crinan
Time	3 to 4 hours
Nearest villages	Crinan and Cairnbaan
Refreshment spot	Cairnbaan Hotel and Restaurant

Crinan

The canal locks

Ardrishaig, 01546-603210 or **www.scottishcanals.co.uk**.

From the large car park at Crinan, cross over either of locks 15 or 14 to reach the towpath which is on the seaward side. The first section has open sea on the left and steep, craggy, wooded slopes on the right, with the canal and the raised towpath hemmed in between. Soon the B841 comes in to run parallel to the canal all the way to Cairnbaan. On the left is a large flat tidal area (the tide was going out on my day) where the meandering River Add reaches the sea.

Soon reach Islandadd Bridge from where the B8025 cuts in a straight line across Moine Mhor, a National Nature Reserve, and one of the last remaining peat bogs in Britain. This flat moss and heather blanket, laid down over thousands of years, is now a special place for plants, insects and other creatures that thrive in the damp conditions.

Dunadd, seat of the Irish and Scottish Kingdom of Dalriada around 1500 years ago, is one of the most important sites in Scottish history. Alas on this occasion

I did not have time to revisit the conical peak and its ancient fort – a long weekend would have been a better idea.

Then reach Dunardry Locks. A tarmac road starts from lock 13 and the beginning of the gentle climb to the canal high point at lock 9, a rise of some 10m. Pass on the left a line of white cottages, some holiday lets, Cairnbaan House and lock 8. Then it is the equally gentle descent to Cairnbaan; the towpath becomes a tarmac way then a minor road. Cairn Ban (*white cairn*) is an area steeped in history. On the hill behind Cairnbaan Hotel and Restaurant are mysterious cup and ring marked rocks.

Just below the hotel is lock 5, signposted Crinan 4½ miles; this is the return point. Further on is Lochgilphead, 2 miles, and Ardrishaig 4 miles. The section from Cairnbaan to Islandadd Bridge is part of cycle route 78.

On the return to Crinan it is surprising how different the scenery looks.

Awaiting a vessel

13 - The Paps of Jura

FACT FILE	
Map	OS map 61, Jura & Colonsay
Distance	8 miles
Height	800m
Terrain	boggy moorland to rough summit slopes
Start point	three Arch Bridge, map ref 544720
Time	6 hours
Nearest village	Craighouse
Refreshment spots	Tayvallich Coffee Shop and Jura Hotel, Craighouse

I last visited Jura over 30 years ago, travelling from Kennacraig to Port Askaig, then by the small ferry to Feolin. This time, Margaret, Rhona, Peter and I used the Jura Passenger Ferry which operates between Tayvallich, Argyll and Craighouse. (David came by car from Feolin.) At the time of writing, the less than one hour journey costs £20 each way (bicycles are free but do advise when booking). There are sailings every day except Wednesdays, generally from Easter until the end of September (please check **www.jurapassengerferry. com).** With seating for only 12 passengers, advance booking is required: phone 07768-450000 or e-mail nicol@jurapassengerferry.com.

A lot has changed in 30 years, many new houses for example, but what has not changed is the Jura terrain – hummocky, muddy moorland and rough quartzite slopes. "Jura lies aslant between Islay and Argyll and is very sparsely populated…there are however zillions of red deer" (Iain Banks, *Raw Spirit, In Search of the Perfect Dram).* Deer stalking is a major job provider (mid-August to September is the main shooting period), as are distilling and tourism. The latter was boosted by the connection with George Orwell (born Eric Blair) who

went to remote Barnhill in the far north, not to die but to write *1984.* He did, however, nearly drown in the world-famous roaring whirlpool, Corryvrecken.

Nevertheless, the island is best known for its three conical quartzite peaks, known as the Paps of Jura. They are instantly recognisable from as far distant as Ben Nevis, and closer to hand from the mainland, and have long been used by seafarers as a navigational aid.

The Isle of Jura Fell Race has a climb and descent of 2370m. Our aim was more modest – the 785m/2575ft *hill of gold,* Beinn an Oir, a Corbett, the central Pap or breast, and the island's highest point. The name likely arises from the occurrences of iron pyrites, better known as Fool's Gold.

It is an easy walk or cycle to the Corran River, map ref 544720, spanned by the Three Arch Bridge, built in 1810 and classified as an ancient monument. The notice board shows a path, not on my map, curving round the shoulder of Cathar an Leargain Bhric; in fact, this is the line used by all-terrain vehicles over boggy ground. Slightly lower and nearer the southern bank of the meandering Corran is a choice of animal tracks that generally give a drier route to Loch an t-Siob, *loch of the spindrift.* (We did not follow the north bank river path shown on the notice board.)

On our muddy traverse I heard my first cuckoo of the year, by which time, and most appropriately, the forecast rain, wind and low cloud duly arrived. It took one hour to reach the loch outflow, forded by extremely useful

The Jura Passenger Ferry

Craighouse and the Jura Distillery

boulders. Cross the stepping stones to the north side and follow a good path which gradually slants away from the water, gently climbing north-west. As the path fades, climb more steeply on grassy slopes to the southern end of the saddle between Beinn an Oir and Beinn Shiantaidh.

Head to Beinn an Oir's eastern face and follow the path that zigzags NNW, easing the climb. The path becomes a bit vague traversing a bouldery area, but then continues more obviously by a grassy strip to reach the north-east ridge by the ruins of a shelter used by OS surveyors in the 19th century. From there, a rock-lined causeway leads to the summit – a trig point amid a very large cairn. There is ample building material!

The summit is a commanding viewpoint, but not on our day! My altimeter was over-reading by 60m, proof, as if any was needed, that we were in the midst of a depression. It was so windy we could scarce stand upright. The only sconsolation was that the next day was forecast to be even worse!

Enveloped in the mist at Beinn an Oir trig point

Dunbartonshire, Lanarkshire & Inverclyde

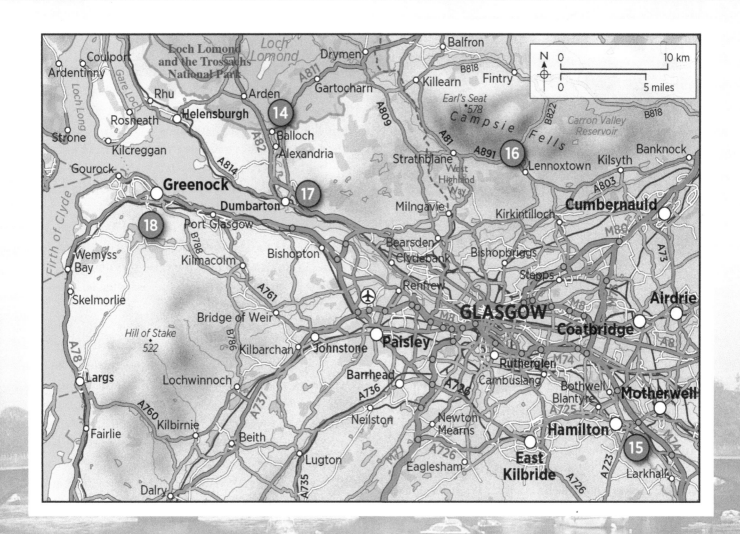

14 - Balloch Castle Country Park

15 - Chatelherault Country Park

16 - Glazert Water

17 - River Leven Heritage Trail

18 - The Greenock Cut

14 - Balloch Castle Country Park

FACT FILE	
Map	OS map 56, Loch Lomond
Distance	2 miles
Height	negligible
Terrain	broad pathway
Start point	Balloch railway station & Tourist Information Office
Time	1 hour
Nearest village	Balloch
Refreshment spot	Tullie Inn, Balloch

With a convenient half-hourly service, it would be hard to imagine a more attractive or idyllic destination than Balloch railway station. Across Balloch Road is the nearby VisitScotland Information Office, situated close to the many small boats moored by the River Leven, the outflow from Loch Lomond. Given its location, Balloch in mediaeval times was a place of great strategic importance. ·

Balloch Castle Country Park, now owned by Glasgow City Council and managed by West Dunbartonshire Council, lies at the southernmost tip of Loch Lomond. The only Country Park within the Loch Lomond & The Trossachs National Park, it was the subject of a £2.5 million Lottery-funded restoration project in 2003-2006. Ordnance Survey map 56, Loch Lomond, is not needed. Go to the VisitScotland Information Office and collect an informative leaflet about the park and the three waymarked circular routes which can be used individually or joined up for a longer walk. The Glasgow to Loch Lomond Cycle Route 7 passes through the park.

Designed to introduce people back into exercise after long periods of inactivity, or those recovering from illness, a Walk in the Park programme within the National Park started in Callander in 2005 and has expanded to Aberfoyle, Killin and now Balloch. But for financial help from the ScottishPower Foundation, supporting volunteers with training and running special events, the Balloch Walk in the Park would not have started. The ScottishPower Foundation only helps fund the Balloch programme but intends to support other walks within the National Park as they develop.

I am grateful to Natalie Stevenson, Project Manager at the Loch Lomond & The Trossachs Countryside Trust, for inviting me to join a recent Walk in the Park Balloch. Admittedly, the walk is a short day at just two miles; for a longer and more rigorous outing, head to the Fairy Glen and climb to Whinny Hill Woods.

Incidentally, the hardest part of the day for me was getting used to the pronunciation of Balloch. After years of living in Inverness, where the close-by village of Balloch is pronounced stressing the last syllable, here, both syllables are equally stressed.

After collecting a leaflet at the VisitScotland Information Office, cross the River Leven by the old Balloch Bridge to enter the park which, despite its relatively modest size, has been included in Historic Scotland's Gardens and Designed Landscapes Inventory. At first by the banks of the Leven, head north through mixed woodland on the Shore Walk. On my visit, after days of rain, the river level had risen but not enough to impinge on the lovely broad track. Pass to the left of a mound and overgrown moat, all that remains of the 13th century castle built by the Earl of Lennox. It was abandoned circa 1390 for a more secure stronghold on Inchmurrin.

A Walk in the Park

Continue as far as the slipway then follow the tarmac path that gently ascends, winding through parkland, to the more modern Balloch Castle, built in 1808, and described as 'a picturesque effusion of mock medievalism.' Once the visitor centre, the castle, surrounded by scaffolding in 2015, is currently unused but is in the process of being made wind and watertight. Nearby is the Chinese Garden.

A long broad driveway leads down through the designed-to-impress landscaped park, passing through impressive varied open woodland including late 19th or early 20th century plantings of rare and unusual trees. Before reaching the South Lodge, a short detour to the Walled Garden is recommended.

15 - Chatelherault Country Park

Chatelherault Country Park, 1½ miles south-east of Hamilton, has a well-signposted entrance from the A72 leading to an extensive landscaped parking area and the Visitor Centre. (Opposite the entrance, Chatelherault Station on the Hamilton–Larkhall line has a daily half-hour train service.) The Centre, which justifiably claims to be a five star visitor attraction, is open daily 10.00am-5.00pm throughout the year except for the Christmas and New Year public holidays; the 500-acre park itself is open dawn to dusk throughout the year.

The Centre is housed in the 18th century hunting lodge and summer house, built by the fifth Duke of Hamilton, and named in memory of his ancestor, James Hamilton, the 2nd Earl of Arran, who was Regent of Scotland during the infancy of Mary, Queen of Scots. For his services, he was created Duc de Châtellerault by Henry II of France. Built on a hill top about one mile south of the former Hamilton Palace, the hunting lodge, constructed from locally-sourced red sandstone, was designed as an eye-catching feature, its grandeur giving the impression of an additional palace at the end of a grand avenue of trees.

The trees were mostly removed in the late 1800s during sand quarrying. The collapse of old mine workings below ground led to subsidence and structural damage. The palace was demolished in the early 1920s. Chatelherault, however, restored from its ruinous state in 1979, is still standing but bears witness to that subsidence.

The meandering 30-mile long River Avon latterly flows through a series of steep, wooded gorges before merging with the Clyde close to Hamilton. One such gorge is the central feature of the Park and is crossed twice on the Green Bridge Trail.

From the Centre, turn right then left as signposted, Green Bridge 3.3km. High above the eastern side of the gorge and the unseen river, the broad leafy track gently rises through lovely mixed woodland, on the left of which is Riccarton golf course. At a junction, stay with the high ground as signposted, Green Bridge 1.5km. (To

Fairholm Bridge

FACT FILE	
Map	OS map 64, Glasgow, Motherwell & Airdrie
Distance	5½ miles
Height	150m
Terrain	broad pathway
Start point	Chatelherault Country Park, 1½ miles south-east of Hamilton
Time	2 to 3 hours
Nearest town	Hamilton
Refreshment spot	Oaks Café, Chatelherault Visitor Centre

The ancient Cadzow Oaks

the right is the way down to the White Bridge, closed on my visit due to landslip.) The track undulates for almost a mile; then a steep stepped path leads through the woodland to suddenly reveal the hitherto hidden River Avon and the lengthy span of the (not so green) Green Bridge.

Do not cross; instead, walk further upstream, signposted to Fairholm Bridge and Larkhall. The beautiful twin-arched stone bridge is quickly reached and a short distance on estate road on the far bank leads back to the Green Bridge.

A gradual climb, passing Millheugh steps on the left, is now required to gain the south-west top end of the gorge. On the west bank return, both gorge and river are less hidden to view. Continue through the broad-leaved woodland, ignore the sign to White Bridge, and cross Divoty Glen. Then gently descend and pass on the left a Site of Special Scientific Interest, Iron Age earthworks and the Cadzow Oaks. These trees are mostly hollow, as a natural process of aging (some are over 500 years old); they have squat shapes that arguably are more impressive when seen on a spooky, murky day. Then there are the famous long-horned Cadzow Cattle, descendants of

the free-roaming white cattle that first grazed there in medieval times. Sadly, I did not see any.

Descend past the must-visit ruins of Cadzow Castle built in the early 15th century and home to the Dukes prior to the building of Hamilton Palace. The extensive ruins, much retained by scaffolding, are surrounded by a high metal fence. Cross the stone-built 1863 Duke's Bridge, 80ft high across the Avon gorge, to return to the Centre.

The Green Bridge

16 - A Stroll by the Glazert Water

As has happened many a time, the day suitable to Jimbo, John and I coincided with bad weather. Heavy rain, albeit forecast to clear later in the day, plus extremely low cloud negated a trip to the Campsie Fells. So, making the best of a grey dreich day, and walking just below the cloud level, we opted for what turned out to be a pleasant, easy stroll by the Glazert Water – from Kirkintilloch to Haughhead then north by the Aldessan Burn to Clachan of Campsie and back again (parallel to but well below our intended hills).

Two Campsie burns, the Finglen and the Aldessan, merge south of Clachan of Campsie to form the Glazert Water which then meanders south-eastwards for some four miles to join the much smaller Kelvin Water a half-mile north of Kirkintilloch. The Glazert is nowadays generally a good quality river with a healthy trout population and its clean water improves the quality of the Kelvin.

Adjacent to the Glazert is the track bed of a dismantled railway which, after a six-year refurbishment programme completed in 2009, provides a well-graded pedestrian

FACT FILE	
Map	OS map 64, Glasgow
Distance	10 miles
Height	negligible
Terrain	path, mostly on old railway line
Start point	north side of Kirkintilloch, map ref 655745
Time	4 hours
Nearest town	Kirkintilloch
Refreshment spot	Aldessan Gallery and Coffee Shop, Clachan of Campsie

Milton of Campsie station platforms

and cycle route from Kirkintilloch to Strathblane. Known as the Strathkelvin Railway Path (Strathkelvin District Council bar horses and motor cycles!), it is also a Right of Way, as is the path to Clachan of Campsie.

Opened in 1848, the Campsie Branch of the Edinburgh & Glasgow railway went at first only to Lennoxtown but was extended in the 1860s by the Blane Valley Railway to Killearn. The line was closed to passengers in 1951

albeit sections continued to be used for freight for over a decade. Beyond Strathblane, part of the old line is now used by the West Highland Way.

From the north-west side of Kirkintilloch, at map ref 655745, a short path leads to the railway embankment. Shortly after, cross a footbridge over the Glazert to head north on the mapped path by the west bank. Later go under a multi-arched viaduct that used to carry the Kelvin Valley Railway. In Milton of Campsie, pass by the remains of the still clearly identifiable station platforms and through a reduced-size tunnel leading to a cutting.

By now in a much more scenic form, the railway line crosses and re-crosses the Glazert, passes Lennoxtown station, now only recognised by the presence of two bridges, and on to Campsie Glen station, map ref 615787, where it is hard to find any remaining traces. Cross a tarmac road to reach the Aldessan Burn, and then cross a wooden footbridge to the west bank and a well-signposted junction (Clachan of Campsie to the right, Strathblane to the left).

Now away from the railway, a lovely path follows the Aldessan (also known as the Kirk Burn). Then cross the

**A multi-arched viaduct that used
to carry the Kelvin Valley Railway**

A891 to enter the lovely grounds of Schoenstatt, a retreat and conference centre, and a lovely woodland walkway adjacent to the water. Leave the grounds by a large metal gate, briefly turn right on Knowehead Road to cross the Aldessan by a stone bridge and so on to Clachan of Campsie, a designated conservation area.

I recommend Aldessan Gallery and Coffee Shop for refreshment before the casual stroll back to Kirkintilloch.

17 - The River Leven Heritage Trail

Derived from *leamhan*, meaning elm bank, Leven is a common Scottish name for many a river, loch and town. I have previously written about the Perth & Kinross Loch Leven Heritage Trail and the loch's outflow, the River Leven, once a source of power for mill owners and textile manufacturers, which enters the Firth of Forth at the town of Leven.

I had an enjoyable December morning visit to Balloch Castle Country Park, at the southernmost tip of Loch Lomond, as a guest of the Balloch Walk in the Park.

FACT FILE	
Map	OS map 63, Firth of Clyde
Distance	7 miles
Height	none
Terrain	mostly tarmac pathway
Start point	Balloch railway station
Time	3 hours
Nearest town	Dumbarton
Refreshment spot	Tullie Inn, Balloch

For the afternoon, Natalie and Eian suggested a seven-mile stroll by the west bank of the loch's outflow through the Vale of Leven to Dumbarton and the Firth of Clyde – the River Leven Heritage Trail, also known as the River Leven Tow Path.

Similarities with its Fife namesake abound. Once one of the most beautiful valleys in the country, the West Dunbartonshire Leven was the focus of a huge textile dyeing and printing industry which lasted for over 200 years until its demise in 1960. At its peak in the 1880s, over 7000 people worked there. In one year, 165 million yards of cloth and 20 million pounds of cotton yarn were dyed and printed. An ancient and secret process brought from Turkey, using bull's blood and other ingredients, the world-famous vibrant Turkey red colours and patterns characterised the industry.

Apart from two loops by the river, the well-signposted Trail, part of the Glasgow to Loch Lomond Cycle Route 7, has a tarmac pathway. Having arrived at Balloch by train, the Trail gave me a superb linear route to Dumbarton Central railway station. Ordnance Survey map 63, Firth of Clyde, is scarcely needed; instead, collect a River Leven Heritage Trail leaflet from Balloch VisitScotland Information Office.

Turn right from Balloch station, and right again, to follow the west bank. The water at this stage is relatively slow flowing, at odds with the assertion that this is the second fastest flowing river in Scotland. All is explained a short distance downstream by the presence of a barrage,

5-arched stone Dumbarton Bridge

beyond which the flow immediately picks up, with some turbulent sections when in spate, only to slow on reaching tidal waters at Dumbarton. Incidentally, which is the fastest river?

A high wall on the right partly hides an old industrial area, but later, despite that industrial heritage, the riverside walk is remarkably secluded. At Bonhill Bridge, Natalie and Eian bid their farewells and returned to Balloch. Pass by Vale of Leven cricket ground, then on

the left a railway bridge of which only the central span remains.

At the first of two loops of the river, originally known as Heron's Point, the cycleway curves to the right. Surely you will prefer to follow the admittedly muddy in places tow path of old. On the right is contaminated land – keep out! The tow path gradually improves then re-joins the cycle way. Pass a sign for Renton station and so on to the second and smaller loop. Again, stay by the riverbank, on a narrow-at-times path weaving through an overgrown area, and so back to the cycle path.

With the distant Kilpatrick Hills as a backdrop, pass under a double row of electricity pylon lines, traverse a meadow and pass under the A82 road bridge. The by now sluggish river passes through the Leven Marshes and finally to a trio of bridges: firstly the rail bridge, the Leven Viaduct, where I met a couple of fishermen, then under the A814 bridge from where is a good view downstream to the five-arched stone Dumbarton Bridge, built in 1765.

Cross the latter bridge to the town centre, signed ½ mile, and so to the railway station.

18 - The Greenock Cut

FACT FILE

Map	OS map 63, Firth of Clyde
Distance	8 miles
Height	100m
Terrain	vehicle track and footpath
Start point	Overton car park, map ref 266749
Time	3 hours
Nearest town	Greenock
Refreshment spot	Cardwell Garden Centre Restaurant, Lunderston Bay, Gourock

It was Derek, fellow marathon runner and rugby player of earlier days, who told me about the Greenock attraction, 'walking the Cut.' As a local boy, and now a retired civil engineer, he was the obvious person to be my guide.

Thanks to the deep offshore waters of the Firth of Clyde, Greenock rapidly developed into a port and shipbuilding centre, home base of the west of Scotland's largest herring-fishing fleet and, in the 19th century, the principal departure point for emigrants.

The high moorland to the south was the source of many a well and stream providing clean water for domestic use, supplemented in 1773 by a piped water system designed by James Watt. However, with an increasing demand for water-powered mills, a further solution was required.

Robert Thom, a civil engineer, prepared a scheme to turn a freshwater lake, Shaws Water, into a reservoir (now named Loch Thom) from which a 5½-mile long canal-like aqueduct would take the water, with an almost imperceptible drop, to Overton, overlooking the town.

The waterfall, the outflow from the loch surging into the glen

Opened in 1827, the aqueduct is now known as the Greenock Cut.

With ever growing domestic demand, the Kelly Cut was constructed in 1845 to bring water from the Kelly Burn; Gryfe Reservoir to the east was built in 1872.

Greenock is accessed by train from Glasgow though the most convenient station, Drumfrochar, has only an hourly service. We arrived by car, saving a ten-minute uphill walk from the station, by Papermill Road and Overton Road, to reach the small Overton car park, map ref 266749.

Head up the tarmac then gravel road, passing on the left an impounding reservoir and the water treatment works, now served by underground pipes. Continue uphill to the gap between White Hill and Jock's Hill. Ignore the tarmac road on the right which leads to the communications mast at 277m and descend to gain the first views of the massive reservoir. Note the warning sign: deaths have occurred at reservoirs. Four fishermen we passed were anxious to show off their recent catch, an 8lb (allegedly) brown trout.

Pass a well constructed by the Argyll and Sutherland Highlanders in 1915, near the white-painted Loch Thom cottage, and on by the loch's outflow that feeds a compensation reservoir. Open daily in summer and at weekends in winter, Cornalees Bridge Visitor Centre has an interactive exhibition about the Cut. There is an independent café open all year round.

At the start of the boarded-off Cut, used until 1971, is a memorial to Robert Thom. Cross a footbridge to reach the beautiful canal-like towpath between the Cut and the wooded Shielhill Glen. At this stage, there is no flowing water in the stagnant and weed overgrown Cut – ironic considering the impressive waterfall on our day (the outflow from the loch surging into the glen). Presumably the cost of maintaining the Cut would be prohibitive. However, on nearing Overton, the aqueduct, collecting some of the water from streams that cross its path, gives a closer idea of what once was.

On the clockwise route round Dunrod Hill, it is mandatory to inspect two stone chambers built to house the ingenious method of releasing surplus water from the Cut. Water flowed down a pipe and filled a bucket which then pulled a chain down over a pulley wheel, so lifting a counterweight and a lever to open the sluice gate. Small holes in the bucket allowed the water to slowly drain out so that, when the inflow stopped, the counterweight eventually pulled the sluice gate lever away and lifted the empty bucket.

We met few walkers on our cold, cloudy blustery day that alas only gave limited panoramic views of the Clyde and north to Ben Lomond. Do go on a clear day!

An 8lbs (allegedly) brown trout - D Chambers

Edinburgh, Lothians and Falkirk

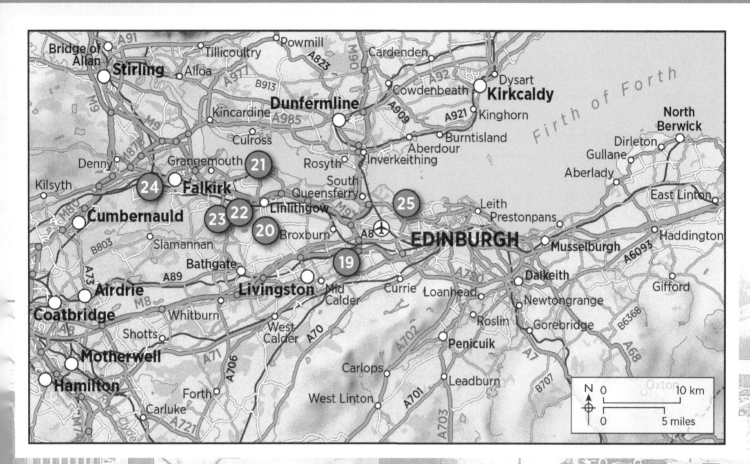

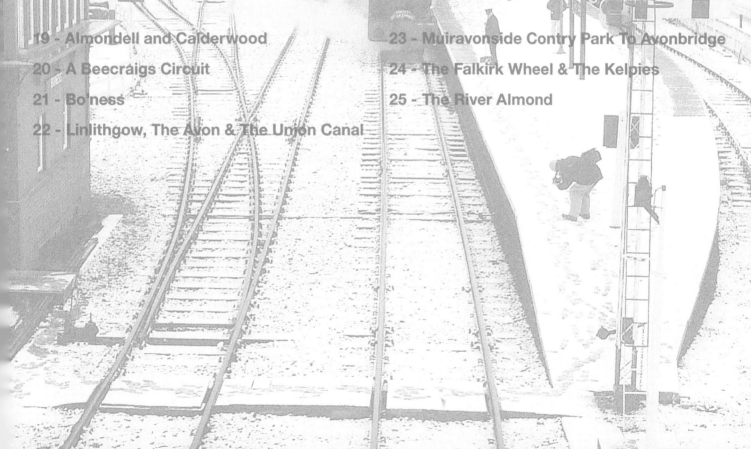

19 - Almondell and Calderwood Country Park

The source of the River Almond is just beneath a 291m trig point on the Cant Hills, one mile north of Shotts. From there the river flows eastwards for 28 miles to Cramond and the Forth. I have previously described a festive season stroll on the River Almond Walkway in December – from Cramond, heading upstream as far as the railway line on the eastern boundary of Edinburgh Airport. An extension of the walkway as far as Kirkliston would be warmly welcomed.

The Almond is quite a significant river, within a steep-sided and partly wooded gorge, by the time it passes through Livingston and the 220-acre Almondell and Calderwood Country Park. Further east, the river flows under the Lin's Mill Aqueduct that carries the Union Canal, then under the M8 and M9 to reach Kirkliston. Once one of Scotland's most polluted rivers, an integrated management plan has improved the water quality in recent decades.

The following walk starts from the East Calder car park, map ref 092682, descends to the valley and the hidden-at-first river, then heads downstream on the east bank as far as the aqueduct. The return is by tow path and minor roads to the Visitor Centre, then upstream on the west bank. Margaret went bird watching, Rhona

An old lade

and I walking, on a day when the car park was closed for renovation. The well-signposted start (Path to Almondell Visitor Centre 0.8 miles and Naysmith Bridge 0.6 miles) is also part of National Cycle Network route 75.

From the ivy-covered archway, a broad tarmac path, ideal for cyclists and wheel-chair users, gently descends to the graceful stone-arched Almondell Bridge, built around 1800 by Alexander Naysmith, then restored and re-opened in 1998. Naysmith is better known as the artist believed to have painted the only authentic portrait of Robert Burns. Do not cross the bridge. Cut up to the right by a path to higher ground, eventually to overlook a more modern suspension footbridge, built by the Royal Engineers in 1970, that gives access to the Visitor Centre on the west bank. Again, do not cross. Instead, follow the path by an old lade (a miniature version of the canal later to be reached), with the aqueduct now coming into view.

Staying above the river bank, follow the waymarked route and many a stile. Continue by the lade, climb steps to a lane, then turn left to reach a car park and picnic area. Take a short walk along the tow path to appreciate the height of the aqueduct, some 35m above the river, then return and descend by steps to pass underneath the canal. Green gates bar the way to Lin's Mill, named after William Lin, reputed to be the last man in Scotland to die of the plague in 1645. Turn right and climb steps to reach the far bank of the canal. Head westwards on the tow path as far as a farm track and cross the first bridge.

FACT FILE	
Map	OS map 65, Falkirk & Linlithgow
Distance	6 miles
Height	200m
Terrain	riverside paths (some tarmac) and minor roads
Start point	East Calder car park, map ref 092682
Time	3 hours
Nearest town	Livingston
Refreshment spot	Almondell Visitor Centre

Continue on the tarmac road to Muirend, and signposted Almondell minor road, and pass a building named Look ye. The noisy M8 is now close by; however, eventually turn left as signposted at the oft-busy entrance way to the Park and Visitor Centre. Open all year and free to visit, the Centre offers limited refreshments.

Head upstream on the west bank, a tarmac driveway passing the suspension bridge and so to Almondell Bridge. Do not cross. Continue, now by path, and pass a weir to reach a metal footbridge just downstream from another viaduct, built in 1820 to carry a feeder stream for the canal. Cross the footbridge, of limited height clearance for taller walkers, and then follow the marked way to return to the initial tarmac path and so back to the start point.

Almondell Bridge

20 - A Beecraigs Circuit

The 913-acre Beecraigs Country Park lies in the Bathgate Hills, two miles south of Linlithgow. The Park, which caters for a wide range of leisure and recreational activities, is open every day from 9.00am and closes at 10.30pm in summer and at dusk in winter; plenty of time, then, to explore its many attractions, including the Balvormie play area and Beecraigs Loch.

In addition, further distant are a number of must-visit places such as Cockleroy, Cairnpapple Hill, the Knock and Witchcraig – all of historical interest and offering good viewpoints. Witchcraig is included in the following walk which, to suit my own purpose, starts from Linlithgow railway station and then heads south to the Park. I am obliged to Derek, my companion that day, for the following composite and well-researched nine-mile walk with a modest 300m climb.

Given the Park's multiplicity of criss-crossing paths, tracks and minor roads, traversing the area may be confusing at times. It is advisable on reaching the Visitor Centre to get a free map, or download it in advance, though the detail shown may still cause some confusion. Incidentally, the Park would be a good training ground for map and compass work.

Start from Linlithgow station. Cross the Union canal and use the pavement by Manse Road to reach the southern end of the town and the speed de-restriction sign. Continue for 100 yards (take care, as there is no pavement), then turn right on the signposted path, Dark

FACT FILE	
Map	OS map 65, Falkirk & Linlithgow
Distance	9 miles
Height	300m
Terrain	waymarked paths and minor roads
Start point	Linlithgow railway station
Time	4 hours
Nearest town	Linlithgow
Refreshment spot	Beecraigs Visitor Centre refreshment spot

Entry, an old road from Manse Road to Preston Road that goes by an attractive wooded area. On reaching Preston Road, turn left as signposted, Beecraigs 1.2 miles, yet curiously with a Beecraigs Country Park welcome sign.

The newish path, initially separated by a dyke from the road, later veers away to pass another Beecraigs sign, notice board and map. The path continues curving southwards to meet a tarmac road. Turn left for the Visitor Centre. Remember to get a map! Head downhill on a broad lane and turn left for Beecraigs Loch at the eastern side of the Park. Stocked with rainbow trout, the fly-fishing loch offers a charming clockwise stroll by embankment and dam, with time to admire swans and fishing boats alike – a must-photo spot.

At the west end of the loch, turn left on a minor road and pass by a sawmill on the left and a former quarry, now a climbing wall, on the right. Continue uphill. The road straightens by the edge of the wood to reach the south-east boundary of the Park. Turn right on the signposted Guthrie's Path which runs in a straight line for 1¼ miles by the wooded southern boundary. After crossing a tarmac road, reach the 260m high point of Guthrie's Path, Wairdlaw Hill, and a copse of ancient beech trees. Descend to a T-junction, the end of Guthrie's Path, and turn left (signposted Refuge Stone, Witchcraig Walk). Cross remnants of a dyke via a stile and so into

Cathlaw Hill Woodland, from where the path climbs to Witchcraig.

The 280m summit offers excellent views over Lochcote Reservoir, Cockleroy and beyond the Forth, but alas not on our hazy day. On top is a fine shelter – a stone semi-enclosure, the wall of which contains samples of many rocks that reflect the geology of the hills around. Just behind, incorporated in a stone dyke, is the Refuge Stone. In the Middle Ages, this stone marked the edge of an area of one Scots mile around Torphicen Preceptory of the Knights of St John, within which debtors and criminals could claim sanctuary from their pursuers.

Return to the T-junction and follow the signs to the attractive Balvormie play area. Later turn left as signposted and at a triple junction follow the middle path. From Balvormie, head to the Visitor Centre and retrace your steps to Linlithgow.

21 - Bo'ness

Bo'ness (which, as every schoolboy should know, is a shortened version of Borrowstounness), is the burgh town on the Ness, the nose of land jutting into the Forth. At odds with the weather forecast, it was one of those black and white days on this visit. The overnight fall of snow, allied to the low grey cloud above the cold waters of the Forth, made the day feel colder than it really was. Nevertheless, when Annie and the Mountain Maid and Hare met me at the Bo'ness and Kinneil Railway centre, there was a cheery feel to the day. Special winter festive season steam train outings that day were fully booked by families with young children, and the station coffee shop was full to bursting.

Bo'ness station is built on a landscaped site previously occupied by railway sidings, timber yards and coal mines; parking presents no problem. Opened in 1981, the railway is operated by the Scottish Railway Preservation Society. Since 2010, the line has continued to Manuel, providing connection with the Edinburgh–Glasgow main line. "Offering a nostalgic day reliving the romantic days of steam," the centre is open on a variety of days from mid-March to October, with special events on certain dates in November and December. For information on the complete timetable, including museum opening times and train timetables, phone 01506-822298 or visit www.bkrailway.co.uk.

FACT FILE	
Map	OS map 65, Falkirk & Linlithgow
Distance	7 miles
Height	negligible
Terrain	good pathways
Start point	Bo'ness railway station car park, map ref 003817
Time	3 hours
Nearest town	Bo'ness
Refreshment spot	Bo'ness railway station coffee shop

Despite the Fife coastline being hidden to view, we had a most pleasant three-hour outing to Kinneil Nature Reserve, then on to Kinneil House. Use the metal footbridge to cross the railway, then go round the east side of Bo'ness harbour to reach the excellent Bo'ness foreshore path which would give a new route for the motorised scooters of the Forth & Tay Disabled Ramblers Group.

Bo'ness railway station

A walk round the harbour gives a hint of the town's rich industrial past. Indeed, Bo'ness in its heyday was the second largest port in Scotland after Leith. Decline followed the collapse of the tobacco trade and completion of the Forth & Clyde canal. Continue west by the Forth towards the site of the former Kinneil Colliery, closed in 1983 and now the man-made Kinneil Nature Reserve, formed from excavated material from the colliery. Turn right for the circular anti-clockwise walk round the reserve before returning to the railway line and a level crossing, still marked as a station on my 1997 map. Go through the metal gates and turn right, parallel to the railway, then curve left towards a parking area. Go up Snab Lane, cross the main road, and straight up the wooded lane on the other side to reach the A993. Cross to the west side of the road, then turn sharp right where signposted on the long straight driveway to Kinneil House.

Pass the museum (which tells the story of the Kinneil Estate from Roman times to the present day) and continue by the stone pillars to the big house, once the country home of the dukes of Hamilton and saved from demolition in the 1930s by the rediscovery of its remarkable wall paintings. Hours can be spent exploring the estate parkland and its interesting aspects. A side wall gateway leads to a bridge above a deep ravine. Follow the path on the far bank to go past the ruins of the 12th century Kinneil Church. An anticlockwise route round the open parkland, traversed by the Antonine Wall, leads to a Roman fortlet and two ponds. National Cycle Route 76 traverses the grounds.

The Factfile for this walk assumes you will be retracing your steps. However, on returning to the A993, we turned right on Wotherspoon Drive, also signposted for the cycle route, to enter a park. We followed higher roads before turning left down Providence Brae to reach the interesting old town centre. Look out for the Hippodrome, Scotland's first purpose-built cinema, opened in 1912 and now recently restored.

Full steam ahead

22 - Linlithgow, the River Avon and the Union Canal

To paraphrase Jane Austen, it is a truth universally acknowledged that a hillwalker in possession of a good weather forecast must be in want of a hill. But such days often coincide with other commitments, with bad weather days then being used for lower level walks. On one such day, the Mountain Maid and I left the ancient burgh of Linlithgow for a river and canal walk, encompassing part of the nine-mile River Avon Heritage Trail, a visit to Muiravonside Country Park and a return on the Union Canal tow path.

From the centre of Linlithgow, go west along the High Street, the A803, for 1½ miles, heading for the railway viaduct over the River Avon. Pass the West Port Hotel, and further on Sainsbury's supermarket, to reach Mill Road on the left, also identified by a River Avon Heritage Trail signpost.

After a few yards, turn right into Burgh Mills lane and descend to the early 19th century viaduct which still forms part of the main line between Edinburgh and Glasgow. Turn left through the gate, again signposted,

FACT FILE

Map	OS map 65, Falkirk & Linlithgow
Distance	8 miles
Height	Negligible
Terrain	pavement, path and tow path
Start point	centre of Linlithgow
Time	3 to 4 hours
Nearest town	Linlithgow
Refreshment spot	Steading Café, Muiravonside Country Park

and pass under the multi-arched viaduct. (On our visit, there was a notice regarding the closure of the Trail beneath Torphicen Bridge, but the bridge is further upstream beyond this walk.)

The Avon on our visit was a swirling muddy spate after days of rain. Follow the signposted east bank sandy path as it weaves its way through a wooded strip. Later on, by now into more open countryside, the path gradually climbs away from the developing ravine. Then the line of the canal embankment appears with the first sight of the aqueduct to the right. The path turns left up steps to reach the canal tow path, then turns right (west) to cross the 1820s Thomas Telford aqueduct – at 810ft, the second longest in Britain.

Despite the reassuring railing, the narrow cobbled path may add a frisson of excitement for those unsure of heights – but do stop midway to admire the views. At the far end of the aqueduct, on the right-hand side, wooden steps come up from the river; this is the point

The early 19th century viaduct which still forms part of the main line between Edinburgh and Glasgow

of return from Muiravonside. Carry on west on the tow path (signposted Polmont 3 miles) to the bridge carrying the B825, reached by path. Turn left onto the road and so on to the park entrance. A tarmac road runs through the park; follow the signs to the Steading Café, a welcoming mid-way rest point (telephone 01324-503746 for opening times).

The café is on the west side, high above a potentially confusing impressive sweep of the river gorge, so it may not be apparent at first which way to continue. From the café entrance, climb very slightly diagonally right. The path, at first high above the noisy flow of water through the gorge, gently descends to the river. (If descending to continue upstream, follow the signpost; however, once at the river, it is not then possible to head downstream. On our visit, the gorge path was closed due to the danger of falling rocks.)

Pass through the small walled graveyard of the Stirling family of Muiravonside and, once back by the river, join a broad track. Go past an outdoor learning centre. Then, with the aqueduct on the right, climb the steps at its western end to reach the tow path as noted earlier.

Turn left over the aqueduct, signposted Linlithgow 3 miles. Stroll along the tow path until reaching an overhead metal pipe bridge. Pass that and immediately cross a burn and road to reach steps on the left descending to the road. Follow the road, then later the path on the left, adjacent to the now underground burn. On reaching the A706 Mains Road, turn right. The road goes under the railway line and so back to the West Port Hotel.

23 - Muiravonside Country Park to Avonbridge

FACT FILE

Map	OS map 65, Falkirk & Linlithgow
Distance	6 miles
Height	200m
Terrain	undulating riverside path, rough in places
Start point	Muiravonside Country Park, off the B825, two miles south-west of Linlithgow
Time	4 hours
Nearest towns	Linlithgow and Falkirk
Refreshment spot	Steading Café, Muiravonside Country Park

In 2011, the Mountain Maid and I walked the first part of the River Avon Heritage Trail, from Linlithgow to Muiravonside Country Park, returning via the Union Canal tow path. At that time, further upstream beyond

our walk, the Trail was closed beneath Torphichen Bridge. On a raw, late January day, a low level, sheltered walk beckoned – a return to Muiravonside to complete the Trail to its end at Avonbridge, this time in the company of the three Js (Jimbo, John and Joe).

The first part of the lovely leaf-strewn path, in the deepest part of the Avon ravine, was a glutinous mess at times, admittedly after a very wet spell. With winter damage, there were also fallen branches to negotiate and some wooden steps were broken. Doubtless after path repair work has been done, and on a dry day, you will wonder at our initial slow progress of less than two miles an hour. Once past Torphichen Bridge, and with the gorge diminishing in depth, easier walking ensues.

Muiravonside Country Park lies off the B825, two miles south-west of Linlithgow. From the car park, follow the signs to the Steading Café (telephone 01324-503746 for opening times). From the café, descend to the path above the impressive sweep of the river gorge, and a signpost (River Avon Heritage Trail, Linlithgow, to the left, and Avonbridge to the right). The path descends to the gorge and the river – a noisy, muddy spate on our day.

Later on, the path, with periodic blue marker posts, rises some 35m above the river, with a new plantation to the right; it then steeply descends by a series of stone steps with a metal handrail in places. Then reach an

The Carribber Bridge

(he of the steamship *Comet*, launched in 1812). Torphichen Bridge is where the busy A801 crosses the Avon, with the Trail passing under the arched bridge but on a boardwalk normally above the water. On our visit, following flood damage, all that was left were the widely separated iron stanchions. We climbed up to the A801, quite narrow at this point, and *most carefully* crossed the road to descend and return to the path on the far side. No problem now – a new boardwalk was installed 2012.

informative plaque at which point the Trail crosses the Avon by the Carribber Bridge. Completed in 2005, it was the first stress-laminated wooden bridge of its kind in the world. A notice on the arched bridge advised us that the Trail beneath Torphichen Bridge was still closed and the damaged boardwalk demolished. The notice suggested no alternative route, as that would require the use of busy roads.

However, we continued, passing on the way a plaque on a ruined cottage, marking the birthplace of Henry Bell

Continue on the south bank through a lovely sylvan area to where a footbridge leads to the north bank. Before crossing, have a look at a sandstone archway on the right, all that remains today of Wallace's Cave, where he allegedly hid after the battle of Falkirk in 1298. Walk through the archway, then head clockwise and so back to the bridge.

The path later climbs up to and under one of the many splendid arches of the Westfield Viaduct, built in the 19th century to carry coal from the local mines, but now impassable. Further upstream by Strath Mill the path crosses back to the south bank. The final section leading to Avonbridge is a gentler affair.

Now, you did organise that pre-placed transport, didn't you?

24- The Falkirk Wheel and the Kelpies

Opened in 1790, the Forth & Clyde Canal became the main highway across Scotland – a route enhanced by the *Charlotte Dundas*, the world's first practical steamboat, and later by the 1822 connection at Falkirk of the Union Canal from Edinburgh.

The Union Inn, once the meeting point of the two canals

FACT FILE	
Map	OS map 65, Falkirk & Linlithgow
Distance	8 miles
Height	negligible
Terrain	mostly tarmac tow path
Start point	Falkirk Wheel, Lime Road, Tamfourhill, Falkirk
Time	3 to 4 hours
Nearest town	Falkirk
Refreshment spot	Falkirk Wheel Cafe

The Forth & Clyde Canal

The 35m/115ft higher Union Canal has been extended one mile further west to link with the Forth & Clyde Canal at the outstanding piece of modern engineering, the Falkirk Wheel, the world's only rotating boatlift and an eye-catching working structure. Operated by Scottish Canals, the Wheel cost £17.5 million to build (Millennium funds well-used). It is Scotland's busiest tourist attraction outwith a city centre location, attracting over 5.5 million visitors between its opening, in 2002, and the end of 2014. Other interests, apart from taking a trip on the Wheel, include a variety of woodland walks – and then there is a stroll along the Forth & Clyde Canal tow path to the Kelpies.

The Helix Park development by the M9, previously an industrial site by the River Carron end of the Forth & Clyde Canal near Grangemouth, won the Saltire Society 2014 Civil Engineering Award. The development contains Scotland's newest cultural landmark, the Kelpies, two majestic 30m-tall horse head sculptures towering over the canal. These, the world's largest equine sculptures, created by the artist Andy Scott and unveiled in April 2014, have quickly become another iconic must-see attraction. A kelpie is a water spirit usually in the form of a horse, though the artist's inspiration came from the working horses which once pulled barges along the canal.

The Kelpies

In the company of Rhona, a stroll from the Wheel to the Kelpies and back, following the tow path of the Forth & Clyde Canal was an obvious low-level winter walk.

From the Falkirk Wheel (Lime Road, Tamfourhill; tourist information 0845-859-1006), cross the footbridge to the far bank tow path, nowadays a tarmac way. Turn right (signposted Carron Sea Lock 4 miles). After one mile, note on the far side of the canal the impressive white building, the Union Inn, once the meeting point of the two canals. The 11-lock connecting flight was dismantled in 1933.

Lock 16 marks the top end of the long flight of locks to Grangemouth; a gradual lowering scarcely noticeable to the pedestrian. Just in case you are tempted, swimming in the canal is not allowed! At lock 15 is the Canal Inn on Canal Street and at lock 11 the A803 passes overhead. Given the busy conurbation the canal now passes through, the way can seem remarkably secluded at times. There is a small detour at lock 9 where the railway crosses the canal.

The lower section is slightly less attractive, as it passes through an industrial area. The canal goes under the B902 then, for a mile-long level stretch, by Bankside. So far no sight of the Kelpies, but eventually go under the A9 and there they are! At lock 3, with the Kelpies enhanced by the distant backdrop of the Ochils, cross by the footbridge to the far side for a closer view of the Kelpies astride the canal.

It is possible to visit the inside of the Kelpies as part of a guided tour. Telephone 01324-506850.

Rhona and I briefly extended the walk, continuing with the canal under the M9, then parallel to the muddy banks of the River Carron, to reach the A905, Glensburgh Road, and Rhona's pre-placed car. I then walked back to the Falkirk Wheel (an out and back outing perhaps more family-appealing if cycled).

25 - The River Almond Walkway

If you are looking for a short and easy low-level stroll, the River Almond Walkway ticks many a box with points of interest for all members of the family. The walk starts from Cramond and follows the river upstream as far as the railway line on the eastern boundary of Edinburgh Airport. A loop by track and minor road then leads back to the river.

The Friends of the River Almond Walkway (www.friendsoftheriveralmondwalkway.org.uk), an independent volunteer conservation group committed to improving the walkway and surroundings for the use and enjoyment of the local community, would welcome your support. They have monthly working parties, carrying out small improvements around the walkway such as removing invasive plant species, tidying ivy from the old buildings and opening up the entrance points to make access easier. They are also involved in some major projects, including the replacement of the Salvesen Steps and the extension of the walkway as far as Kirkliston.

Ordnance Survey map 65, Falkirk & Linlithgow, covers the route (Map 60, Edinburgh, does not extend far enough west). The more detailed Spokes West Lothian and Edinburgh cycle maps (2 inches: 1 mile) may be

FACT FILE	
Map	OS map 65, Falkirk &Linlithgow
Distance	7 miles
Height	100m
Terrain	riverside path, track and minor road
Start point	car park, Cramond Glebe Road, map ref 190770
Time	3 hours
Nearest city	Edinburgh
Refreshment spot	Cramond Gallery Bistro

Weir on the River Almond on a bright Autumn day

useful, but are not essential. On this well-signposted route, it would be difficult to get lost. Follow the river!

On a glorious blue sky, cold but crisp day, I met Sally and Derek, old running friends, at the large free car park, map ref 190770, at the foot of Cramond Glebe Road. Close by are the remains of one of the best-preserved Roman bath houses in Scotland, only discovered in 1975 when the car park was built. Adjacent is the site of the Roman Fort. Descend through the village to the mouth of the river. If tempted to extend the walk to Cramond Island, do bear in mind that the causeway is tidal. Take due note of the warning signs: it is safe to cross between two hours before and two hours after low tide.

Head upstream, past the once passenger ferry point, to Cobble Cottage and where the Cramond lioness was recovered in 1997. This statue depicts a bound male

prisoner being killed by the lioness. Enter the lovely wooded river valley by the fast flowing water, then ascend the concrete Salvesen Steps and follow a walkway high above the river. Wooden steps then descend to the river and so to Dowie's Mill Lane. By the end of the 18th century, the river was industrial with four other mills along the banks.

Turn right very briefly on Brae Park Road, then left at a Walkway sign. (Do not cross the old Cramond Brig.) Dip down to the river and under the A90 concrete bridge. One-and-a-half miles from the start, steps lead to a tarmac road. Turn right then later right again (not left), signposted Cammo Estate, to descend to the river. The next section stays close by the river, passing Grotto Bridge and by another wooded stretch with fields on the left. Continue into open country with a narrow path,

The trees are resplendent in their autumnal cloaks

muddy on our day, leading to the railway line (map ref 156749).

Earlier, you may have expressed regret about low-flying planes and by now the noise from the airport and railway is all too apparent. Turn left along a lane. The next section under the flight path of descending planes, not so high above, may be of interest to boys of all ages. More excitement is gained by waiting under the flight path for the arrival of the next plane.

At the end of the lane, turn left on the minor road, then left again on the track to Nether Lennie. A grassy track by the right of the house leads back to the riverside path.

Stirlingshire and Clackmannanshire

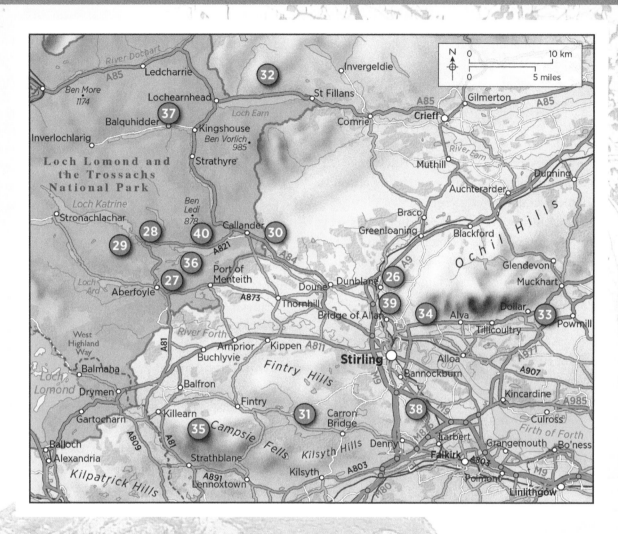

26 - A Dunblane Allan Water circuit

From its source in the Ochils, the 22-mile long Allan Water flows through Dunblane to join the River Forth just south of Bridge of Allan. I had previously walked downstream from Dunblane with Rhona, following the Darn Road (an ancient track way thought to have been used by the Romans) that links Dunblane and Bridge of Allan, then back by the west bank. This time, with Jimbo and two Springer spaniels, it was an upstream east bank walk to Kinbuck then a return by a minor road overlooking the west bank. The upstream rise is only some 50m but, with many undulations on both path and return road, the overall climb is closer to 150m.

Although Ordnance Survey map 57, Stirling, covers the signposted walk, I recommend the more detailed local pamphlet, *Dunblane Community Paths*, available from the public library in upper High Street. Dunblane is readily accessed by a frequent train service, so flaunt your green credentials.

Start from one of Scotland's oldest buildings, Dunblane Cathedral, built on the site of a much earlier building which may have been constructed as early as the 9th century. David I established the bishopric in 1150.

A gentle climb up the Braeport leads to one of the oldest parts of the town, Ramoyle, home in the early

The Faery Footbridge

19th century to artisans, especially weavers, and where many of the houses still betray their origins. Turn left by Northend Garage (signposted Public Path Ashfield 1½ miles, Kinbuck 2½ miles) to reach the Scouring Burn which is followed for a short distance. Later turn right as signposted for Ashfield. The path gently rises then descends to the railway and the Allan Water, then passes under the massive concrete bridge of the A9 and into open country by the undulating river.

On our day, a minor landslip had washed away part of the path but this can be avoided. We simply walked straight on. An underpass leads to the west side of the railway and a path junction. Ignore the branch to the left (Auchinlay Road ½ mile) and continue straight on, as signposted, for Ashfield. Pass a white bridge over the railway and stroll through Ashfield, a model village built in 1866 to house workers employed in the mill. The mill started as a bleach works then converted into Pullar's Dyeworks before closing in 1975.

Beyond Ashfield, the path follows the line of the railway, albeit with a loop by the river, at this stage more like a canal. On reaching the Craigton Farm track, a small detour may be required if the field ahead is flooded. It was on our day. Simply head east on the lane to reach the B8033 (which has a pavement, apart from the bridge over the railway) and so into Kinbuck. At the north end of the village, cross the beautiful twin-arched and much-buttressed Kinbuck Bridge over the river and turn left (signposted Cromlix).

FACT FILE	
Map	OS map 57, Stirling & The Trossachs
Distance	7 miles
Height	150m
Terrain	riverside path and minor road
Start point	Dunblane Cathedral
Time	3 hours
Nearest town	Dunblane
Refreshment spot	Choices Delicatessen and Coffee Shop, 21 High Street, Dunblane

The much buttressed Kinbuck Bridge

In 1813, a chalybeate spring was discovered on the Cromlix Estate. The waters, impregnated with iron salts, were believed in those days to cure a variety of illnesses including rheumatism, alcoholic-related diseases and depression. 'Taking the waters' became a fashionable trend and led to the building of a health spa resort, the Dunblane Hydropathic Establishment in 1878 (nowadays the DoubleTree by Hilton Dunblane Hydro).

Follow the quiet Auchinlay Road which, being higher above the Allan Water, gives more panoramic views. Later, pass under the A9 to reach the outskirts of Dunblane and over a bridge above the once railway line to Doune and on to Callander. Turn left (signposted Cycle Way 765), cross the Allan Water by the 1911 ferro-concrete arched Faery Footbridge, then bear right to return to the Cathedral.

27 - Aberfoyle to Callander over the Menteith Hills

The weather forecast, heavy morning rain easing by noon to give a two-hour dry spell, was sufficient for Rhona to meet me in Aberfoyle, one of the settings in Walter Scott's novel, *Rob Roy*. Appropriately, our intended traverse of the Menteith Hills, a range of hills on the Highland Boundary Fault, follows part of the Rob Roy Way. Waymarked with yellow arrowheads within small green circles, it would be difficult to get lost and, with a south-westerly wind at our backs, the return of rain by the time we were descending to Loch Venachar and Callander was of little concern.

Nevertheless, given that forecast, we opted for the seven-mile traverse to the East Lodge car park by Loch Venachar, and a pre-placed car, rather than continuing a further three miles by minor road to Callander. The entire route is within the Loch Lomond & The Trossachs National Park. The loch side area, and the curiously named Loch Drunkie, had previously been explored with Jimbo; we had noted a green sign at the East Lodge car park – footpath to Aberfoyle via Menteith Hills – a route immediately added to my list of walks to do.

From the very large car park, once the site of Aberfoyle's railway station, head east on the pavement by the A821 to the signposted tarmac drive that leads to the Dounans Outdoor Centre. As an alternative, that point can also be reached by following a short section of the old railway line, now part of National Cycle Route 7 from Glasgow to Inverness.

FACT FILE	
Map	OS map 57, Stirling & The Trossachs
Distance	7 or 10 miles
Height	250m
Terrain	track, path and minor road
Start point	Aberfoyle large car park
Time	3 or 4 hours
Nearest towns	Aberfoyle and Callander
Refreshment spot	The Harbour Café, north shore of Loch Venachar

Pass the Centre on the left, then turn right on a good gravel track that heads by the top end of Aberfoyle golf course. With steep slopes on the left and the golf course to the right, the track steadily rises to give lovely open views over Flanders Moss. Continue to a signposted T-junction. From the right is the approach from Braeval car park.

Turn left on the gently rising track to reach a new gate and a sign – Malling Forestry Estate, Please Prevent Fires. No chance on our sodden day! The very new track quickly comes to an end, but on its left is the mapped path of old. Cross a burn to enter a lovely area with trees on the right and an escarpment on the left. Unsurprisingly, after days of rain, the path was exceedingly muddy in places and it was amusing to meet two mud-bespattered mountain bikers, constantly coming off but obviously enjoying themselves.

Eventually clear the forest by a new gate (put dogs on lead) and traverse the open moorland, heading north-east. Midway through the open area, cross one burn (quite substantial on our day). Exit the moorland by

Heading north-east over the open moorland

another new gate by a dyke, from where a short rise leads to the high point of the traverse, followed by a slight descent to the narrow, secluded and charming Lochan Allt a' Chip Dhuibh (not named on my map).

The loch-side path leads to a forestry track. At this point, a small path climbs to a nearby mound with a picnic table, giving views to Ben Ledi and the north. Continue by track to the north end of the loch, cross its outflow by a causeway dam and pass a padlocked boathouse on the right.

The track slants down north-east, later through a large cleared area giving the first views of Loch Venachar, and so to the East Lodge car park; a rewarding walk with a few hours grabbed from a very wet day. If continuing by foot, allow another hour to reach Callander.

Charming Lochan Allt a`Chip Dhuibh

28 - Ben A'an and The Trossachs

Resting at the summit

Originally applied to the narrow pass between Loch Katrine and Loch Achray, the name 'Trossachs' derives from the Gaelic for bristly, an apt description of this craggy territory. The tourist industry was launched following the publication in 1810 of Sir Walter Scott's classic work *The Lady of the Lake* (the water being Loch Katrine), nowadays a poem that many are aware of but few have read.

Queen Victoria's visits to the Trossachs in 1859 and 1869 (the first occasion being for the opening of the Loch Katrine waterworks, still the main water supply for Glasgow) further boosted tourism; the area's popularity is maintained to this day. Hemmed in between Loch Katrine and Glen Finglas is a rocky area whose high point is 564m Meall Gainmheich. To the south of that,

FACT FILE

Map	OS map 57, Stirling & The Trossachs
Distance	2 miles
Height	400m
Terrain	path all the way
Start point	signposted car park, south side of A821, north-west bounds of Loch Achray, map ref 509070
Time	2 to 3 hours
Nearest towns	Aberfoyle and Callander
Refreshment spot	The Harbour Café, north shore, Loch Venachar

form higher up – eases the way and the effort is well rewarded.

The path goes through lovely mixed woodland to reach a ravine and stream, at first on the left bank of the burn. Later on, the path crosses to the far side by a wooden bridge, with a gap in the trees giving a tantalising sight of the conical summit. Then return by stepping stones to the left bank, being aware of the many wet tree roots and polished boulders.

The path suddenly clears the forest and, at this stage, our forecast was spot on. The heat of the day was gradually burning off the low cloud to reveal the awesome summit cone, or as Scott wrote "Ben-an heaved high his forehead bare." The obvious question at first – how on earth to get up there – is simply resolved. The superb improved path, now that stone staircase, eases the steep gradient by another burn and ravine, efficiently gaining height on the right hand (east) side of the summit cone. The path leads to a col with sudden dramatic views down Loch Katrine and possibly of the steamship *Sir Walter Scott*.

The path then curves left to the small rocky summit, with steep slopes all around. The clarity of our day was disappointing, not ideal for distant photographs, which was a pity because, with Ben Ledi to the north-east as well, this is a superb Trossachs viewpoint, arguably better than Ben Venue.

The only excitement on the way down was on meeting a couple vainly shouting for their Lurcher, a dog they admitted had gone astray before. But this was holiday time and the couple were due to return home the following day!

mapped at 461m/1512ft, lies Ben A'an. However, a short distance to the WSW overlooking Loch Katrine is a rocky outcrop at 454m/1490ft, usually accepted by visitors, and the path, as the summit of Ben A'an.

Often described as a mountain in miniature, there is no danger of it being confused with its Cairngorm namesake Ben Avon (pronounced A'an), a big mountain both in area and height that demands a long, full day. Its name may simply derive from the Gaelic word for a river, *abhainn*, with the early OS surveyors writing it as Avon, a common word for many a river further south.

However, the Trossachs Ben A'an probably has nothing to do with the River Achray and is more likely a mistake by Sir Walter Scott. The original name *binnean*, meaning a small peak, has a similar pronunciation.

Being a short hill day and the weather forecast to improve, Jimbo and I had a leisurely start from the signposted car park on the south side of the A821 by the north-west bounds of Loch Achray, map ref 509070. Carefully cross the oft-busy road for the start of the uphill path. A 100m starting height, plus a few undulations on the way, gives almost 400m to climb over less than one mile, but the good path – in almost staircase

Ben A`an

29 - Ben Venue

FACT FILE	
Map	OS map 57, Stirling & The Trossachs
Distance	7 miles
Height	700m
Terrain	excellent path/track to grassy hillside
Start point	Ben Venue car park, west end of Loch Achray, map ref 505069
Time	4 to 5 hours
Nearest hamlet	Brig o' Turk
Refreshment spot	The Harbour Café, Loch Venachar

Originally just the area of wooded hills between Loch Katrine and Loch Achray, the Trossachs are forever associated with Queen Victoria and Sir Walter Scott who, referring to Loch Katrine, wrote:

High on the south huge Ben Venue
Down on the lake in masses threw,
Crags, knolls, and mounds, confusedly hurled,
The fragments of an earlier world…

an apt description of the craggy hillsides. Indeed, the name Trossachs, derived from the Gaelic, means the bristly country.

Ben Venue is the commanding twin-peaked height above Loch Katrine. The name means the small mountain, from *A' Beinn Mheanbh*, pronounced in Gaelic much like the anglicised *Venue*.

Go past the Ben A'an car park at the west end of Loch Achray, to a junction on the A821. Straight on leads to the Loch Katrine pier head and the steamship *Sir Walter Scott*. However, turn left for the well-signposted Forestry Commission Ben Venue car park, map ref 505069.

A bridge across the Achray Water allows footpath access all the way from car park to hill. The convenient

notice board, with a map, shows the path which traverses south-west into the forested Gleann Riabhach. The path, not shown on my 2004 map, avoids the short road walk of old, though the latter gives a pleasing variation on return.

The waymarked posts have coloured stripes: blue, green and red to begin with, although blue is the one to follow.

Bridge across the Achray Water

The excellent path, well-suited to the area, undulates westwards through a semi-wooded area as if heading direct to the forbidding craggy north-eastern face of the hill. The path gently descends towards the Achray Water and the Loch Katrine pier road. However, follow the minor road on the left (this leads to the Katrine Dam), then shortly afterwards look out for the blue sign on the left, with the path descending to the arched wooden bridge spanning the Achray. Just over the bridge, at a path junction, turn right on to a broadish gravel track though pleasing woodland. A little while later, leave the track and turn left by two large boulders (the point again signposted). A short descent leads to another track junction; turn right, again signposted for the hill (to the left leads down to the Achray Hotel).

Thereafter, with the new unmapped path crisscrossing then climbing well above the track, a description of the route into Gleann Riabhach may seem quite complicated. It is not – simply follow the signposted way. At the only possibly confusing section, where the path climbs right from the track, is a well-sited high wooden signpost.

Brian and one dog at the summit

Continue through a newly planted area, with the path eventually clearing the forest, at map ref 474052. A few duckboards then lead to the open hillside.

The wet unmade mapped path goes NNW towards a distant waterfall, then curves to approach the summit from the west. However, we opted for the direct climb, north-east at first, to reach the grassy southern shoulder. Traverse a minor bump, by now following a vague path, then climb again to reach the 727m/2385ft trig point, square-shaped, stone built and nowadays slightly crumbly.

The highest point (by some 2m) is actually a separate top 300m to the north-west; however, given the implied authority of the trig point and its commanding position overlooking Loch Achray and Loch Venachar, it is little surprise that many go no further. We lingered by the trig point, taking photos and admiring the views, then headed downhill.

For a variation lower down, we followed the signs for the Achray Hotel, then returned with care along the road.

Loch Achray - B Lobodzinski

30 - The Bracklinn Falls, Callander

Over countless years, the fast-flowing Keltie Burn, in a series of dramatic waterfalls, has cut a high-walled gorge into the hillside that is impressive even in a dry spell – and truly awesome when in spate. Such a spate occurred in August 2004 when severe flash floods swept away the iron bridge that spanned the 100ft-high gorge. Now, though, the Bracklinn Falls above Callander – one of Scotland's most famous waterfalls – can again be crossed by bridge, thus re-opening a popular circular walk.

A few days after the 2004 spate, on an approach to Ben Vorlich from Callander, we saw at first hand the ravages of the floods, including the demolition of a northern concrete bridge over the Keltie. At the same time, a landslip barred the Glen Ogle road and the south-side Loch Earn road was closed when parts of the bridge by the Falls of Edinample were washed away. It took two years to rebuild the 1859 Grade B listed bridge and re-open the road.

FACT FILE	
Map	OS map 57, Stirling & The Trossachs
Distance	5 miles
Height	200m
Terrain	pavement, minor road, path and track
Start point	public car park behind Dreadnought Hotel, Station Road
Time	3 to 4 hours
Nearest town	Callander
Refreshment spot	The Atrium Cafe, 79-81Main Street, Callander

The Bracklinn bridge - G Cantley

It took even longer to replace the Bracklinn bridge, and for good reason. With no cranes or helicopters able to access the site and the nearest road about a mile away, the component parts had to be dragged over a specially-built track, then assembled by hand on location – a six-month job. Then engineers had to build temporary steel rails across the 60ft-wide gorge so that the 20-tonne bridge could be hand-winched across.

After four years of remarkable effort, the bridge, designed using locally sourced larch and four 12m-long Douglas fir trunks, was formally opened on 16th November 2010 – all at an unbelievably modest cost of £110,000.

On a glorious day of blue sky, with no breeze and with reasonable warmth in the sun, the Mountain Maid and Hare, plus Margaret and I, just had to have a look at the (then) new bridge. It is far too short a walk to the Falls from the upper car park on Bracklinn Road, so we started from the old railway station, now a large public car park behind the Dreadnought Hotel.

Walk east along Main Street to Bracklinn Road then, via a steepish ascent, pass a lower car park to reach the upper car park. Turn right by the green lamp-post sign, Bracklinn Falls ¾ miles, along what was for us a snow-covered and slippery track. However, on the way the Mountain Maid found a £1 coin lying in the snow.

To the sound of surging water, the pathway descends by the edge of the rocky ravine. Later, the water can be seen but, at first, there is no sign of a bridge spanning the gorge. Then, as the path turns right, suddenly there it is:

impressive, triangular-shaped and copper-roofed. The views from the centre of the bridge are quite something.

Now for the circular walk. Heading north on the east bank of the Keltie, the water-side path was, on our visit, slightly overgrown, indicative of the lack of use by walkers during the time before the new bridge was built. Later, however, the path climbs away from the water by a lovely side ridge to meet a broad forestry track which is then followed. On approaching a track coming in from the right, a felled area allows distant views of the eastern flanks of Ben Ledi.

An easy descent leads to a broad wooden bridge across the Keltie with a short climb then to the upper Bracklinn road. On return to Callander, pass on the left a signposted Wishing Well. The well held a couple of coins, left undisturbed of course, just in case. The newly-found £1 coin, to be saved for a more charitable purpose elsewhere, was not splashed in. Further on is the Red Well, signposted on the right. Its chalybeate

waters, impregnated with iron salts, were once believed to have healing properties. We opted instead for coffee in Callander.

A glorious day of blue sky, no breeze and reasonably warm in the sun - G Cantley

31 - Cairnoch Hill

Some years ago, Rhona and I visited the Carron Valley Reservoir area, climbing 570m/1870ft Meikle Bin. This time, after an usually heavy dump of snow on a late March day, we had a more modest target: the less commanding 413m/1355ft Cairnoch Hill on the north side of the reservoir and on the southern slopes of the Gargunnock Hills.

The extensively forested slopes enclosing Cairnoch's small summit dome offered shelter on our day of persistent snow and sleety rain. Despite its modest 200m

A wintry day

FACT FILE	
Map	OS map 57, Stirling & The Trossachs
Distance	7 miles
Height	200m
Terrain	track, then short clear-fell traverse to open hillside
Start point	B818 car park, map ref 672859, west end of Carron Valley Reservoir
Time	3 hours
Nearest towns	Denny and Balfron
Refreshment spot	Carronbridge Hotel, east of Reservoir

height, the B818 Balfron to Denny road was snow covered on our day and almost devoid of traffic.

There was, at the time of writing, a large area of felled trees above the B818; however, our route was from the west via tracks. Weather forecasts indicated a deep depression and my altimeter was grossly over-reading. However, purely by chance, we were bang slap in the midst of that depression and enjoyed a calm day with minimum wind chill.

From the Meikle Bin car park at the west end of the reservoir, briefly head east on the B818 and pass a track that leads to Todholes. Continue to the minor road that heads north-east towards Stirling, then turn south onto the forestry track to reach a large open grassy clearing on the right.

This is the site of very impressive and visible earthworks which maps of the 1920s show as Sir John De Graham's Castle (ruins). A relatively rare type of medieval earthworks, the square motte, the site is thought to have been the residence of Sir John who was killed at the battle of Falkirk in 1298. However, the castle itself may be of earlier date, probably the stronghold of the Barony of Dundaff. Access to the castle must have been by wooden drawbridge but now wooden steps lead down to the moat then up to the central raised part.

Continue on the track to a junction and turn left (north). The track later curves to the right; from here, clearing and replanting allow more open views, including one gigantic wind turbine. Head south at the next junction, with the track later curving eastwards. Pass a quarry on the left, then (on our day) large stacks of felled timber behind which is a tall radio mast. To the south, another large cleared area gives views down to the reservoir and over to Meikle Bin, the latter sadly not visible on our day.

Continue eastwards as the track dips and, just before its end, climb diagonally north-east through clear-fell

Cairnoch Hill trig point - R Fraser

to reach a line of trees by which there is easier walking. Cross the remnants of a fence and stone dyke to reach the modest dome of the hill, unforested as mapped apart from a few escapee trees, and so to the moss-covered trig point. At this stage the snow was a foot deep.

Return to the track and retrace your steps to complete the walk.

However, we decided to explore a fire break by the line of the dyke. With many wind-blown trees to climb over and under, and with a few deviations along the way, this route is not recommended! We eventually staggered down to the cleared area, with a grassy strip leading to the track east of Carnoch. That track, not shown on my 2004 map, goes parallel to the B818 and this gave us an easy return.

After our wintry 'spring' outing, it was a welcome return to the highly recommended Carronbridge Hotel, east of the reservoir, to enjoy coffee and scones by a warming coal fire. Other walkers and cyclists staggered in later to escape the clutches of a poor day.

32 - Creag Each

Overlooking Loch Earn, 672m/2205ft Creag Each, *hill of the horse*, lies north-west of St Fillans from where it is well-seen. It is a Graham, one of over 200 hills in Scotland with a height of between 2000 and 2499ft and with a drop of at least 150m on all sides. With 4½ miles to walk and only 600m to climb, it offers a short but most pleasant outing.

I met Rhona at St Fillans and there was time to enjoy coffee and scones before setting off for the hill – and indeed again on return. On the way to the village, the temperature was -6c so I welcomed that mid-morning refreshment. Nevertheless, it was a well-chosen day, with blue skies, sunshine and no wind chill.

Use the car park on the loch-side of the A85, two miles west of St Fillans, map ref 668246. Carefully cross the road to reach the start of a track with the welcoming Public Footpath sign. The beautiful estate track slants through the trees to the track bed of the old Caledonian Railway line from Perth. The section from St Fillans and finally to Balquhidder was only completed in 1904, then closed in 1951.

FACT FILE	
Map	OS map 51, Loch Tay & Glen Dochart
Distance	4½ miles
Height	600m
Terrain	track then grassy slopes to craggy summit
Start point	car park by A85, two miles west of St Fillans, map ref 668246
Time	3 to 4 hours
Nearest village	St Fillans
Refreshment spot	The Four Seasons Hotel, St Fillans

Loch Earn

The track, by now in rougher form, crosses the railway line, passes two old cottages, runs beneath electricity transmission lines and then climbs north into Glen Tarken. Ignore an unmapped track on the left and continue past the next junction on the right, where a grassy track leads to a distant cottage.

A little later, circa map ref 666253, leave the track and follow a fencepost line slanting westwards. Cross a wall

and so on to the open grassy slopes below the crags of Meall Reamhar. Gradually turn north-west to reach flatter ground at 550m, on our day with just a dusting of fresh snow, and a good spot to look back to Loch Earn and St Fillans. A slight ATV track eases the way through the higher heather-clad slopes and so on to the craggy summit area (possibly confusing on a poor day).

Immediately beneath the rocky summit, we suddenly came across a very strange sight: one well-wrapped-up man sitting in the snow by a radio mast and extended wires. Explaining his apparently bizarre presence, Andy MM0FMF, an amateur radio operator, told us about Summits on the Air (SOTA), an amateur radio award programme launched in 2002. SOTA is an ideal way to combine exercise with radio, getting people to go out into the wonderful countryside rather than being inside all the time. The idea is you take your radio to the top of the hill, set up and have some contacts with people. On our day, Andy had contacts with fellow amateurs from nine European countries. Participants are encouraged by an award scheme with prizes based on points garnered on the hillsides. There are 57,329 mountains worldwide in

The craggy summit of Creag Each

Summits on the Air

the scheme, now including most of Europe and indeed Creag Each.

After chatting to Andy and taking time to appreciate the superb views from this detached hill, it was time to head down. In bad weather, it is best to retrace your steps; however, Rhona and I sped downhill, navigating south-west over tussocky terrain for the long-time hidden gap in the trees above Derry Farm. We then followed the railway track bed east – safer and more pleasant than returning by road.

33 - From Dollar to Muckhart and back

Making the most of yet another damp, dreich and cold late March day, Rhona and I 'explored' a new-to-us, low-level six-mile walk, from Dollar to Pool of Muckhart and back. The latter, though mapped as Pool of Muckhart, is usually referred to as simply Muckhart. The attractive village has consistently performed well in Scotland's best-kept village competition.

With the River Devon to the (at times distant) right, there is a gentle upstream rise of 100m, albeit with undulations. However, once back in Dollar, I assessed that there is an overall ascent of some 250m. The first brief part of the walk is on the old Alloa to Kinross railway. The well-preserved section between Dollar and Tillicoultry, known as the Devon Way, had given me a thoroughly enjoyable walk previously, despite similar weather conditions.

Start from Park Place on the east side of the Dollar Burn and go past Strathdevon Primary School, Dollar Health Centre, and then playing fields to reach the railway track bed. Turn left and pass on the right the steadily rising, massive, grassy embankment where the railway curved southwards across the strath to reach the Devon. (The bridge is no more.)

A burn, once forded but nowadays spanned by a wooden bridge

Follow the embankment for a few yards to join a track leading to a muddy track/worn path across fields. (Alternatively, curve left on a path beside houses, then turn right to a horse-rider-friendly gate.) On our day, the field edge track clearly showed its popularity for walkers, cyclists and horse riders. Normally at this stage, there are good views to the Ochils.

FACT FILE

Map	OS map 58, Perth & Alloa
Distance	6 miles
Height	250m
Terrain	well-made pathway, mostly signposted
Start point	Park Place, Dollar
Time	3 hours
Nearest town	Dollar
Refreshment spot	Café des Fleurs, 44 Bridge Street, Dollar

Later, a superb path leads to Wester Pitgober, map ref 973979. Turn right at the farm lane, with a slight dip then rise to Linnfield Farm close to the Devon. Turn left as indicated by the Public Path sign, passing a gate signed 'Dogs must be kept on a lead.' Head towards Pitgober and the now closer A91.

The track curves by Pitgober House; then turn right on a minor tarmac road that goes to the Vicar's Bridge across the Devon. One mile walked so far! Go past Devonbank Cottages but, as the road curves to the right, look out on the left for a sunken path, signposted Muckhart 2 miles. This is an old road from the 18th and 19th centuries, its age evident in places: the amount of traffic has eroded the surface so that sections are much lower than the surrounding land.

Follow the charming sunken way and cross a burn. Half way across the next field, take care to turn right as mapped, map ref 986986 (there is no sign); follow the vaguer path to reach a minor road and turn left. Another Public Path sign shows Dollar 1½ miles. The minor road leads to a junction and more green signs. Straight on is the old road, once the principal way to Muckhart, 1½ miles, and our route. (To the right is another old road to Muckhart Mill and Rumbling Bridge.)

Head north-east, gently climbing on the broad farm track past Cowden Farm. A muddy cutting dips to a burn, once forded but nowadays spanned by a wooden bridge. Climb through an open grassy area, though the way is still obvious, then leave the sunken way on either side to reach the brow of the hill and so on to Leys Farm. Pass another Public Path sign, then by tarmac road to reach a crossroads. Cross over as signposted, ½ mile to Muckhart.

Pass on the right Muckhart School and by a charming path (known locally as the Cinder Path) to School Road. At Coronation Hall on the left, reach the A91 at the west end of Muckhart.

Later retrace your steps for the slightly faster return to Dollar.

34 - Dumyat

Although mostly rounded grassy hills, the most dramatic aspect of the Ochils is the southern escarpment (caused by a natural break in the earth's crust, the Ochils Fault) overlooking the fertile flood plain of the Forth. The prominent hill at the western extremity of the escarpment, north-east of Stirling, is Dumyat (pronounced doo-my-at, stressing all three syllables). The name is thought to originate from Dun (hill fort) of the Maeatae, a confederation of tribes who lived in Roman Britain, possibly in an area between Dumyat and Myot Hill, west of Denny. Dumyat qualifies for Marilyn status – hills of any height, but with a drop of at least 150m all round. Although of modest height, considering its position by the edge of the escarpment, it is not surprising that the 418m/1373ft summit boasts a trig point, beacon and memorial.

Erected by the Menstrie Scout Group, the metal basket beacon was part of the UK chain of beacons lit as part of the Queen's 1977 Silver Jubilee celebrations. Once filled with stones, representing wishes made by summiteers, republicans or otherwise, the beacon was empty on our visit. The memorial is in commemoration of all ranks who served in the 7th Battalion Argyll and Sutherland Highlanders, from its formation in 1908 to its disbandment in 1967. Their regimental museum is housed in Stirling Castle.

Somewhat bizarrely never having climbed Dumyat before, it was my pleasure to have the locally-based Dave (who has climbed it over 100 times) as our guide, plus the company of Jimbo and John. We decided on an east/west traverse, from Menstrie towards Bridge of Allan, then a pavement return by the A91. The popular route is from

Determined Jimbo

FACT FILE

Map	OS maps 57, Stirling & The Trossachs, and 58, Perth to Alloa
Distance	6 miles
Height	400m
Terrain	path, track, minor road and pavement
Start point	Park Road, Menstrie
Time	3 to 4 hours
Nearest village	Menstrie
Refreshment spot	Blairmains Farm Shop & Coffee Bothy, Blairlogie

the west, then returning the same way.

Start from the Holly Tree Inn on Main Street East, Menstrie, and go up Park Road. Turn left on Ochil Road, pass the Menstrie Scout Group Activity Centre on the right and cross the Menstrie Burn. Turn right up a sloping pathway, then by gate to the open hillside on the west side of Menstrie Glen. The path splits immediately with the left branch giving the most direct line. Cross a track at a stile and continue westwards steadily up the hillside. Pass a fenced-off area – Central Regional Council Water and Drainage Dept, public water supply (private property, danger, keep out).

With the recent thaw moving snow but leaving overnight icy patches, just as Dave had warned, the path was slippery in places, though not quite enough to justify putting on crampons.

We said goodbye to Dave at the summit then headed west on the undulating very obvious path popular with runners, cyclists and local strollers. It was a surprise on a superb wintry day to meet only three other walkers. We skirted past the aptly named Castle Law, on the summit of which are the still-discernible remains of an ancient hill fort.

On reaching the western minor road there is a warning sign: 'Private ground, dogs not under control will be shot.' Someone had added: 'This is not private ground.' Descending on the ice-covered road became 'interesting' until common sense prevailed – both walking rate and safety were increased by putting on crampons. We met an on-coming JCB and tractor having difficulties attempting to clear the road. At a junction, turn left and pass a gate to Broomhill to reach Logie Old Graveyard,

The three amigos

closed at the time of writing due to unsafe structure and memorials. However, with assistance from the Heritage Lottery Fund, conservation and refurbishment is underway. The Parish of Logie is one of the oldest parishes in Scotland, dating from 1124 and 1153.

Continue past the modern Logie Kirk and cemetery and turn left by the roundabout to reach the A91. Go past the charming Blairlogie, a cluster of 17th to 19th century cottages beneath Dumyat's great cliff, and Witches Craig Caravan Park. It is a pleasant two-mile pavement walk by the A91 to Menstrie. There is however a regular bus service (contact Traveline, 0871-200-2233).

The summit beacon

35 - Earl's Seat

At 578m/1897ft, the highest point in the Campsie Fells, Earl's Seat lies on the border between the Stirling and East Dunbartonshire council areas. It is a Marilyn (hills of any height, but with a drop of at least 150m all round) and, allied to its position at the western end of the Fells, that relative height and drop make it a contender for the best Lowland viewpoint. I last visited the area with Jimbo and John on a stroll by the Glazert Water to Clachan of Campsie, parallel to but well below the Fells. This time with Rhona, Earl's Seat was the target.

The walk starts from Ballagan Farm by the A891, opposite Dunglass, a volcanic plug with a crag-and-tail feature and perhaps a good marker if descending on a misty day. This southern ascent overlooks Strath Blane, the Glazert Water and the Strathkelvin Railway Path, a pedestrian and cycle route on the track bed of the dismantled railway from Kirkintilloch to Strathblane. Beyond Strathblane, part of the old line is used by the West Highland Way. Higher up there are good views eastwards to the Forth and the Pentland hills, south-east to Tinto and west to the Clyde and Arran. Being not too distant from Glasgow airport, expect to see many a plane. On the way up you may think that the views are impressive – indeed they are, but just wait until you reach the summit!

From an off-road parking spot, map ref 589791, on the south side of the A891, it is a half-mile roadside walk west to Ballagan Farm and the start of a stony/grassy track. The zigzag track eases the initial 300m ascent; however,

FACT FILE	
Map	OS map 64, Glasgow, Motherwell & Airdrie
Distance	9 miles
Height	600m
Terrain	zigzag track then undulating, wet at times, grassy way
Start point	off-road parking spot, map ref 589791, south side of A891, ½ mile east of Ballagan Farm
Time	5 hours
Nearest villages	Strathblane and Lennoxtown
Refreshment spot	Aldessan Gallery and Coffee Shop, Clachan of Campsie

given the undulations on the out and back route, there is still another 300m to climb.

At the hint of a track junction, keep to the left to reach the track high point, then climb north to meet a grassy way and a line of fence posts which follow the county

Loch Lomond and the Arrochar peaks as seen from Earl's Seat - R Fraser

boundary all the way to the summit. Navigation could not be simpler.

Now coming into view to the east is 570m Meikle Bin, the highest of the Kilsyth Hills. According to an enthusiast I once met at its summit, it is one of the best viewpoints in Scotland. Earl's Seat is even better!

On the undulating semi-moorland traverse over 508m Dumbreck (with trig point), then Owsen Hill and Little Earl, the grassy way is, from time to time, indistinct and may be rather boggy; it's a traverse perhaps best done on a frosty but snow-less day.

Yet another fence comes in from the left, and both fences merge right to the nearby trig point of Earl's Seat; for the first time, the magnificent views are revealed. The trig point is but a short distance from the northern spectacular basalt escarpment which, breached only

by the Endrick Water and the B818 at Fintry, extends some 14 miles eastwards over 511m Stronend and 485m Carleatheran. Both peaks, plus Meikle Bin, are superb viewpoints but, given its location at the western end of the escarpment, there is no doubt that Earl's Seat reigns supreme. On our admittedly crystal clear day, we had glorious views to the islands at the southern end of Loch Lomond and north to the Arrochar peaks and Ben Lomond. It may perhaps be at times a tedious traverse, but the effort is well rewarded.

On return, take care to leave the grassy way at the same point, i.e. after passing by a gate. The immediate descent on a misty day may require care – the convex slope hides the top end of the mapped track.

36 - Invertrossachs and Loch Drunkie

FACT FILE	
Map	OS map 57, Stirling & The Trossachs
Distance	9 miles
Height	100m
Terrain	private road, track and path
Start point	parking area, east end of Loch Venachar, map ref 599061, on minor road south-west of Callander
Time	3 to 4 hours
Nearest town	Callander
Refreshment spot	The Harbour Café, north shore, Loch Venachar

The dogs are gasping to go

With twin objectives in mind, we met for coffee at Kilmahog. Jimbo and Joe wanted to investigate a route on the southern shores of Loch Venachar possibly suitable for the motorised scooters of the Forth & Tay Disabled Ramblers Group. Being a blustery, showery day, not ideal for the high tops, the Mountain Lamb and I, whilst very happy to go along with that, wanted a slightly longer circuit to visit the curiously named Loch Drunkie. After an uneventful but enjoyable outing, both targets were achieved.

As it happens, Invertrossachs Estate, lying within the Loch Lomond & The Trossachs National Park, has a plethora of paths, mapped and unmapped, ideal for my purpose and the private tarmac estate road of level gradient is ideal for scooters. Furthermore, the scooter route could be extended by continuing west on a smooth track, part of National Cycle Route 7, Lochs & Glens (North), that goes from Glasgow to Inverness.

Start from the parking area at the east end of the loch, map ref 599061, on the minor road south-west of Callander. Enter Invertrossachs Estate by the warning sign 'Cyclists keep left, beware, cars and pedestrians use this road.'

Stroll through a lovely mixed woodland, albeit predominately coniferous higher up on the flanks of the Menteith Hills – a lovely sheltered walk on our blustery day but with frequent open views to the loch. Pass on the right Venachar Sailing Club, then a Scout campsite and activity centre.

Continue to the junction, map ref 565050, where the cycle way turns right on to the newish, broad smooth track – our return route. Straight on is Invertrossachs House, graciously vacated in 1869 by the owner to allow Queen Victoria to stay.

However, turn left up a gently rising gravel track going south-west adjacent to the Drunkie Burn. After passing a small loch on the left, turn right (north) on a forestry track which then becomes a pleasing, curving old estate route. Go right at a wide turning point, then immediately left on the small, grassy mapped path through a forestry clearing.

The clearing is long and the path, at least on our day, was somewhat wet after days of rain. With lovely views to the conical peak of Ben A'an, the path descends north-west to reach the northern end of Loch Drunkie, a hillside loch at 125m/416ft above sea-level, and the smallest of the five Loch Katrine lochs. The loch is not entirely natural. It was raised 25ft by the (then) Glasgow Corporation to supply compensation water for the River Teith on which Deanston Cotton Mill near Doune depended. Nowadays, it is an excellent brown trout stretch of still water. With a picnic table by the charming dam, this is a beautiful tranquil spot, ideal for a food stop.

Loch Drunkie is a corruption of the Gaelic *Drongaidh*, meaning loch between the ridges. One such ridge can be clearly identified from the map, namely the line of the Menteith Hills. Indeed you will have earlier passed a sign – Footpath access across Menteith Hills (Highland Fault Line) – a five-mile approach to Braeval on the A81, and on to Aberfoyle, which I kept in mind for a future walk.

Notwithstanding the mapped path (now gone), go to the far end of the dam and turn right on to a well-made, old unmapped estate path that descends through semi-open lovely woodland. Regain the loch-side cycle track, circa map ref 548054.

To extend the walk we turned left (west) for an out and back visit to where the cycle route meets a gate and a tarmac road (mapped Forest Drive). We then strolled back by the loch side.

Loch Drunkie

37 - Kirkton Glen to Glen Dochart

The Kirkton Glen, Balquhidder to Glen Dochart public footpath, generously signposted as seven miles, is six miles at most. With the 580m mid-point offset by a starting height at either end of circa 140m, that makes for an easy three-hour outing – ideal during the stalking season and/or when the weather is too blustery for the high tops.

I met Rhona at Ledcharrie by the A85 and, leaving one car there, we had a south/north traverse, starting from the considerably more attractive Balquhidder. Not that two cars are essential. Apart from two miles on the narrow Balquhidder road, a curving cycle route to the east via Glen Ogle gives a pleasant bike ride before or after the walk.

Arguably the best way to go, the Kirkton Glen ascent has an excellent track and path, whereas the descent to the A85 has a poor path, vague in places and usually wet. The Library Tearoom in Balquhidder only opens May to September. We made it with a few days to spare and over home-baked scones Rhona indulged in a trip down memory lane. Her first and only traverse was as long ago as 1977 – on the back of a pony. This time it was to be shanks' pony.

Balquhidder has associations with the famous, or notorious, MacGregor chieftain, Rob Roy, and with the

FACT FILE	
Map	OS map 51, Loch Tay & Glen Dochart
Distance	6 miles
Height	450m
Terrain	good track and path, then a wet and vague at times descent
Start point	Balquhidder Old Kirk
Time	3 hours
Nearest village	Balquhidder
Refreshment spot	The Library Tearoom, Balquhidder (not open in winter) or the Golden Larches Restaurant, Balquhidder Station

The Kirkton Glen ascent

MacLaren clan. At the tearoom, we met a Canadian family researching their clan roots. The nearby Creag an Tuirc, the Boar's Rock, was traditionally the rallying place and the war cry of the MacLarens.

Start from Balquhidder Old Kirk (built in 1631 on the site of a pre-Reformation chapel) or slightly to the west via a slanting path from the road. A lovely path by the east bank of the Kirkton Burn climbs north through the wood. After making a short detour to a waterfall, head right as signposted. The path joins a narrow forestry track, just one of many in a possibly confusing area. However, simply stay with the track on the burn's east bank to gently climb through the partially open forest, with clear views to the craggy ridge on the east side.

Continue to a wooden bench and the start of the Glen Dochart path, map ref 523238, clearly identified by a green signpost with white letters. Then clear the trees, cross a fence by a stile, and head towards what is known as Rob Roy's Putting Stone, by far the most massive of many a boulder from the fractured south-west face of

Leum an Eireannaich, *The Irishman's leap* (no, I don't know why). The 580m bealach contains the surprisingly large and well-hidden Lochan an Eireannaich.

It is then a steep descent into the tree-less glen, redeemed only by good views west to Ben More and Stob Binnein. Lower down, traversing a very wet and rough area, the line of the path is marked by periodic marker posts. The notice board by Balquhidder Kirk stresses that good navigation skills are needed in misty weather, most certainly true here even on descent.

The fractured south-west face of Leum an Eireannaich

Pass an old shieling and eventually reach a narrow grassy track of old, most welcome after the rough passage from one post to another. Thereafter, the path gets somewhat vague and, despite our clear day, we drifted a bit too far NNE. We crossed the railway track from Glen Ogle (part of the Caledonian Line – Callander to Oban – axed as part of the Beeching cuts of the 1960s). Then, going through a cattle-churned area, we lost all traces of the 'path.' We headed straight for the road rather than doing what we should have done – searching out the mapped way by the east bank of the Ledcharrie Burn. The path goes beneath the railway by an underpass and so to the west side of Ledcharrie Farm.

Lochan an Eireannaich

38 - Plean Country Park and Torwood Broch and Castle

FACT FILE	
Maps	OS map 65, Falkirk & Linlithgow, or map 57, Stirling
Distance	5 miles
Height	100m
Terrain	paths and minor roads
Start point	Plean Country Park car park, map ref 827868
Time	3 hours
Nearest village	Plean
Refreshment spot	Carronbridge Hotel, Carron Valley, Denny

Ideas for walks come from a variety of sources: previous knowledge, suggestions from friends, news items scanned from the press or, in this case, by chance encounter. Travelling back home on the London train, I found myself sitting beside Hazel and Ian Greenhalgh and their daughter. We got talking such that the journey seemed to take less time than usual. Noticing my Ordnance Survey Stirling map, Ian suggested that Plean Country Park could offer a good walk.

Ian had heard of Torwood and a nearby signal station, which name suggested Roman origin. A glance at the map established that Torwood, with a nearby broch and castle, lies just south of the village of Plean. And, yes, the course of a Roman Road runs close by to the south-west. A few weeks later, Rhona and Jimbo joined me on an exploratory short winter walk, covering country park, minor road and ancient broch and castle. The successful outcome is described below – serendipity indeed!

Situated within the triangle of land enclosed by the M9, M80 and M876, the 200-acre park is adjacent to Plean, from where it is well-signposted. Plean House was built in the early 19th century by a wealthy East India trader. Later, coal was mined until 1963. Stirling Council bought the estate in 1988 and turned the once industrial land into a country park, nowadays with beautiful and varied woodlands. The remains of two once-barren coal bings are now showing healthy regeneration of native trees. Plean House was inhabited until 1973, but soon after was vandalised and only the skeleton remains.

The park is criss-crossed by a number of marked and unmarked trails for walkers, bikers and horse riders – routes shown in the informative leaflet map, available at the large car park, map ref 827868. Follow the Horse Trail that weaves south through the mixed woodland and crosses a burn, heading to the South Bing. Note the brown wooden markers and fingerposts. As to be expected, some sections of the Horse Trail can be rough and muddy. At the curve on the trail look out for the leaflet path, mapped but not signposted. If you meet a broad track and the canter section then you have gone too far! A short descent leads to the Roman Road, map ref 824860.

Torwood Iron Age Broch

Head south-east on the minor road, passing on the left Glen Road, to reach the village of Torwood. On the right is a broad lane with a Public Right of Way signpost, Denovan 3km. Go up the lane a short distance to a large cleared area on the left. On the right, a plank of wood spans a ditch and leads on to a path that slants to the right through mature trees. A modest 65m climb suddenly leads to the highest point in the area, graced with the impressive Torwood or Tappoch Iron Age Broch, one of the best preserved in the Lowlands. First excavated in 1864, the walls at ground level are 20ft thick; part of the internal stairway is still visible, with the remaining walls being about 7ft high. Although surrounded by trees that limit distant views, it is a lovely spot in a clearing.

Descend south on a charming weaving path, one of many, to reach the lane, map ref 833844, west of Torwood Castle. Once the seat of Clan Forrester, the castle, built around 1566, is undergoing a slow restoration under the auspices of the Torwood Castle Trust, but is not open to the public.

Return by the lane to Torwood then to the junction with Glen Road and so by the latter towards Plean. Just before the village, turn left at the gates and follow the gradually rising lovely South Drive.

Resting at the Torwood Broch

39 - A Darn Good Walk

Linking Dunblane and Bridge of Allan, the Darn Road is an ancient track way that mostly follows the east bank of the Allan Water. (Dobhran is the old Gaelic for water.) Thought to have been used by the Romans, unlike the modern road, it does not cross the Allan Water. Ordnance Survey map 57, Stirling, covers the well-signposted walk but it would be sensible to have a more detailed local map.

Rhona, arriving by car, met me at Dunblane railway station. Strolling up High Street, we passed the Andy Murray golden post box then turned right into upper High Street and so to the public library. Here, the staff were most helpful in plying us with informative leaflets and maps of the area.

Dunblane and Bridge of Allan are readily accessed by a frequent train service, so flaunt your green credentials. My day was completely car free. We started from Dunblane on a there-and-back walk, a distance that can be halved by using the interconnecting train.

From Dunblane railway station, follow Stirling Road, cross the Allan Water, and turn right by the Riverside Hotel to Beech Road. Cross with care the very busy B8033 dual-carriageway and turn left for 50 yards to the signpost, Heritage Public Path, the Darn Road. On our December day, affixed to the signpost was a warning of closure to a railway bridge, despite improvement completions being expected by August 2013. Worry not if

FACT FILE	
Map	OS map 57, Stirling
Distance	5 miles
Height	100m
Terrain	mostly riverside path
Start point	Dunblane railway station
Time	2 to 3 hours
Nearest towns	Dunblane and Bridge of Allan
Refreshment spot	Choices Delicatessen and Coffee Shop, 21 High Street, Dunblane

the sign is still there – that bridge is not required on this walk.

At first, walk by the perimeter of Dunblane New Golf Club course on the left. To the right, being high above the Allan Water, there are lovely open aspects overlooking Kippenross (Gaelic, *Ceapan Ros*, the promontory on the small hill). As the walk progresses beyond the golf course, it becomes more obvious that this is indeed an old road. On the right is an attractive high old wall, to the west of which is Kippenross House, a Georgian mansion.

Weir on the Allan Water

A gentle, though stonier, descent by a line of beech trees leads to Kippenrait Glen (a Site of Special Scientific Interest) and a footbridge over the Wharry Burn. On the far side is a three-pointed sign: back the way, Dunblane 2 miles; to the left, Dunblane via Glen Road; and straight on, Bridge of Allan 2 miles. The burn joins the Allan Water, a noisy bustling river on our day, and a most attractive and secluded section. Ignore the footbridge on the right (the return route) then pass on the left a hillside cave known as Robert Louis Stevenson's cave, thought to be the inspiration for Ben Gunn's cave in Treasure Island. A path, stepped at first, climbs high above the river then crosses Cock's Burn (no footbridge), with a cutting leading to the far bank.

Pass on the left the outskirts of Bridge of Allan to reach a tarmac road and another sign, back the way, Dunblane

2½ miles. Head down the road, which turns out to be Blairforkie Drive, then turn right and cross the river and impressive weir to reach the A9. Continue by pavement and pass Bridge of Allan railway station on the left. Immediately turn right at a children's' nursery, Lecropt, and a sign, Dunblane 2½ miles. Continue to the road end and another sign. The path goes left of Milsey Bank House whose garden gate has a sign: 'Shut the gate, the penalty is 40 shillings for leaving this gate unlocked.'

The walk continues high above both railway and river, hidden to sight but not to sound. A high footbridge spans the railway line, and then a gentle rise leads through charming mixed woodland. Descend to the Allan Water, crossed by footbridge, and so back to the three-pointed sign and on to Dunblane.

Autumn on the Darn Road

40 - The Great Trossachs Path

Starting from Inversnaid Pier on the eastern shores of Loch Lomond (a point crossed by the West Highland Way), the Great Trossachs Path heads east for 30 miles to terminate at Callander. Jimbo and I opted to explore the 6½-mile section from the Glen Finglas Visitor Gateway, near Brig o' Turk, to Callander.

Much of the Way is through lovely mixed woodland, with the path contouring the northern slopes high above Loch Venachar and the mostly hidden A821, then reaching Callander by the track bed of an old railway.

It is a secluded walk on an excellent path, such that the overall 200m ascent is scarcely noticed. Going west to east with the wind on our backs, the partly sheltered

route was a good choice for our blustery day, although this linear walk alas involved taking two cars.

Start from the Little Druim Wood car park on the south side of the A821, by the western end of Loch Venachar and just east of Brig o' Turk. There is an informative notice board: 'Welcome to the Great Trossachs Forest and Path.'

Head east by pavement for a short distance, then carefully cross to the north side of the road and the start of a path, signposted with two arrowheads, blue and brown. Climb the steep, wooded lower slopes of Lendrick Hill, with the lovely well-graded grassy path easing the ascent with gentle zigzags. Rest if you will at a bench

FACT FILE

Map	OS map 57, Stirling & The Trossachs
Distance	6½ miles
Height	200m
Terrain	superb path, then tarmac old railway track bed
Start point	Little Druim Wood car park, by the A821, just east of Brig o' Turk
Time	3 hours
Nearest town	Callander
Refreshment spot	The Harbour Café, north shore, Loch Venachar

provided by Royal Mail employees in the woodland, part of the Royal Mail grove of trees.

The path eventually slants right, eastwards, to reach a T-junction and a new broad gravel path, the Trossachs Trail, indicated with a 'T' sign. The bulk of the climb is over. The two arrows point left, uphill; however, time for a change in direction – eastwards. The path rises slightly higher on its undulating and twisting way well above the loch and the periodic trail signs are scarcely needed. Ignore a path that descends to the right and continue east.

There are some metal gates, with horse-rider/mountain-biker-friendly latches. The Great Trossachs Path is also designed for mountain bikers and, interestingly, the sole person we met was a cheerful mountain biker, Chris Ryan, who preferred the path to the busy A821.

Now for the gentle descent. Pass by water treatment works on the right and briefly follow the broader track used for works access. The track crosses Milton Glen Burn by a wide planked bridge then cuts down right to

Chris Ryan on the Trossachs Way

the road. However, continue on the signed path, though taking care at a junction to keep going eastwards.

Reach a triple wooden signpost: back the way, Brig o' Turk; to the right, Invertrossachs; to the left, Callander and Samson's Stone. A few yards later there is a sign to the Stone. Clearly seen from the path, this is an erratic deposited on Bochastle Hill by a retreating glacier in the last Ice Age. Descend to the Woodland Trust Bochastle car park.

Cross the A821 with care and turn left to reach a parking area and a triple blue sign: Brig o' Turk 6 miles; Route 7 of the National Cycle Network to Strathyre; and Route 7 to Callander 1.25 miles. Turn left on the tarmac track bed of the old Caledonian (Callander to Oban) railway line. The line was due to be closed in November 1965 as part of the Beeching cuts, but a rock fall in Glen Ogle in September accelerated that decision. The track bed on an embankment curves round the flood plain

High above Loch Venachar

of the River Leny then crosses the river by a metal footbridge that has replaced the old railway bridge, and so to the Meadows car park in Callander.

Fife

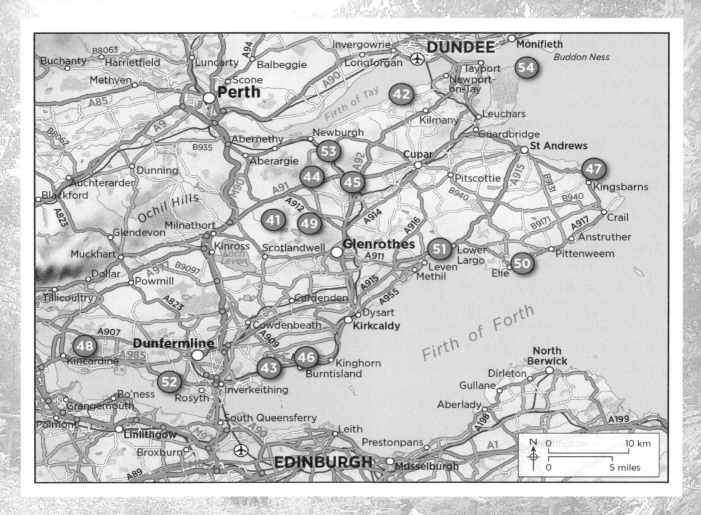

41 - West Lomond and the Bunnet Stane

The Lomond Hills have two clearly identifiable landmarks, the twin volcanic peaks of East and West Lomond, the latter, at 522m/1713ft, being Fife's highest point. On a cold grey February day of considerable wind chill, Jimbo, John, Alan and I, all clad as if bound for the high tops, had a short Lomond outing – a new-for-me approach to West Lomond, passing the Bunnet Stane, then a return by Glen Vale. It was an interesting drive to the mapped car park by the minor road at the foot of Glen Vale, map ref 172069. With pot holes gouged by heavy rain and floods, the road was more like a rough farm track. However, council workers were undertaking the necessary ditch improvements, preparatory to attending to the road surface.

Walk north-east along the road for one mile to reach the start of the mapped path, map ref 185082 (and another car park, smaller and not mapped), just before Nether Urquhart Farm. The path heads south-east as if direct to the summit. On gaining height to some 200m, the way smacks of an old narrow road between low

FACT FILE	
Map	OS map 58, Perth & Alloa
Distance	5 miles
Height	400m
Terrain	minor road, paths and grassy slopes
Start point	mapped car park by minor road at foot of Glen Vale, map ref 172069
Time	3 to 4 hours
Nearest town	Kinross
Refreshment spot	RSPB Vane Farm cafeteria

dykes. Straight ahead is an intermittent rocky horizontal line – strange outcrops of calciferous sandstone that have resisted erosion.

On top of the largest outcrop, and looking like a mighty mushroom, is the unmapped Bunnet Stane (bonnet stone), measuring 20ft by 10ft and nearly a metre thick. Climbing to the base of the bonnet is easy enough but none of us were tempted to climb any further. Tucked away to one side behind a metal cage is a small man-made chamber, the Maiden Bower, around which has been cast a story of a tragic Romeo and Juliet style romance. The less romantic truth is that the bower may have been some sort of bothy built by a landowner, probably in the early 1800s.

The path of old climbs and slants to the left to meet a grassy track which heads right over the summit cone and so to the remains of an Iron Age fort, the trig point and its eroded base.

A quick descent and tussocky traverse leads towards Glen Vale, the gap between West Lomond and Bishop Hill, also known as Covenanters Glen. We bypassed the Devil's Burdens, heading for the rocky bluff which overlooks the glen. A careful descent, easier to the east

John Knox's pulpit

A big bunnet

at first, leads to the Glen Burn. Cross the burn and climb to the higher track on the south bank from where the rocky bluff is best viewed. The crag, or rather a cleft in the rocks, is the 'pulpit' from which preached John Knox, and the point at the top end of the secluded glen where local people, who believed in the Reformation, would congregate secretly. However, for safety reasons, the rocks which formed the pulpit were removed in 2004.

Follow the track west a short distance, then slant down as signposted, cross the burn and rejoin the north bank path. Lower down, the glen gradually widens. The path continues through a planted area, re-crosses the burn by a wooden footbridge and continues through a wooded strip. Turn right on reaching the road to return to the car park.

After refreshment at the RSPB Vane Farm cafeteria, my outing came to a premature stop. Car trouble! Following conversation with the driver of the breakdown vehicle on the way to the garage, I now know more about

crankshafts, power steering and alternators. I then got a bus. Alas, it too broke down, leaving me with another two miles to walk. It had been an interesting day and four hours longer than expected to return home!

The Bunnet Stane

42 - Wormit to Balmerino Abbey

FACT FILE

Map	OS map 59, St Andrews
Distance	5 miles
Height	100m at most
Terrain	mostly path
Start point	parking area, end of Bay Road, Wormit, map ref 391259
Time	3 hours
Nearest town	Wormit
Refreshment spot	The View Restaurant, Naughton Road, Wormit

The Tay Bridge

It was not the best of starts when Margaret queried why I was up at 7.00am. I had forgotten to adjust the alarm clock following the end of British Summer Time! No matter, for I managed an hour of desk work before heading off to meet Jimbo and Joe at Wormit for a walk on part of the Northern Extension of the waymarked Fife Coastal Path (FCP) to Balmerino Abbey. Surprisingly, this was a new route for all of us on what turned out to be one of the most attractive sections of the FCP. (The extension west to Newburgh is most definitely not a coastal path.)

From the western end of Wormit, turn down Bay Road, going under the large, high brick archway of the rail bridge to reach a parking area by the edge of Wormit Bay. Here there are lovely views of the Tay railway bridge and across the wide Firth to Dundee.

A public Right of Way path goes by the coast, signposted Balmerino 2 miles. Odd, then, that another Right of Way sign further west says 'Path to Balmerino and the Abbey 2½ miles.' Confusing! I reckon the second sign is more accurate. The following walk assumes a return to Wormit from Balmerino, a distance of five miles, for which two hours would suffice were it not for stoppage time at the Abbey.

(At the time of writing, the car park Right of Way sign was slightly twisted, possibly giving the impression that the way is by a narrow path heading south-west to Peacehill. It is not!)

The first part of the walk stays close to the bay and the mud flats, valuable feeding grounds for waders such as curlews. The path then gently climbs away from the coast line, undulating through a mixture of trees and gorse. There are plenty of FCP brown posts with coloured discs and white arrows, arguably more than are necessary, indicating the way. A lovely grassy track above the shore then goes through a wooded area, a mixture of old oak, sycamore and beech.

Then reach a large grassy area with a sign indicating that the path runs between white houses and the shore – a delightful approach to the charming village of Balmerino, designated a Conservation Area in 1987. Traverse a cobbled area then follow the shore-side track to the village, looking out for Samson's Stone on the way. The 'poet' McGonagall refers to Balmerino as "Beautiful Balmermo on the bonnie banks of Tay" – and indeed it is.

Pass by the Old Mill and stream to climb away from the shore by a gravel track. Ignore a path to the right which one might imagine to be the obvious way (most surprisingly the FCP does not continue by the edge of the Firth past Birkhill House, but instead cuts inland) and continue uphill. Pass a community notice board to reach Balmerino Abbey.

Founded in 1229, it was overthrown in 1599 by protestant reformers and the community dispersed. Because of conversion into a private residence in about 1600, parts of the abbey still survive today. It is now under the care of the National Trust for Scotland.

The abbey became a home for James Elphinstone, the first Lord Balmerino, a title that lasted until 1746 when the 6th Lord was executed for his part in the Jacobite uprising. Before heading back to Wormit, look out for the old Spanish chestnut, core borings of which in 1988 indicated that it was between 400 and 435 years old.

Balmerino Abbey

43 - An Aberdour Circuit

Sharing a simple harbour, Aberdour (from Obar Dobhair, mouth of the water) originally consisted of two villages, Wester and Easter Aberdour, separated by the Dour Burn. The village developed as a seaside resort in the 19th century; a development enhanced from 1890 with the building of the railway line east from the newly-opened Forth Bridge, offering a convenient half-hourly train service to Edinburgh.

I too arrived by train, to be met by the waiting Jimbo. Aberdour is crossed by the Fife Coastal Path, but we were bound for an eight-mile hinterland circular walk, more demanding than might be expected because of an overall climb of 300m, some of it over roughish terrain. Fife Core Paths map 58 may be more useful than Ordnance Survey map 66.

From Aberdour railway station car park, follow a tarmac pathway between the railway and the semi-ruined Aberdour Castle, of which the oldest part constitutes one of the earliest stone castles in mainland Scotland.

Reach a road, turn left over the railway, then right on Main Street, the A921, which is followed to the east end of the village. The A921, with a pavement on the right, heads up Mains Brae. When the road curves right, cross

FACT FILE	
Map	OS map 66, Edinburgh
Distance	8 miles
Height	300m
Terrain	tracks, paths and minor roads
Start point	Aberdour railway station car park, map ref 191854
Time	4 hours
Nearest village	Aberdour
Refreshment spot	McTaggart's café deli, 21 High Street, Aberdour

Cullaloe Temple

most carefully (note the Fife Core Path purple sign), then immediately right (signposted Dunearn).

A gently rising path through a charming wooded strip (known locally as Kamal's Cut) leads to Long Gates cottage. Now into open country, showing to the right is the top of the Craigkelly mast and the Binn, the 193m/632ft volcanic plug that overlooks Burntisland. A farm track heads directly to the A909, by now at a height of 170m. Fife Core Paths map 58 indicates a diversion to avoid the road descent towards Stenhouse Reservoir. This diversion had yet to be developed on our day, so we descended on the oft-busy road.

Turn right towards the 35-acre Stenhouse Reservoir, a trout fishery centre, but for 90 years part of the Fife water supply until decommissioned in the 1990s. Leaving the loch behind, take the higher lane, later a grassy track between fields, to reach Balmule Farm. Cross the B9157 to a minor road, Puddledub ¼ mile, then turn left on the signposted historic Old North Road.

The next mile, curving westwards to reach the A909, may take longer than expected. Pass through a rougher section to enter a wood where the path is not overly obvious. There are a couple of green ScotWays signs; at the time of writing, there were also some white plastic strips periodically tied to trees – a novel approach! The Old Road eventually becomes a broad grassy way, finally with a sharp turn to the left and so to a stile by the A909.

Enter the Forestry Commission Cullaloe mixed woodland. The forestry track steadily rises to the Cullaloe Hills, with views of the route so far walked. Pass a listed building – the distinctive Cullaloe Temple, a 19th

The 19th century Goat Quarry, re-opened in 2004

century octagonal folly constructed from locally-quarried sandstone. The track curves to the left and descends past danger signs surrounding the 19th century Goat Quarry, closed for over 50 years then re-opened in 2004. Its pale-buff sandstone is an exact match for Craigleith stone, from which much of Edinburgh was built, hence solving the problem of restoring the city's crumbling sandstone buildings. The path/track follows the perimeter of the fenced-off massive quarry, which is more than 1km long with high, hewn rock faces surrounding the flooded centre.

It is then an easy descent to a minor road, then left past Old Whitehill cottage and the remains of a dovecot, to reach the crossroads with the B9157. As this is a well-known vehicle accident site, cross with extreme care. A pavement, later by the Dour Burn, leads back to Aberdour.

44 - Auchtermuchty to Weddersbie Hill

The record for the hottest ever March day in Scotland was broken in 2012; the residents of Aboyne sunbathed in an unprecedented 23.6C. That day, though, was quickly followed by a return to winter. An Arctic blast brought a 21-degree drop in temperature and more than six inches of snow in places. With plans to head to the north-west put on hold, I met up with Jimbo and Arthur to explore a route taking in Auchtermuchty Common and Weddersbie Hill – ideal for winter or inclement weather. The walk requires two OS maps (58 and 59) and a self-printed map is recommended.

King James V granted the Common Lands to the Burgh of Auchtermuchty in 1517. Certain of the town's householders, the 'Small Heritors', still have the right to graze animals, fly falcons and cut turf. Most of the local Royal Burghs have now lost their common lands, making this one a very precious wildlife refuge and an irreplaceable leisure resource for the town. The Common was formally granted to the people of Auchtermuchty in the 1970s by the Town Council before it was disbanded. The Macduff (Auchtermuchty) Trust owns and manages the Common, to conserve, preserve and protect its

FACT FILE

Maps	OS maps 58, Perth & Alloa, and 59, St Andrews
Distance	8 miles
Height	200m
Terrain	Right of Way, minor road and forest tracks
Start point	Auchtermuchty
Time	4 to 5 hours
Nearest town	Auchtermuchty
Refreshment spot	The Tannochbrae Tearoom, High Street, Auchtermuchty

A wintry walk

wildlife, flora and fauna for the benefit of all. To help save this tiny but important fragment of ancient meadow for future generations to enjoy, why not become a Friend of the Common? Contact the Trust Secretary, c/o Auchtermuchty Community Centre, 1 Distillery Street, Auchtermuchty, Fife KY14 7BY.

From Burnside, turn right by the Cycle Tavern into Bondgate and so to Broombrae Farm. Follow the track slanting left, an attractive old Right of Way which might once have been part of a coach road from Falkland to Scone. Pass on the right two of the three areas comprising the Common – The Whitefield and The Mairs – but I would suggest first continuing to the small, not too well signposted, car park off the B936. Read the notice board and then retrace your steps for a pleasant wander round the fenced-off but well-gated area.

Return to the B936, head north, then east on the minor road, passing Lumquhat Farm to reach a wooded strip, map ref 247134. (The mapped path from the Common to the farm scarcely exists nowadays.) A path winds through the strip, on our day with yellow gorse and snow. Cross a fence, then descend gently to the edge of Weddersbie Hill, a Forestry Commission managed woodland. Pass through the old gap in the wall and follow the obvious path to reach the forestry track. With the lower slopes felled, there are good views south to the Lomonds. Follow the track, east then curving north, to reach a junction of tracks on the east side of the quaintly-named Red Myre, an overgrown reedy pond. On our day there were a colossal number of trees down, many of which blocked the tracks for some distance. This involved lengthy and time consuming detours, but the way has since been cleared.

Turn sharply right for an anti-clockwise circuit of the northern end of the forest, passing close by the site of the 196m trig point, map ref 258144. A short ascent through partially wooded slopes leads to the trig point on the small heathery dome. Although the dome is not wooded, a lower rim of trees cuts out distant views. Return to Red Myre, head west by its northern edge and so to the west end of the forest, from where a broad track descends to Lumquhat. Then retrace your steps back to Auchtermuchty.

On top of Weddesrbie Hill

45 - Birnie and Gaddon Lochs

Desperate for even a wintry short stroll, Margaret and I met all the Js – Jimbo, Joe and John – at Birnie Loch: Margaret for bird watching, the rest of us for a figure-of-eight walk round Birnie and Gaddon Lochs Nature Reserve, managed by the Fife Coast and Countryside Trust on behalf of Fife Council. On a day of thaw after yet more snow, the entrance was closed off. It was possible, however, to park in the small roadside area, albeit more like a skating rink. Most of the paths were icy, making for slow progress. Not that this was really a problem, for on a glorious day we took plenty of time to admire both views and bird life. No swimming, boating or fishing is allowed – and dogs must be kept on leads – but with ice-covered lochs there was no thought of indulging in those activities and Jimbo's dogs had been left at home.

However, going round in circles can be confusing, especially as my 1996 1:50000 Landranger map 59 showed only Birnie Loch. However, I returned at a later date with the Mountain Hare, this time armed with a 2007 1:25000 Explorer map 370, showing Gaddon Loch and its extent to the east. With Birnie on the west and Gaddon on the east, and a path in between, all confusion was resolved. Whilst the larger scale map obviously shows more detail, in truth neither map is essential.

It is a short walk, no doubt (the circuit of both lochs is 1½ miles), but include time for bird watching (though please keep to the paths so as not to disturb the wildlife).

The area of the twin lochs was used to extract sand and gravel, but quarrying below the water table meant that the workings flooded as they were dug. Each site, sold to Fife Council for £1, quickly attracted wildlife and in August 2000 Fife Council declared it a local nature reserve.

From the picnic area, go first in a clockwise direction round Birnie Loch, passing close to the now and then noisy A91. At the north-east corner of the loch, ignore the signposted path leading the few yards to Gaddon Loch and continue south on the path between the two lochs. Cross a wooden bridge over the outlet of the Birnie Loch, to return to the edge of the starting picnic area.

To the left (east) is the second of the two entrances to Gaddon Loch, now taken on an anti-clockwise circuit.

The north-east side of Gaddon Loch, where the path develops into a broader track, is close to a not too intrusive railway line. On reaching slightly higher ground, look out for the electric fence, part of the Gaddon Loch grazing project. To manage the grassland areas, a flock of sheep had been borrowed from the Scottish Wildlife Trust to increase the value of the meadow area for wild flowers and ground-nesting birds.

FACT FILE	
Map	OS map 59, St Andrews, Kirkcaldy & Glenrothes
Distance	2 miles
Height	negligible
Terrain	well-pathed
Start point	Birnie and Gaddon Lochs car park off the B937, map ref 283126
Time	1 to 2 hours
Nearest town	Auchtermuchty
Refreshment spot	Pillars of Hercules Organic Farm Shop and Café, off the A912, map ref 241083

Birnie Loch

At this vantage point, there are lovely views of the Lomond Hills to the south-west. It is also interesting to observe the more immediate water-covered low-lying area. One thousand years ago, there were many more lochs and wetland areas in the Howe of Fife. As the glaciers retreated after the last ice age, they left behind an old glacial ridge on the west bank of Birnie Loch, used by the minor road, and more importantly a patchwork of small water bodies, now mostly drained over the last few centuries. The best example is that of Rossie Loch which was emptied in the 1790s by digging to the south the Rossie Drain, traditionally known as the Drain Burn.

Complete the anti-clockwise Gaddon circuit by returning to the path between the lochs and so back to the picnic area and the numerous swans.

A slippery loch for this swan

46 - A Circular Burntisland/Kinghorn Walk

I travelled by train to Burntisland (possibly a nickname from the burning from fishermen's huts on an islet, now incorporated into the docks) for a new-to-me (and partly new for Jimbo) varied and interesting walk: over The Binn to Craigencalt and Kinghorn Loch, then a return partly following the Fife Coastal Path (FCP). Rather than following the FCP via the A921, we ended with a lovely stroll along Burntisland beach.

My thanks go to the staff at Craigencalt visitor centre who, on hearing of our hoped-for beach return, confirmed that high tide was due at 4.45pm. Look up the tide tables before you leave! I was also kindly given a booklet, *Kinghorn Pathways*, with a choice of short to longer distance trails for walkers, cyclists and horse riders (widely available elsewhere; £1 donation appreciated).

From the west end of the Links, head up Cromwell Road (yes, his forces were here in 1651). Cross East Toll roundabout, by the school, then follow the pavement of the gently rising A909, the Cowdenbeath road. On the north side, map ref 226867, is a sign (its message only shown on the distant side): 'Public Footpath to Standing Stanes Road.' The lovely path of old cuts through a wooded strip then zigzags to reach a stile. Traverse open country by a grassy path to meet another backside-first sign (map ref 226870): 'Public Path to Kinghorn by The Binn.'

Passing Binn Pond on the left, a broad grassy track steadily climbs towards the 125m high Craigkelly

FACT FILE	
Map	OS map 66, Edinburgh
Distance	7 miles
Height	200m
Terrain	pavement, path and sandy beach
Start point	Cromwell Road, Burntisland, west end of Links
Time	3 to 4 hours
Nearest towns	Burntisland and Kinghorn
Refreshment spot	Potter About, 253 High Street, Burntisland

broadcasting and telecommunication mast. Turn right as signposted and so to the craggy escarpment face leading to The Binn, a 193m/632ft volcanic plug graced with a viewfinder and a glorious viewpoint to the south.

Descend eastwards to a path crossroads. (To the left is Binnend, founded by James 'Paraffin' Young in 1878 to house those employed in shale-oil production. The last

Kinghorn Loch

inhabitant left in 1954 and little now remains.) Cross the remains of a metal barrier and continue eastwards. The enclosed spoil heap on the left is a reminder of the town's former plant for the refining of alumina, opened in 1917 but closed in 2002.

Continue by track and path to reach the B923, map ref 251872. Head east past Whinniehall landfill site, then turn left (signposted Public Path to Kinghorn Loch), onto a stony track (Bramble Lane) that descends to the charming Craigencalt Farm and Ecology Centre.

Follow the east end of Kinghorn Loch, cross the outflow by metal footbridge and so back to the B923. Cross the road for the signposted Burnside Path. The sign rather suggests cutting through wasteland. Not so! Go as far as the edge of the fields from where the excellent path leads to the outskirts of Kinghorn.

Cut up to the right and follow the perimeter of the golf course, then descend left by the edge of the school to reach the A921, then followed westwards. Later, pass the entrance to Kinghorn Golf Club; on the left, the FCP comes in from Pettycur. The FCP continues by pavement all the way to Burntisland, passing a roadside cross commemorating Alexander III who fell to his death from the cliff top in March 1286.

However, on reaching Pettycur Bay Holiday Park, we turned left, crossed the railway line by road bridge and followed a narrow path by the Park's perimeter to reach the beach. Head west, at first by a bouldery area beneath the rocky headland, then along the glorious sandy beach of Blue Flag status. Due to the tide, we used the tunnel under the railway at the east end of Burntisland, and then walked by pavement back to the Links.

47 - Cambo Sands to St Andrews

FACT FILE	
Map	OS map 59, St Andrews, Kirkcaldy & Glenrothes
Distance	8 miles
Height	200m
Terrain	coastal path and minor road
Start point	Cambo Sands car park, map ref 602125
Time	4 hours
Nearest town	St Andrews
Refreshment spot	Con Panna Coffee Shop, 203 South Street, St Andrews

The waymarked Fife Coastal Path (FCP) extends from Kincardine in the south to Newburgh in the north. Crossing at times rough coastal terrain, arguably the most remote section is from Cambo Sands to St Andrews. Indeed after only ½ mile on the way there is a sign, St Andrews 7½ miles, with such a cautionary warning.

Having pre-placed a car in St Andrews, Jimbo and I drove back to Kingsbarns, from where a narrow lane, Back Stile, leads to the car park at the golden Cambo Sands. (The hourly St Andrews/Crail Stagecoach 95 bus service passes by Kingsbarns: phone Traveline 0871-200-2233.) The village name derives from the barns used for storing royal household grain when the King was in residence at either Crail Castle or Falkland Palace.

A narrow path goes between fenced-off fields and the rocky shoreline, but later descend to the water's edge at Airbow Point and a significant beach. Later, sandy strips are few and far between. Pass by the rocky promontory,

A wooded gorge

Follow the grassy track, then fork right to approach the south side of the Kenly Water. On our day, the muddy fast flow crossing was not appealing. No matter, for the FCP takes a long loop upstream before crossing. The track leads to buildings (please keep dogs on lead); descend by the stepped path to the river's edge. The path, in what is now a wooded gorge, gives a delightful stroll to a metal footbridge, crossed to reach Burnside Farm on the north bank. A track, then a minor tarmac road, leads towards Boarhills; however, turn right as signposted on a track (by now, quite a distance from the sea). Reach a farm track, turn left briefly, then right on another track by a doocot – confusing perhaps, but all as signposted. After 100 yards, turn right on a narrow grassy path between fields and so back to the coastline.

Babbet Ness, to reach a sandy inlet with a high wall to prevent erosion from the sea. On the far side is a ruined house (danger, keep out), from where an old slipway runs down to the sea.

Soon pass Buddo Rock, a prominent sandstone stack, once part of the cliffs behind. Its natural arch gives it a distinctive appearance. Later, the path goes by a drystane

Buddo Rock

dyke with a golf course beyond. The next two miles may take longer than imagined from a quick glance at the map. A high escarpment overlooks the rocky coastline and the FCP alternates between the two features resulting in many a climb and descent, albeit by good stepped paths. Reach a burn by the beach which is easily crossed; nevertheless, there is a small footbridge just yards upstream.

Later, a high wooden footbridge crosses a ravine; descend to the water's edge and a notice: 'Caution, at high tide wait for tide to recede.' We had no watery problem but there was one mini scramble over the rocks to help the two Springer spaniels. Beyond this scrambly area is another warning sign: 'This area is winter grazing for cattle and may be uneven and muddy.'

St Andrews is now tantalisingly close but it may be slow progress on a wet day through the churned-up area. Just beyond the muddy area is the Rock and Spindle, a tall stack, the remains of a volcanic vent and with a structure at its base which closely resembles a spinning

Where is Jimbo?

wheel. The final climb high above the water give views overlooking St Andrews; then a gentle descent by a large camping and caravan area leads to the very popular East Sands. It is then a pleasant stroll into the centre of the ancient university town.

48 -Devilla Forest

Devilla Forest, north-east of Kincardine, is an open coniferous habitat. Its lochs, burns, meadowland and broad-leaved areas support rich and varied wildlife.

Since retiring, local historians Bob and Meg Smith have extensively researched the area's varied history, from ancient sites and battles to the development of coal mining, and have prepared a detailed informative map, smaller laminated copies of which are attached to trees at key points in the forest. With a plethora of paths, cycleways and tracks, it is prudent to have OS map 65 to hand but also take time en route to study Bob's maps.

Bob has also produced two amateur DVDs and a book about the area, copies of which he kindly forwarded to me.

OS maps of the 1930s show Tulliallan and not Devilla as the name of the forest. The Forestry Commission (FC) bought Tulliallan Estate after the 2nd World War. On the estate was a farm called Devilla (meaning bad farm, referring to poor agricultural land); cue change of name. Produced by the FC and Bob, leaflets containing a small map and other information are available from a box in the car park on the north side of the A985, map ref 964871.

Keir Loch, a large reedy pond

Go along the broad track for a few yards to a green sign on the left: 'Red Squirrel Walk to Bordie Loch.' A path, under two miles long and suitable for children and push chairs, goes around the loch, taking in the Standard Stone (marking the 1038 Battle of Bordie between King Duncan and Macbeth and the opposing Danes) and the Pulpit Stone where Covenanters held their Conventicles. Return to the track, then, at the first junction, turn left.

FACT FILE

Map	OS map 65, Falkirk & Linlithgow
Distance	6 miles
Height	negligible
Terrain	track and path
Start point	car park, north side of A985, map ref 964871
Time	2 to 3 hours
Nearest town	Kincardine
Refreshment spot	The Biscuit Café, Culross

The outflow of Moor Loch

Continue in a straight line west for two miles (crossing a junction en route; north goes to Keir) to reach a broad north/south clearing carrying a double line of electricity pylons.

Turn north by the pylons, then left at the next four-way junction (the mapped path continuing north was overgrown at the time of writing). At the next junction, leave the track for a rhododendron-lined pathway on the right to reach the southern tip of Moor Loch and a white house, formerly the estate boathouse. A curling pond by the south-east end of the loch once provided excellent sport.

Curving right all the while, a clockwise half-perimeter route goes round the loch. Look out for a short path that gives a charming detour through the trees to the water's edge and the cobbled outflow of the loch. Of the four Devilla lochs (Bordie, Keir, Moor and Peppermill Dam), this is the best stretch of water for wildlife.

Continue to the loch's northern side, then follow the mapped old path north-east through the pylon-cleared rhododendron area to join a narrow track. Turn left on this to skirt the western end of the forest by Windyhill Farm. Then curve east to reach Peppermill Dam, a one-mile loch created as the water supply, via the Pep Burn, for the local paper mill, now closed. A side track leads to the water's edge and what is left of an old boat house – a delightful spot, the water level on our visit very high after days of rain. It is then a lovely walk on a good track by the forest edge. Ignore a side track from the right. The track gradually edges away from the water to reach a five-track junction, from where either of two tracks go south.

Head east, passing a rectangular area, once a tree nursery, now an overgrown thicket. At its east end, a path leads to Keir Loch, a large reedy pond. Return to the track, head east, then south for the car park.

Moor Loch

49 - East Lomond

FACT FILE	
Map	OS map 59, St Andrews, Kirkcaldy & Glenrothes
Distance	5½ miles
Height	275m
Terrain	good path to summit
Start point	Pitcairn Centre car park, north Glenrothes
Time	2½ to 3 hours
Nearest town	Glenrothes
Refreshment spot	Balgeddie House Hotel, Balgeddie Way, Glenrothes

Footbridge over the Conland Burn

The readily accessible Lomond Hills Regional Park dominates the centre of Fife. Seen from miles around, on the northern flanks lie two very clearly identifiable landmarks also known as the Paps of Fife: the twin volcanic peaks of 434m/1424ft East Lomond, also known as Falkland Hill, and 522m/1713ft West Lomond, the highest point in Fife. By contrast, the south-eastern flanks are gentler, falling away to rolling moorland terrain and a number of reservoirs close to Glenrothes. The Lomond Hills share the same name and meaning (beacon hill, from the Gaelic laomainn) as the admittedly much higher 974m/3192ft Ben Lomond.

I have climbed East and West Lomond with Jimbo many a time: from Falkland, a short but brutal approach, and from the west by a number of routes. However this time, surprisingly after all these years, it was a new route for me, and just to East Lomond: a longer albeit more gradual well-pathed approach from Pitcairn Centre car park by the northern suburbs of Glenrothes. For the locally-based Jimbo, this approach had been trodden hundreds of times, usually with his two Springer Spaniels.

Taking just two-and-a-half to three hours of gentle exercise, this approach is ideal for the winter festive season. Ordnance Survey map 59, St Andrews, Kirkcaldy & Glenrothes, covers the area. However, a more detailed map of all the paths in the Lomond Hills Regional Park can be found in a leaflet, *Accessing the Lomonds*, published by the Fife Coast & Countryside Trust. Of the four mapped car parks by the edge of a wooded area at the northern end of Glenrothes, the Pitcairn Centre car park, off Pitcairn Avenue, gives the most direct route to East Lomond. A signboard clearly shows the way and the path is waymarked at critical points with circular blue, yellow and green signs with white arrows.

Ignoring a path that slants to the right by the back of houses, head north and pass through a lovely wooded strip to Formonthills Community Woodland. A slight descent leads to a stepped dip and a footbridge over the Conland Burn, after which the path gently rises by the wood on the left and a fence on the right, beyond which are open fields. There were cattle there on our day so Jimbo was obliged to put the Spaniels on the lead.

It is then into more open country, by now with the easily identified summit cone of East Lomond in sight. The path swings left then right to enter a new plantation. Once clear of the trees, the path, which follows the line of an old stone dyke, steadily rises through open heathery moorland, heading for the less than attractive communication masts on Purin Hill and the East Lomond car park (where I collected the leaflet, *Accessing the Lomonds*). The car park (with toilets) is approachable by tarmac road from the east but surely that is too easy, even on a wintry day, for serious walkers.

Then follow the worn boot path on the steep grassy summit cone. The actual height of East Lomond is usually taken to be 424m as shown on the Ordnance Survey map, but this presumably refers to the trig point which is situated a short distance away to the south-east below the summit. The leaflet gives the hill a height of 434m. No matter, for both summit, with its informative plaque, and trig point are superb viewpoints. By the summit are the remains of an Iron Age fort.

On a good day there is no reason why the walk should not be extended to West Lomond.

On return it is easier to admire the southern aspect over the Forth and beyond, perhaps studying the viewfinder at the East Lomond car park.

On the way to east Lomond

50 - Elie to St Monans and back

FACT FILE	
Map	OS map 59, St Andrews, Kirkcaldy & Glenrothes
Distance	5 miles
Height	negligible
Terrain	mixture of coastal path, railway track bed and beach
Start point	car park, east side of Elie
Time	3 hours
Nearest towns	Elie and St Monans
Refreshment spot	The Pavilion Café, Golf Club Lane, Earlsferry

At a wedding reception at Kilconquhar Castle, just north of Elie, I got talking to a staff member about the outdoors. She was astonished to know that I had never walked on the nearby section of the Fife Coastal Path (FCP) and, in particular, by St Monans. The prettiest village in Scotland she opined – then admitted to being a local.

During the coldest March for 50 years, with high pressure north of Scotland, and Siberian winds from the east, mountain weather forecasts were regularly indicating temperatures of -5C at 3000ft, even before adding significant wind chill. Nevertheless, the short stretch of the FCP from Elie to St Monans and back gave Jimbo and me a short bracing outing to clear the cobwebs. With a stormy sea, surging waves and a bitterly cold wind, it was a brisk walk; the gently undulating route was made more varied by returning on parts of an old railway line and with a short stretch on the seaside sands. A well signposted route, it would be impossible to get lost.

Start from the east side of Elie, mapped as East Links, using the car park by Ruby Bay, so called after the garnet or red gemstones sometimes washed up there. Elie grew up around the natural haven of the bay, then protected

Newark Castle

St Monans

by an island with a causeway, and by the 19th century the town had developed as a seaside resort.

A short detour to Elie Ness leads to Lady's Tower, 'built' by Lady Janet Anstruther as her summerhouse and changing room for use when she went sea-bathing. We were not tempted. There is also a lighthouse.

The well-worn FCP follows the slightly undulating ground above the beach. Also parallel to the coastline is an old railway track bed. The line was extended east in 1857 to Kilconquhar, then further extended in 1863 past St Monans to Anstruther. The line was closed in 1966. One mile beyond Elie is an impressive arch of the railway and a signposted circular route. However, we continued by the shore.

Continue to the fragmentary ruins of Ardross Castle. Much of what is left today dates back to the 1400s or 1500s. Later it is likely that much of the stone was recycled into nearby buildings in what is now the hamlet of Ardross. Further on are the more impressive and substantial ruins of Newark Castle. Alexander III (1241-

1286) spent some of his childhood there.

Approach St Monans by a concrete path at the water's edge (the tide was far enough out at this point; otherwise take a higher path). Then cross the Inverie Burn. A stepped concrete path leads to Braehead and so to the harbour. Take time to wander round St Monans. Now that I have been there, I am inclined to agree it is surely a contender for the prettiest village in Scotland.

For a change on the way back, we headed inland on the high tide alternative path by the Inverie Burn to reach a bridge, all that is left at this stage of the railway. Turn left as signposted by the field edge then left again by a lane to Newark Castle.

We then stayed above the coastal path, following the old track bed for some distance before crossing the FCP and continuing to the beach for a lovely sandy walk. The Springer spaniels frolicked in the sea. They don't mind cold water!

51 - Letham Glen to Lundin Links and back

Amid a period of stormy wintry weather, it was prudent to have a change of tack – in this case, a short walk from Letham Glen to Lundin Links and back. The area covered had been a boyhood stamping ground for Jimbo and, during the walk, Joe and I were entertained by his nostalgic memories.

Accessed from the roundabout on the A915 at the northern end of Leven, map ref 382017, the attractive wooded glen was donated to the people of Scoonie and Leven in 1925 by the then land owner, Mr Letham. The old glen footpath, originally part of a drove road, was also used by monks to collect fish from the harbour. The glen once had an ochre mine (the yellow pigment used as paint). The area is also mapped as Sillerhole – 'siller' perhaps meaning 'silver'?

To reach the hidden-at-first car park, drive under the archway then over a narrow bridge that spans the Scoonie Burn. A tarmac (at first) drive is on the west side of the burn; later, stone bridges give access to a path on the other side if so wished. All ways, however, meet at the top of the glen, by then a small ravine. A slanting path leads south-west to a mapped track. Head north towards a farm and follow the track, curving left round farm buildings. There are a couple of confusing public footpath signs.

Turn right at a junction and cross the burn to reach the B927, known locally as Dangerfield Road. Go past Blacketyside House on the left and continue in a straight line on a track. There are good views of Largo Law.

FACT FILE	
Map	OS map 59, St Andrews, Kirkcaldy & Glenrothes
Distance	5 miles
Height	negligible
Terrain	mixture of tracks, paths and minor roads
Start point	Letham Glen car park, map ref 382017
Time	2 to 3 hours
Nearest towns	Leven and Lundin Links
Refreshment spot	Blacketyside Farm Shop and Tea Room (closed Sundays)

Pass by an extensive growing area for strawberries and raspberries. Follow the track as it turns SSE then ENE to reach Lundin Wood. Ignoring the perimeter track, enter the wood. Look out for the sharp turning to the north where the broad grassy track (wet, I suspect, on many a day) crosses between two small ponds. The rhododendron-fringed track clears the wood and leads to Lundin Tower, once the seat of the Lundin (or Lundy/Lundie) family. The main mansion was demolished in 1876. The tower now has an attached private residence.

Pass the tower on the southern side, though this involves a short detour by the edge of the field, to join a track. Turn right on Kilmuir Road and so to the outskirts of Lundin Links. Cross the A915 with care, go down Links Road and straight over to the site of the former Lundin Links railway station. The line, extended in 1857 from Leven to Lundin Links and beyond, was closed in 1966. By now on the Fife Coastal Path (FCP), briefly follow the line, then turn left following the FCP signs. Take heed of the warning notice when crossing the golf course and so reach the coast.

The Scoonie Burn

A paddle in the Scoonie Burn

The tide was out so we had a lovely sandy walk round Largo Bay, with the dogs frolicking in the water. Leave the beach at the small Silver Burn, map ref 398019, cross the high tide alternative FCP path and the line of wartime defence concrete blocks. Follow the burn by the Mile Dyke that marks the boundary between two golf courses.

Enter Silverburn Park, turn left and pass by cottages (not uphill) to reach a stonework-fringed path that winds by the edge of the golf course. On the right is a bing, a reminder of the mine once here. Pass by Scoonie Golf Club car park and cross the Scoonie Burn. Immediately turn right on the west bank path which is followed all the way to the pedestrian crossing on the A915.

The dogs enjoy a day at the beach at Largo Bay

52 - Limekilns

FACT FILE	
Map	OS map 65, Falkirk, Linlithgow & Dunfermline
Distance	5 miles
Height	negligible
Terrain	path, minor road and estate track
Start point	car park by old pier, Limekilns, map ref 075834
Time	2 to 3 hours
Nearest town	Dunfermline
Refreshment spot	Limekilns Hotel & Bistro

Ideal for winter (a wet, raw day for Jimbo and me), this five-mile walk of no hills has many features of historic interest. The old settlement of Limekilns lies west of Rosyth and east of Broomhall, the latter home to Lord Elgin, whose ancestor – saviour or vandal – is forever associated with the Parthenon Marbles. The village can trace its history back to the 14th century when it served as the main port for Dunfermline and was the northern terminus for a ferry linking it to Bo'ness across the Forth. The oldest building, the Kings' Cellar, dates back to 1362. The main industries were the exportation of lime, coal and wool, with the natural harbour providing docking for small and medium sized vessels of the time. From 1750, the limekilns industry moved to nearby Charlestown where it continued to operate until 1956.

Head east from the car park by the old pier, map ref 075834. The shore-side walk initially follows the Fife Coastal Path and National Cycle Route 76. Pass by Capernaum Pier and the Forth Cruising Club. Beyond a Scout Hall and by now on a narrower path, pass a metal gate with a sign: 'Please do not walk on the gabions' (stone-filled cages built to prevent further damage to the sea wall).

Then look out on the left for a green sign, Windylaw Heritage Path, used for many centuries as a Coffin Road, where people carried their dead, possibly from as far away as Dunfermline, to Rosyth Church, the remains of which lie further east. For those carrying the heavy coffins, it was downhill to the coast and a return uphill, fortunately by then empty-handed. Head inland on a tarmac then narrower path, a muddy strip on our day, and into open fields with another green sign, Pattiesmuir. At this stage, climbing gently, look back to the right to Rosyth Dockyards. A fence with a stile leads into a wooded strip (with a few trees marked with a white arrow). Curve east to clear the trees to meet a tarmac path. Turn left to reach the A985 – cross with care.

Continue to Douglas Bank Cemetery and slant left (signposted Leckerstone and Grange Road). The good mapped path climbs by the edge of a wood and over Bellknowes. Leave the short section of rutted grassy track as signposted and reach a broad farm track. Turn left for the B9156 (do not turn right for Leckerstone) and

Rosyth Dockyards on a misty day

use the narrow pavement on the left-hand side to reach the junction with the very busy trunk road, the A985. Walk a bit further left before crossing, *with extreme care*, to the lodge and entrance to the beautiful parkland of Broomhall Estate. Dogs are to be kept on leads at all times here. The tarmac driveway quickly leads past Gellet Cottage to a sign: 'Broomhall Privacy Zone.' Please use the alternative route and follow the arrows directing walkers through a gate into grassland to avoid the curtilage of the impressive mansion.

Follow the arrows to a path, then a smaller tarmac drive which, curving through a wooded area, runs on the escarpment overlooking the Forth. Pass the Queen's Hall (built to celebrate the 50th jubilee of Queen Victoria's reign in 1887, and now Charlestown's village hall) to exit Broomhall Estate by metal gates. Turn left and continue by steps to the coastal road and a signpost, Limekilns ½ mile. Head east on the pavement, cross over to the esplanade and so back to the old pier.

Patiently waiting by Douglas Bank Cemetery

53 - Around Lindores Loch

This was a completely new walk for Jimbo and me – a wide circuit of Lindores Loch, following Fife Core Paths 211 and 206 that Jimbo had downloaded. Sandwiched between the Perth-Ladybank railway line and the B937, the tranquil shallow loch is a Site of Special Scientific Interest. From the Middle Ages up to the 20th century, the loch was an important source of water for powering mills in the Lindores valley. The walk starts and finishes in Collessie, the beautiful conservation hamlet in

North East Fife. There is a car park, map ref 287134, by Collessie Victory Hall, a facility upgraded in 2001.

Walk downhill, turn right by the green signpost (Public Path to Grange of Lindores via Collessie Den, 3 miles) and continue by a play area with the Den Burn on the left. Pass on the right Station House. The station was closed in 1955. A narrow grassy path steadily climbs to overlook both railway and burn and there are good views south to the Lomonds.

At a junction just beyond the first house, slant left, signposted Path to Grange of Lindores (to the right leads to Woodmill Mains, part of the return route). The path, in fact a narrow tarmac road, descends by a high gorse hedge on the right to reach a stone-arched bridge over the railway line and so to the B937. Continue north a short distance (but be aware of traffic), then turn left on the minor road, signposted to Goldenloch Fishery, a private loch for fly-fishing enthusiasts. The road rises by the Black Burn to reach the Black Loch situated beneath Weddersbie Hill.

Ignore the sign to the left (Footpath to Red Myre), pass by Golden Loch and continue to Berryhill Farm, overlooked by Golden Hill. After a slight ascent, pass Berryhill House to reach a sign on the right to Abdie Old Kirk. The path follows the line of telegraph poles, a narrow strip between fields, and for the first time Lindores Loch comes into view. Pass Abdie House, then the churchyard and the remains of the old kirk. At the entrance, within a small building, are three carved stones of Pictish origin, one of which had at some period been converted into a sundial with Roman numerals.

Continue by lane to Abdie and Dunbog Parish Church, built in 1827 to replace the old kirk, turn right and cross the railway line. Turn right on the A913, lacking a pavement until reaching the hamlet of Lindores. Turn right on the B937 for some 100 yards (no pavement again), then left as signposted on a path. Overlooking road and loch, this gives a wooded stroll to join the track from Inchrye and return to the B937. Just before the pier area at the east end of the loch, turn left up the farm track.

FACT FILE	
Map	OS map 59, St Andrews, Kirkcaldy & Glenrothes
Distance	7½ miles
Height	200m
Terrain	paths, minor road and grassy slopes
Start point	Collessie Victory Hall car park, map ref 287134
Time	3 to 4 hours
Nearest town	Auchtermuchty
Refreshment spot	Pillars of Hercules Organic Farm Shop and Café, off the A912 by Falkland, map ref 241083

Continue to a sign on the right from where a lovely path climbs through a plantation.

Once clear of the trees, and crossing a stile, continue in a straight line as indicated by a ScotWays sign. On reaching the edge of the higher plantation, map ref 277159, turn southwards with an easy grassy descent high above Cairneyhall to reach the track, map ref 274153, that comes in from the B937, opposite Woodmill Mains.

Follow the mapped path and waymarkers, climbing and undulating to reach the small plantation, map ref 275147. Ignore the mapped path and skirt to the west side of the plantation as waymarked. Continue to the green signpost, Public Path to Collessie. Turn left for a few yards, then right by a swing gate and follow the waymarkers to Braeside and rejoin the starting route.

Lindores Loch - J Wyllie

54 - Tentsmuir

After a period of wet weather, Jimbo and I went to Tentsmuir in search of drier conditions. Notice boards passed on the walk indicate that the area was so named following the shipwrecking of a Danish fleet in the 1780s when some of the sailors settled there, living in tents on the moor. This is also referred to in a booklet, Tentsmuir Time Line Trail, A landscape through time, published by Scottish Natural Heritage.

However, even in 1791, the parish minister was pooh-poohing stories about shipwrecked Danes, explaining that the tents used by shepherds on the muir could be seen by inhabitants of the inland part of the parish, leading them to coin the name Tentsmuir.

We had several targets – a first-time visit to Morton Lochs, an inspection of an old railway line, then a stroll around the coastline before returning west through the forest.

Morton Lochs, created in the early 1900s, soon became an important habitat for wildlife. In 1953, the area was declared a National Nature Reserve, only the second NNR in the UK. By diverting the Lead Burn, originally known as Ninewells Burn, and flooding the dune slacks (hollows) and surrounding wet lands, three lochs

Sand bank covered by over 100 grey seals

were created, North, South and the smaller West Loch. Signposted off the B945, map ref 464263, the car park, by an attractive stone-built arched bridge, utilises part of the double track bed of the old railway line from Burntisland to Ferry Port on Craig, later named Tayport. The Leuchars to Tayport section was closed to passengers in January 1956.

Go west to North Loch, then north (parallel to the hidden railway line) on the signposted footpath to Tayport. Continue past Garpit, then through Scotscraig golf course, giving consideration to golfers. To the right is the grassy railway embankment. Exit the golf course and turn right on Shanwell Road South to reach Lundin Bridge. Continue east along the Tay foreshore, a pedestrian access to Tentsmuir. Pass by the line of large concrete blocks, constructed in 1941 by Polish troops as defence against enemy tank landings. At this point, we experienced a hailstorm and then the heavens opened. Luckily, shelter was on hand at one of the old lookout points and by the afternoon we were enjoying blue skies.

Do not enter the Reserve; stay by the shoreline. On our day, the tide was well out and the vast expanse of exposed firm sand made for easy, delightful walking. Further on, follow the mapped path by the edge of the trees to a signpost to Tentsmuir Point, a National Nature Reserve. Jutting out are the Abertay Sands where the Tay, disgorging more water than any other river in Britain, meets the sea's currents and tides. The resultant sediment helps form the Sands' glistening curves and channels,

FACT FILE	
Map	OS map 59, St Andrews
Distance	7 miles
Height	negligible
Terrain	paths, sandy shore and forest tracks
Start point	Morton Lochs' car park, signposted off the B945, map ref 464263
Time	4 hours
Nearest town	Tayport
Refreshment spot	The Harbour Café, Broad Street, Tayport

Looking at the sun-bathing seals

only fully revealed at the lowest of tides – the best time to go. Purely by chance, we had such a day. We were lucky enough to see a sand bank covered at one end by over 100 grey seals. The seals and the many species of birds that use the area are vulnerable to disturbances. Do not let dogs roam off the lead.

The land around the Point is constantly moving and changing, making it one of the fastest growing parts of Scotland and one of the most dynamic coastlines. The line of concrete blocks, marking the high water line of the 1940s, is by now well inland.

Continue curving round the coastline on a grassy path. Look out for a green corrugated hut on concrete legs, map ref 504267, not readily apparent at first, from where a sandy track leads into the forest to an icehouse. Built around 1852, this stone building was used to store ice within its thick dark walls; the ice was used to preserve locally-caught salmon before shipping the fish south. Nowadays, it is home to a colony of Natterer's bats.

Turn right (north) up the broad track, then left at Junction 5, map ref 499272, signposted Morton Lochs 2¾

miles. Continue south-east, curving left past another sign (1¼ miles to go), then soon turn right on a smaller track (1 mile to go). Reach a junction just north of Fetterdale and head west, north, then south-east. Confusingly, these last few junctions have no signs pointing the way back to the car park.

The Abertay Sands

Perth and Kinross

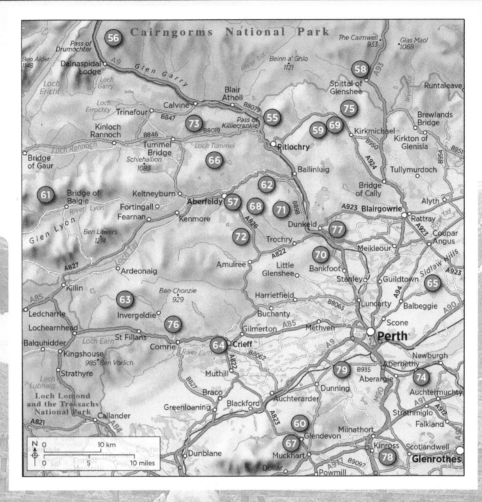

55 - A Killiecrankie circuit

The following walk is a circuit of the slopes on the east side of the Pass of Killiecrankie – an attractive and varied composite of two waymarked walks (Killiecrankie, blue, and Bealach, green) where it would be difficult to get lost. The walk straddles two Ordnance Survey maps, 43 and 52 – a difficulty eased by self-printing a map for the area concerned. Even better is to obtain the Pitlochry walks leaflet, Explore Pitlochry Path Network, from the VisitScotland Information Centre in Atholl Road.

Being at the back end of the lambing season, Jimbo decided not to take his two born-to-run Springer Spaniels, which, when on the lead all day, give less pleasure to either man or dog.

Leave the A9 just north of Pitlochry and follow the old A9, now the B8079, to the National Trust for

Resting on the way - J Wyllie

Scotland Killiecrankie Visitor Centre. The Visitor Centre is generally open from April to October (check **www.nts.org.uk/Property/Killiecrankie** for details). At the time of writing, there was a £2 fee for the car park. An exhibition area details the history of the Pass (through which General Mackay led his troops in 1689 to face the forces of Graham of Claverhouse), which is now a Site of Special Scientific Interest.

Start with the green waymarked Bealach Path. Most carefully cross the B8079, head up a tarmac road, then by tunnel pass under the A9. Go past Old Faskally House, continue uphill then leave the road before reaching the Scottish Water plant. Turn left as signposted to a grassy

FACT FILE	
Maps	OS maps 43, Braemar & Blair Atholl, and 52, Pitlochry & Crieff
Distance	8 miles
Height	600m
Terrain	well-graded tracks and paths
Start point	Killiecrankie Visitor Centre car park by the B8079, map ref 917627
Time	4 hours
Nearest town	Pitlochry
Refreshment spot	Ballinluig Motor Grill

farm track, then later right to leave the track. Cross a stile and follow a superb track of old cut into the hillside. By then we had good views west to the snow-capped Schiehallion.

With grass gradually giving way to heather, a slight dip leads to a ford over the Allt Eachainn. There is however a small footbridge. A wetter planked area, then an eroded section of the track, leads to a broad renovated path and a signpost, from where a side path gives an optional extra walk to Loch a' Choire and the ever popular Ben Vrackie.

It took us 1¼ hours to reach the highest part at 570m, the Bealach na Searmoin, *pass of the sermon*, a broad heathery way between 633m Meall na h-Aodainn Moire, *mountain of the big face*, and 627m Meall Uaine.

A gentle southerly descent through the open heathery moorland leads to the Ben Vrackie path and then to a gate to enter the mixed and partly-felled woodland by the Moulin Burn. Continue to the car park, often full at weekends and during busy holiday times, then follow the small lane towards Moulin. Do not go as far as the A924. Turn right (west) on the minor road and follow the now blue Killiecrankie waymarkers.

Pass Balnacraig and the entrance to Pitlochry Golf Course. The tarmac road then becomes a gravel track, steadily rising through the golf course to reach the edge of the forest. The way then swings north-west by the partially-felled forest to meet a forestry track. Pass on the right a path to the summit of Craigower but head straight on with a gentle descent towards the 2½ mile-distant Killiecrankie.

Later on, where the track curves left, continue straight on as signposted on a smaller track by the edge of the forest, heading north, parallel to and steeply above the A9.

Eventually cut down by steps to the left as signposted, minding your head as you go under the motorway, impressively supported by multiple concrete pillars. Cross the old A9 with care and follow the pavement to return to the Killiecrankie Visitor Centre car park.

56 - A' Bhuidheanach Bheag

It was a five-year traverse over 282 Munros (plus the two since found to be under 3000ft) to complete a tenth round, ending on A' Bhuidheanach Bheag (A'BB) in 2012. It would have been quicker, though less exciting, had I not included the 227 subsidiary Tops, a 4th round completion, with the main challenges being in Skye, Torridon and on An Teallach.

Unfairly regarded by some as one of the dullest Munros, this small *yellow hill* lies east of the Pass of Drumochter, although the top is not visible from the road. On the lower slopes, it is impossible to avoid the noise of the A9. So, not an exciting hill to mark the

completion of a round? Maybe so, but the reason for selecting the hill is that a not-too-long outing is required (important if there are adverse weather conditions on the chosen day). The climb of only 500m over two miles and a bit fits the bill. In addition, A'BB has a certain distinction in matters Munro, being the first in the alphabetical list; hence there was a certain perverse appeal in finishing there. My first visit was unashamedly as a Munro bagger: a late evening swoop, getting back to the car in two hours, feeling pleased but not quite fulfilled. I wonder how many others have done something similar.

There is a subsidiary Top, 928m Glas Mheall Mor, some distance from the main summit (a separate Munro in the original list, though downgraded to Top status in 1921). It has a more attractive summit than the 936m/3071ft Munro, though linking the two involves a traverse over a rolling plateau where strict navigation is needed on a poor day – not a good idea for that final party. That is why Rhona and I, studiously ignoring the Munro, had earlier climbed the Top via the attractive long ridge on the south-east side of Coire Mhic-sith.

From any of the parking areas at Drumochter (crossing the A9 with care), climb steeply north-east near the south bank of a stream or by the line of fence posts; this is the only demanding part of the day. The gradient eases once at 650m on the broad south-west slopes; a feint path by the fence posts also helps.

(Alternatively, once at a height of 600m, and above the gulley, a pleasant way is to follow the green grassy rill of the stream on the north side of the boundary as far as 900m then slant over to the fence posts.)

Once at 900m, a diversion to 916m Meall a'Chaorainn may be of interest. In the original 1891 listing (as Meall

FACT FILE

Map	OS map 42, Glen Garry & Loch Rannoch
Distance	5 miles
Height	500m
Terrain	grassy slopes to moorland
Start point	parking areas at Drumochter, map ref 631760
Time	3 to 4 hours
Nearest villages	Dalwhinnie and Blair Atholl
Refreshment spot	House of Bruar, north of Blair Atholl

Not much of a summit

the summits is higher, both points should be visited by those in search of a clear conscience – no problem on this approach from the west. Head east over the plateau to the forlorn trig point amid flat cheerless ground. This final stretch can be boggy or icy, depending on the season.

I have been blessed with a number of hillwalking companions over the years and it was a pleasure that Rhona, Jimbo, Peter, the Mountain Maid and Hare, the Mountain Lamb, Dave, Tessa, Graham and Richard were able to accompany me. We did not linger too long at the top; champagne, cake and photos, then down to Dunkeld for drinks and dinner.

a'Chaoruinn), it was credited as the main summit, with A'BB (listed as Fuar Bheinn) as a Top. The 1921 revision saw the 'polarity' reversed, with Meall a'Chaorainn retaining its Top status until 1981.

Continue by the fence posts to a mapped 936m spot height, map ref 654774, 600 yards west of the summit trig point. The dip between the two 'summits' is not exactly cavernous, around 10m or so. Various same-height problems have cropped up elsewhere over the years and with A'BB it is perfectly possible that the western point is marginally higher. For all that, the be-trigged summit has traditionally and understandably been regarded as the 'official' top. Until re-surveying clarifies which of

Well done team

57 - Aberfeldy to Kenmore Riverside Walk

The General Wade Bridge, Aberfeldy

Jimbo, Rhona and I had intended to go to the high tops, but with widespread low cloud forecast there was a last-minute change of plan. Jimbo's brother, John, a resident of Aberfeldy, had mentioned the new-for-us eight-mile Aberfeldy to Kenmore Riverside Walk – a well-signposted, though unmapped, route which follows the northern banks of the River Tay.

The quick change of plan, and John's absence on holiday, gave us little time to check on the infrequent public bus service for the return from Kenmore. There are school buses serving Breadalbane Academy in Aberfeldy but the school was on holiday on our day. (The Ring of Breadalbane Explorer Bus may be useful at certain times of the year; it may be best, however, to contact Traveline, on 0871-200-2233.)

FACT FILE

Map	OS map 52, Pitlochry & Crieff
Distance	8 miles
Height	negligible
Terrain	riverside path and track, plus minor road
Start point	Tayside Drive, Aberfeldy, by Wade Bridge, map ref 852493
Time	3 to 4 hours
Nearest town	Aberfeldy
Refreshment spot	Kenmore Hotel

Start from Tayside Drive in Aberfeldy, the town side of the General Wade Bridge. First opened to traffic in 1733 at a cost of £3,596 (over £1,000,000 in today's terms), for many years it was the only bridge spanning the Tay. It is now the only one of Wade's 35 major bridges to remain as a public highway, albeit single track and with traffic lights.

Cross the bridge and immediately turn left (signposted Riverside Path, Kenmore 8 miles) and follow the riverbank. One mile later, a path forks to Castle Menzies, the spectacular 16th century renaissance castle restored by the Menzies Clan Society. Straight on in any case is signposted, Kenmore 7 miles. Reach a track, map ref 805481, which continues west by the riverside then, according to the map, comes to an end. However, it does continue by electricity transmission lines which cross the river at this point.

There were many anglers by the water on our day. The Upper Farleyer beat, at the junction of the Tay and Lyon, is reckoned to be one of the best beats in the upper Tay

Kenmore Bridge

though, with depleted stocks at the time of writing, the salmon were thrown back. Continue past fields on the right, then by riverside path through a lovely wooded strip and so to the B846 at Tirinie. Turn left to reach the unattractive bridge over the Lyon, signposted Kenmore 3 miles. On the left is Comrie Castle, a small tower house, originally the seat of the Menzies family.

Continue south on the minor road, passing the Peeler Gate parking area for Drummond Hill and on the left Kenmore Quarry. Immediately turn left and follow the path that briefly goes parallel to the road, then turn left as signposted on the broad track, Kenmore 2 miles.

Pass a Taymouth Angling Club sign affixed to a tree and, when the track forks, stay with the higher one, a lovely way through the old estate. Still on high ground above the river, pass through a lovely beech tree avenue.

It is not possible to cross the Tay to Taymouth Castle. The Chinese Bridge, actually of cast iron, has been closed since 2011 for maintenance work and was still closed at the time of writing. However, continue on the north bank, pass a golf course on the right, and then arrive at a 30ft-high memorial, erected as a tribute to Mary, Countess Breadalbane. Known as Maxwell's Temple, its spiral staircase leads to a small arched gallery.

A lovely beech tree avenue

Descend past holiday lodges and so to the A827 and Kenmore Bridge (not built by Wade, though there are obvious similarities, but by the Earl of Breadalbane).

Taymouth Castle, built by the 2nd Marquess of Breadalbane, was completed in time for the visit of Queen Victoria in 1842. It took 656 horses to convey the entourage to and from Taymouth. We departed in more modest style, by taxi. The next bus would have left us with a three-hour wait.

58 - Ben Gulabin

Jimbo having admitted that he had never been up Ben Gulabin, we set off on this walk on a late January day. John and Alan and two Springer Spaniels came along as well, none of them caring which hill they went up.

Ben Gulabin is the high point of the triangular area bounded by the A93 and the private Glen Lochsie road to Dalmunzie Castle Hotel. Although the summit is further to the north-west, its south-eastern craggy shoulder overlooks Spittal of Glenshee.

With a starting height of over 300m, Ben Gulabin is one of the easiest Corbetts (hills between 2500 and 2999ft with a drop of at least 500ft all round). With a track leading most of the way to the 806m/2644ft summit, it is a short hill-day, even in winter. As neither crampons nor ice-axes were required on our visit, we extended the walk by descending into Coire Shith, then down to Dalmunzie Castle Hotel and so back to Spittal of Glenshee.

In a must-read book for hillwalkers, *Scottish Hill Names*, Peter Drummond states that the name Ben Gulabin

appears in varying spellings and several localities. "All these hills are reputed to be places connected to the Fingalian legend of the hunter Diarmaid, his lover Grainne, and their two hounds, lying buried on the slopes." A 16th century poem, set in Glen Shee, tells of

The wooden footbridge over the Allt Ghlinn Thaitneich

Ben Gulabin as seen from Spittal of Glenshee

FACT FILE

Map	OS map 43, Braemar & Blair Atholl
Distance	6 miles
Height	500m
Terrain	track/path, then heathery slopes to private road and the A93
Start point	one mile north of Spittal of Glenshee, map ref 114715
Time	3 to 4 hours
Nearest hamlet	Spittal of Glenshee
Refreshment spot	Dalmunzie Castle Hotel , by Spittal of Glenshee

the hunter dying "after being tusked by a boar after spitefully denying Fionn a sip of the hill's life-saving water." It is thus ironic that Spittal of Glenshee (hospital or place of shelter) lies at the base of the hill.

One mile north of Spittal of Glenshee on the A93, map ref 114715, is a small parking area from where a track climbs northwards. With a starting height of 370m and a steady track gradient, it is a relatively easy ascent towards the 600m level ground between Gulabin and Creagan Bheithe to the north. With the 'twa dogs' (not Caesar and Luath, but Angus and Hamish) pulling on their leads, Jimbo stormed on ahead.

Just before the 600m col, follow an unmapped gravelly track through heather that heads SSW to the twin-bumped summit plateau. The bump to the south-east is at 780m. A narrow path, going right (north-westwards) and passing a few minor knolls, leads to the main summit. On a day of limited visibility, it may seem further to

the summit cairn than imagined. We were lucky in that Gulabin was cloud-free and distant views to the north were gradually developing, though on a day of zero temperature we did not linger too long.

Descend NNE through heather – an easy pathless way down to the aptly-named sheltered Coire Shith. We crossed the burn fairly high up, knowing from a previous visit that there is a reasonable unmapped path on the north side. The south side is steeper and pathless. It is then an easy descent to Gleann Taitneach and the wooden footbridge over the Allt Ghlinn Thaitneich at map ref 089724.

A grassy track on the west bank then leads to the Dalmunzie Castle Hotel and, joy of joys, it was open. Relaxing in comfort, we certainly enjoyed our coffee and scones.

It is a pleasant carefree walk of just over a mile on the private road back to Spittal of Glenshee where Jimbo and Alan stayed with the dogs. John and I went back up the A93 to collect the car – this time a careful walk facing oncoming traffic, especially at the bends just before the car park. We returned to collect the others and, like Burns' twa dogs, "resolv'd to meet some ither day."

A standing stop at the summit

59 - Blath Bhalg

FACT FILE	
Map	OS map 43, Braemar & Blair Atholl
Distance	4½ miles
Height	400m
Terrain	track and heathery slopes
Start point	Dalnacarn by the A924, map ref 002631
Time	3 to 4 hours
Nearest town	Pitlochry
Refreshment spot	Moulin Inn, Moulin by Pitlochry

At a red corrugated roofed hut
Photo by R Fraser

An unremarkable hill at first glance, 641m/2103ft Blath Bhalg is often scarcely noticed when passing by on the A924 Pitlochry-Kirkmichael road. Nevertheless, as a Graham (hills with a height of between 610m/2000ft and 761m/2499ft and with a drop of at least 150m all round), it does attract attention from Grahamists ticking off their outstanding tops. With a sizeable 265m drop allied to its relatively isolated position, Blath Bhalg's pleasing double summit makes an excellent viewpoint and is hence attractive to those other hillwalkers not worried about lists.

The name could be translated as *warm bag*, a possible reference to the sheltered northern slopes east of Dalnacarn Craig. Another reference to *bhalg* can be found in the neighbouring Munro to the north-west, Braigh Coire Chruinn-bhalgain, which has been translated as *height of the round bag-shaped corrie*.

Blath Bhalg's southern and eastern slopes are heavily forested, so the usual approach is from the A924 to the north-west.

On the way to meet Rhona in Ballinluig, the temperature was -6.5C, albeit warming up to -3C at the start of the walk, but it was a sunny blue-sky day of glorious visibility and little breeze. With the highest

point being 384m, it was a careful drive on the A924 to Dalnacarn, itself at a healthy starting height of 300m. With a distance of just over two miles to the summit, the hill lends itself to a short winter's day. The time range indicated, 3 to 4 hours, makes allowance for slow going if there is deep fresh snow.

Park a short distance north-east of Dalnacarn then walk back to a gate that marks the start of a mapped path, in fact a grassy track. The track immediately slants to the left (ignore what might be a path straight ahead) then gently climbs southwards by the east side of a burn. On our day, there was a slight covering of snow with many an icy patch underfoot but the track eases the way through the heathery slopes, with the double-breasted hill gradually coming into focus.

Later, the track heads easterly to terminate at a red corrugated roofed hut. Little height is gained in heading east and away from the hill and it may be tempting to leave the track for a more direct approach. However, it is worthwhile continuing to the hut with its benches and table – an obvious resting point on a poor day.

A rough all-terrain vehicle track does continue eastwards heading for the west end of Kindrogan Wood. As the track fades away in crossing two burns, the climb cannot be put off. Head SSE over rough heathery ground. Higher up, the heather is less vigorous and the way is also eased by following animal tracks and rivulets.

On reaching the first bump, a small plateau, come across a line of fence posts which is then followed south-east into a dip then on to the high point with its small cairn. We enjoyed superb views to neighbouring Kindrogan Hill and, to the north-west, Ben Vrackie and the snow-capped Beinn a'Ghlo trio of Munros, plus, to the south, the more sheltered Loch Broom.

Rather than retrace your steps, follow the line of posts to the second bump, some 600 yards distant and just 4m lower, but graced with no cairn. Descend west, still following the fence line but, when it turns south-west, cut over to the high ground leading to Dalnacarn Craig to come across an unmapped narrow track between the clipped heather. Follow the track until it fades away, then curve right to follow the ridge line. A short descent over rough heathery ground regains the original track at around 400m.

It was then a short drive for us to refreshments at Moulin Inn where diaries were scanned for possible future outings.

A happy summit day - R Fraser

60 - Cadgers' Yett and wind turbines

With overnight snow then gale force winds forecast for the west, it was an easy decision not to go to the high tops. Jimbo, Joe and I wisely opted for a shorter lower-level outing on the eastern Ochils, a route Jimbo had long been keen to explore. Leaving one car at the Tormaukin Hotel in Glendevon (after an early coffee), we drove up the narrow and partly snow-covered B934 to the signposted Littlerigg parking space on the east side of the road, map ref 016083, just south of Corb Bridge. (This is one mile north of the mapped cottage, Littlerig.) By now at 300m, it was a speedy change into full walking gear on such a snell day.

A few yards to the north is a gate, from where a lovely track, initially hemmed in by trees, goes north-west, gently ascending through a forested area. The track, curving westwards above the south bank of the burn, enters Corb Glen and rolling grassy countryside. Heading into the strong wind with occasional flurries of hail, it was a bit of a struggle to reach the surprisingly narrow defile at the head of the glen and the first sight of the wind turbines on Rowantree Craig.

A gate marks the high point at 360m, after which the track is fairly level before a steady descent on the north side of the Coul Burn heading towards Coulshill Farm. Some 250 yards before the farmhouse is a gate bearing a large red sign: 'Strictly no admittance.' At this

FACT FILE	
Map	*OS map 58, Perth & Alloa*
Distance	*6 miles*
Height	*250m*
Terrain	*mostly all-track route*
Start point	*Littlerigg car park, east side of the B934, map ref 016083, south of Corb Bridge*
Time	*3 hours*
Nearest village	*Glendevon*
Refreshment spot	*Tormaukin Hotel, Glendevon*

point, leave the track and follow the drystane dyke that descends south-west to the Coul Burn.

The track up to this point, and the descent left, is part of the Perth & Kinross core path network. However, a footbridge across the burn, to avoid encroaching on the immediate environs of the farm, had still to be erected at the time of our visit. Crossing the burn and the water-gouged gully may pose a problem. If so, simply head upstream by the east bank, an interesting stroll in any case, and cross higher up.

The mapped path on the west bank is not only a track but an old right of way from Auchterarder to Borland and Glendevon. The track becomes grassier as it easily undulates up the hillside and then in a straighter line traverses a wet reedy area. Aim for the left-hand side of the turbines, heading for the gap between Green Law and a mapped 474m spot height. The ground at this point was covered with a heavy dusting of overnight snow.

A vandalised wooden gate on the ground marks the 440m high point, a crossing point known as the Cadgers' Yett, used by travelling packmen (cadgers) to transport goods and cattle. Yett, as in nearby Yetts o' Muckhart, is an old Scots word for a gate.

On descent into Borland Glen, initially the track is somewhat wet and passes very close to the wind

On descent into Borland Glen, close to the wind turbines

turbines, attractive in a modern art sort of way and well sited. I appreciate that my opinion is likely to be a minority one. Steadily turning, earning their corn as it were, the noise being made was oddly satisfying.

The track improves, now more of a grassy way. However, further on it forks – right to Borland and left for the muddier right of way beside a dyke. Follow the latter, then continue through open fields to reach a white cottage, Glenfoot.

Turn left on reaching the A823 but be careful on the short road walk through Glendevon. Use the pavement, at first on the right then on the left, to reach the 18th century Tormaukin Hotel. Tormaukin means *little hill of the hare* and a painted billboard of two mountain hares advertises the inn.

It had been a rewarding walk, albeit a bit of a battle at times, but that only enhanced our enjoyment of more coffee and scones beside an open fire.

Narrow defile at the head of Corb Glen

61 - Cam Chreag

There are two Corbetts called Cam Chreag, one near Bridge of Orchy and the other north-east of Bridge of Balgie, halfway up 'the longest, loneliest and loveliest glen in Scotland,' Glen Lyon. I judged that the latter hill should be free of the cloud and rain forecast for the west and so it turned out to be (just). It was a vast improvement on a previous visit when I experienced a

very heavy hailstorm, sore on the face, that turned the hillside white in minutes – and that was in late May!

Cam Chreag, *crooked crag*, consists of a long ridge that runs north-east from Glen Lyon, then north from the slightly craggy summit towards Loch Rannoch – hence the 'crooked' reference. The eastern slopes form an escarpment, easily breached however at one point, and

FACT FILE

Map	OS map 51, Loch Tay & Glen Dochart
Distance	9 miles
Height	700m
Terrain	track to heathery slopes, then grassy plateau
Start point	War Memorial car park, Innerwick, Glen Lyon, map ref 586475
Time	5 hours
Nearest town	Killin
Refreshment spot	Glen Lyon Tearoom, Bridge of Balgie

The sun came out as I was sitting by a small burn, its cool babbling water pleasant to hear and refreshing to drink. Just before the track end hut (a rusty corrugated shelter, its side kept closed by a small boulder), note the All-Terrain Vehicle (ATV) track that heads west over heathery then grassy slopes to reach the plateau. The ATV track makes light work of the 200m climb to the plateau. Before reaching a wooden post, slant right for the summit cone, its cragginess at odds with the grassy plateau.

To vary the return, head south-east along the plateau following a vague path that later becomes more developed as an ATV track. Descend to the flat area north of the 754m spot height and follow the stream into Coire Odhar, at the steepest part staying high on the west bank. Periodic deer tracks lead through the heather to meet another ATV track which curves left to join the ascent track at 585m as previously noted.

Once back at the car park, why it just has to be the ever-popular Glen Lyon Tearoom at Bridge of Balgie.

the south-eastern flanks are drained by the Allt a' Choire Uidhre that joins the River Lyon at Innerwick.

At 862m/2828ft, the hill is not much short of Munro status and is commonly climbed on the same day as the Munro to the west, Meall Buidhe.

The War Memorial car park at Innerwick had a few visitors, but I met not a soul on the hill. A broad gravel track gently rises by the forest edge then dips to cross the Allt a' Choire Uidhre. (Ignore unmapped tracks going off on the right.) Stay with the mapped track that heads west, passing the ruins of an old settlement, then dips back to the south bank and the first sight of the hill, its plateau rimmed with snow on my day.

Later, a side track leads to a water abstraction point on the charming Allt a' Choire Uidhre, but continue west, now on a narrower track undulating through the heathery terrain. There is one briefly confusing point, circa 500m, where apparently another track appears on the north bank of the river. The track you are on dips to the right and crosses a side burn, at which point you discover that what was previously seen is in fact the same mapped track you are on – and still on the south bank. At 585m, take note of an obvious vehicle turning point on the left, the return point later in the day.

The War Memorial at Innerwick

62 - Castle Dow

FACT FILE	
Map	OS map 52, Pitlochry & Crieff
Distance	4 miles
Height	230m
Terrain	well-graded forestry track then path
Start point	forestry car park, map ref 932523, 250 yards off the B898
Time	2 hours
Nearest village	Grandtully
Refreshment spot	Ballinluig Motor Grill

More accurately known as An Caisteal Dubh, the black castle (or possibly Caisteal Dubh Baile nan Ceard, black castle of Balnaguard), Castle Dow, now a scheduled monument, is a prehistoric fort which overlooks Grandtully and lies within the Tay Forest Park. It was built by the Picts, the Celtic tribes that the Romans called Picti, meaning painted. Regretfully, though perhaps understandably, for over 1000 years Caisteal Dubh's tumbledown ramparts have been plundered to build walls, cairns and sheep pens.

On a sunny day, albeit very cold in the shade, Jimbo and I had a short, easy but most enjoyable walk to the fort – new ground for all of us and the Springer Spaniels. Most bizarrely, thanks to a sudden change of plan following an adverse weather forecast, we returned a few days later, this time with John. The two Js visited the fort (sorry John, no views this time) while I had a look at the dismantled railway by the B898. This Ballinluig to Aberfeldy spur line, built by the Inverness and Perth Junction Railway, opened in 1865 and operated for exactly 100 years.

From Ballinluig, after the mandatory bacon butty, drive towards Grandtully on the A827 but, once over the River Tay, head east for one mile on the B898, part of National Cycle Network route 7, to the signposted start of a forestry track, map ref 934523. Some 250 yards up the track is a small car park, map ref 932523. There were two other parked cars and they were still there on our return. Where the folk had gone was a bit of a mystery. Even with a lengthy spell on top looking at the views, the walk should only take two hours.

A well-graded track heads west then curves south-eastwards, all the while gently rising through the mixed broadleaved woodland to give developing views of Strathtay. The track makes light work of the 200m ascent to a waymarked post with a red stripe by a small cairn, from where an unmapped but obvious path slants up to the right.

By now at a height of 300m, the path follows the side of a dyke, and then both path and dyke take a sharp turn to the right to lead to the small open summit and the remains of Castle Dow. At 340m, it is a glorious spot and an obvious place on which to build a fortified viewpoint.

Overlooking the north-east side, and accessed by a gap in the dyke, is a peculiar line of towering stone pillars. These well-built cairns, the equivalent of a rambler's folly, date back to Victorian times, yet apparently serve no purpose. I would suggest that the readily available supply of building material from the old fort led Victorians to do what modern man still does – fall

One of the peculiar line of towering stone pillars

victim to an insatiable urge, especially when the required material is to hand, to build small cairns or snowmen. In a slightly sheltered spot on the west side, and at a lower level, are the very obvious sheep pens.

For those with hawk eyes such as Jimbo, to the south can be seen the tips of the wind turbines of the Griffin Wind Farm. To the north-east is the craggy outline of Farragon Hill and Meall Tairneachan and, further west of these two very fine Corbetts, is the distinctive mass

of Schiehallion. The Cairngorms lie on the northern horizon.

The castle walk can be extended by continuing along the forestry track which undulates southwards for a further 2½ miles. Alternatively, once back on the B898, head eastwards to Balnaguard Glen Wildlife Reserve – a juniper and birch woodland trail by spectacular landslips round the highly-dissected gorge of the Balnaguard Burn.

63 - Creag Ruadh

It was -2C at the start of the walk, a crisp, sunny blue-sky day of glorious visibility and no breeze – January days don't come any better. I met Jimbo, broken-wrist-John (don't ask why) and the two Brians in Comrie, bound for Ben Chonzie. Having already climbed this Munro on the current round, I was not so keen to join them but, in truth, the real reason was that I was recovering from a fortnight's very heavy cold (no, it really was much worse than man flu). I knew that on this first outing it would be prudent to tackle a lesser climb.

My alternative was Creag Ruadh which stands in the fairly featureless moorland area between Loch Tay to the north and Loch Earn to the south. At 712m/2336ft, it comfortably qualifies as one of the Grahams (hills in Scotland between 610m/2000ft and 761m/2499ft, with a drop of at least 150 metres on all sides).

A four-mile drive from Comrie up Glen Lednock leads to the public road-end by Coishavachan, map ref 743273, at a height of 200m and our common starting point. Two Scottish Rights of Way Society signposts at the car park indicate public footpaths to Ardtalnaig and Ardeonaig, hamlets on the southern shores of Loch Tay. It is the latter footpath (in fact a mapped track that is metalled) that is followed initially. The straight road, heading north-west, passes through Invergeldie estate.

After one mile, the tarmac road forks. Straight on leads to Loch Lednock. Dammed in 1957, the reservoir supplies water via a tunnel to St Fillans power station on Loch Earn. However, slant left, still signposted for Ardeonaig, to cross the River Lednock. The road steadily rises by the Allt Mathaig, then heads west still following the burn.

At around 350m, ignore the track that comes in from the left and shortly later reach a junction, map ref 708287. It could be all too easy to curve right at this point,

FACT FILE	
Map	OS map 51, Loch Tay & Glen Dochart
Distance	11 miles
Height	550m
Terrain	track then rough summit terrain
Start point	Glen Lednock road-end car park by Coishavachan, map ref 743273
Time	5 hours
Nearest town	Comrie
Refreshment spot	Café Comrie, Drummond Street, Comrie

Creag Ruadh, the high point of some very broken terrain

Lochan na Creige Ruaidhe

following the tarmac road which heads north-east, then descends to the reservoir. Instead, continue westwards, now on a good grassy track, still following the Allt Mathaig.

The rocky summit of Creag Ruadh, the high point of some very broken terrain, can now be identified – albeit Lochan na Creige Ruaidhe remains tucked away. Continue to the track end, map ref 688288, at 520m. With the summit now hidden to view, it would be essential on a misty day to take a compass bearing. Even on my superb day I did that; it is difficult to describe just quite how confusing the terrain can be. Head north-west, aiming for the north shore of the still-hidden loch. As you gain height, the summit gradually appears and, after traversing a flattish tussocky and peat haggy area, suddenly so does the surprisingly large lochan, nestling beneath the south-eastern side of the craggy summit cone.

A line of rusty fence posts can be followed over the undulating summit area but, as they veer away north-westwards, head slightly south-west to reach the small cairn on the summit tor at the western end of the hill. On the way up, I traversed large patches of firm névé – a delight to walk on – and that day the hill was particularly well-named, its heathery slopes reddish-brown in the wintry sunshine. There are lovely views northwards to Ben Lawers and Schiehallion.

Other than a handful of well-known and popular hills, it is still unusual to meet anyone else on a Graham, so it was quite a surprise to meet a fellow explorer, David Heyes from Ratho. We put the world to rights during the walk back to the car park, returning at the same time as the Ben Chonzie four.

64 - From Crieff to Muthill to rescue a sheep

With afternoon rain forecast, we had an early start from the Stuart Crystal Visitor Centre by the A822 on the southern boundary of Crieff. There was still time of course for coffee and scones before setting off for a walk to Muthill and back, a short outing that was to involve rescuing a sheep lying on its back, its legs vainly thrashing about in the air. Jimbo and I leapt to its rescue while Joe grabbed a camera. Jimbo got a cut to his hand for his troubles before we managed to upturn the shorn sheep. It staggered to its feet, moved away a short distance, then stopped and turned. The look on its face I could only interpret as a silent appreciation of our good deed!

At the entrance to the car park, map ref 858203, is a green sign (Footpath to Strageath via Templemill 3

Quiet flows the Earn

miles). The walk, though, continues to Muthill – a total of four-and-a-half miles or nine miles there and back. There is also a sign (The River Earn Walk) with a map which gives the outline of the stroll by the meandering river that traverses the rich farmland of Strathearn, then continues by an old railway line and through a wood to reach Muthill. Pronounced 'mewthill,' the name comes from the Gaelic, *maothail*, possibly meaning 'soft place' i.e. a comfortable place to be based.

Head east to the river bank and a gate, with a notice: 'Keep your dog under control at all times.' Small yellow signs, River Earn Walk, show the way. It is a lovely start to the walk, with a short drop leading to the fast-flowing water's edge then through a woodland strip. Later, a

somewhat shoogly wooden bridge crosses a burn and leads back to the side of the open fields.

We were disappointed to come across an area churned up by cattle, with part of the riverside path now a lengthy stretch of glutinous glaur. On meeting a fisherman later on, he explained that cattle normally came down at this time of year to the water. All this made for a slower plod than anticipated by the delightful start.

The path eventually improves. A short wooden bridge then crosses the outflow from Pond of Drummond to approach the farm buildings of Templemill. Past the farm is a footpath sign to the right, but carry straight on as indicated, Strageath 1 mile. Along the way, you will have come across a series of old wooden sculptures, 'six hands waving at the river', reflecting elements of the river's influence on the local landscape and its people. One such sculpture at Templemill, the Miller's Flow Stone Kit, tells how an ingenious miller could gauge the speed of the water flow.

The stretch from Templemill to Strageath is particularly attractive, a good path in a good setting. Leave the

FACT FILE	
Map	OS map 58, Perth & Alloa
Distance	4½ or 9 miles
Height	negligible
Terrain	riverside path (possibly muddy in places), track and minor road
Start point	Stuart Crystal Visitor Centre by A822, southern boundary of Crieff, map ref 858203
Time	2 to 3 hours one way
Nearest towns	Crieff and Muthill
Refreshment spot	Stuart Crystal Visitor Centre, Crieff

Tight lines

right, then shortly later left by the signpost, to enter Sallyardoch Wood. Once into the wood on a track (in fact the line of the old railway), look out for the signpost on the right and the path that wends its way through this charming woodland and so back to the minor road and into Muthill.

Rescuing a sheep

riverbank when reaching the old piers of the former viaduct where the Crieff to Auchterarder railway crossed the river. Head south, at first on the left-hand side of the embankment, then climb to reach the railway track and so under a bridge. Noting another yellow sign, continue in a straight line on the railway, now a grassy way, as far as the parapets of an old bridge.

Turn left by track for Strageath Hall, then turn right on the farm road to reach a minor tarmac road. Turn

65 - Dunsinane Hill and King's Seat

With more harsh weather in the west, it was another retreat to the east with Jimbo and John, this time to the Sidlaws that extend north-eastwards from Perth to Forfar. Despite living in Auchterhouse for many a year, I had never explored the section nearer Perth – 377m/1105ft King's Seat and the lower, but more interesting, 308m/1012ft Dunsinane Hill.

Before planning the walk, I would recommend reading *Off the main road, a history of Collace Parish*, available at the time of writing at a cost of £10.95 (including p&p) by phoning 01821 650521. All proceeds go to Kinrossie & District Recreation Club. There are chapters on Collace Quarry, Dunsinane and the much-maligned Macbeth.

Dunsinane is bettered rendered 'Dunsinnan' since this is supported by early documentary evidence and by local pronunciation which stresses the second syllable. The hill fort is known locally as Macbeth's Castle: "...not an edifice of turrets and towers, but the ramparts of the already ancient hill fort ... strengthened for defence and there may have been wooden buildings within the ramparts for shelter."

FACT FILE	
Map	OS map 53, Blairgowrie
Distance	6 miles
Height	400m
Terrain	path, heathery hillside and minor road
Start point	south-east of Collace, map ref 207322, parking space at sharp turn in road
Time	4 hours
Nearest village	Balbeggie
Refreshment spot	Macdonald Arms Hotel, Balbeggie

The clipped green grassy summit terraces of Dunsinane

Macbeth's throne was said to be secure until Birnam Wood came to Dunsinnan Hill. In 1054, Malcolm ordered his 10,000-strong army to cut trees from Birnam Wood for use as camouflage during their attack on Macbeth's castle. Macbeth retreated but was killed in battle three years later. The ramparts are still very obvious though the interior was much disturbed in the 19th century by antiquarians attracted to the site by its Shakespearean connections. Little of value was learned about the history of the monument from these unscientific excavations.

Leave the A94 at Balbeggie, following the B953 for three miles, then turn north on the road to Collace, passing on the right the vast Collace Quarry (an extent best revealed from aerial photos), gouged from the western flanks of Dunsinane Hill. At the sharp turn in the road, just before reaching the village, is a small parking place and an informative plaque by a gate at the start of the grassy path.

On our dry but very cold day, the warmth generated by the initial, steep 140m south-east climb direct to the summit fort was most welcome. The fort is perhaps better appreciated once on top of the neighbouring and well-named 360m Black Hill, its dark heathery slopes contrasting with the clipped, green grassy summit terraces of Dunsinane.

On the way to King's Seat we made a small diversion to the mapped broch, map ref 223326. We found what looked like the obvious small conical bump, but no signs of any ruins. Make use of any animal tracks on the traverse over heathery ground to King's Seat, graced with a prominent white trig point, from where can be seen Birnam Wood, 12 miles to the WNW.

Then descend NNE to the mapped path, in fact an old grassy track. However, the track quickly degenerates into a vague path. In curving westwards, it is important to stay close to the south bank of the stream, and its gradually developing small gorge, until reaching map ref 221335 opposite a small plantation. (Do *not* follow a small path that leads SSW. Later this will entail a descent north-west to the southern edge of the mapped small triangular wood, then an ungainly route to reach the start of a farm track.)

Leave the stream and follow the line of the mapped path, scarcely extant at first. Traverse rough ground; eventually, in curving through gorse, the grassy track of old gradually redevelops. Reach a gate from where the mapped track goes by the north end of the triangular wood. A tree-lined farm track between fields, passing Ledgertlaw Farm on the right, easily leads to the minor road and so back to Collace.

66 - Farragon Hill

I first climbed Farragon Hill (St Fergan's hill), with Frances and Eleanor, on 3rd January 1982 – golly gosh, all those years ago! With soft deep snow, cloud at 1500ft and an icy conical peak, it was a physically demanding day only eased by the track from Loch Tummel which passes just half a mile east of the summit.

On the second visit, this time solo, to this 783m/2658ft Corbett, the weather forecast predicted westerly gales of 40mph, gusting to 60mph, plus extensive low cloud and a wind chill temperature at 3000ft of -15C. Not a day for the very high tops. Later the wind was due to 'ease' to 35mph

and the cloud to lift, so, rather than following a high-level track from the west, a long sheltered walk in from the south made more sense. Not surprisingly, I met just two others, local lads Duncan Pepper and Tom Edwards.

From Weem, head east for half a mile on the minor road to reach a broad track on the left, map ref 854498, signposted Cuil and Glassie. There is also a green sign: Glassie circular, Weem 3 miles.

The track curves right past a number of houses and Cuil Farm to enter the Glassie section of the Tay Forest Park. There are good views down to Aberfeldy as the steady-

Loch Glassie with Farragon dominating the skyline

gradient Forestry Commission track eases the climb to the junction at map ref 861510. To the left is signposted Glassie Bunkhouse and Glassie circular walk; however, follow the track on the right. At the next junction, curve sharply left, and go past another junction, ignoring turns to the right, to clear the forest at map ref 859514 by a padlocked gate.

Traverse the grassy field to its northern end at map ref 860519, to meet a stone wall and a wide fire-break on the left. Cross the dyke and follow the fire-break, the mapped boundary between the Forestry Commission land and Edradynate Estate.

I was curious to find the nearby mapped 433m trig point but there was no way through the dense growth. The fire-break gives a pleasant north-west approach to the hidden-at-first Loch Glassie with Farragon dominating the skyline. Follow a grassy path of old round the loch (grey-coloured, partially ice-covered and with some swans on my day) and cross the outflow at the north end.

Continue anti-clockwise to the east bank of a stream to enter the mapped fire-break and head NNW to reach open country at map ref 847540. Traverse wet ground to reach the base of the hill, then continue by heathery slopes to the south-east ridge and easier terrain. The summit area is craggy but that presents no problem on a clear dry day.

Despite the wind having eased, I had quite a battle to reach the cairn. Once back at Loch Glassie, follow the water's edge south-west, then a short distance west over rough ground, to reach an obvious break in the forest and another track at map ref 846528. At the first junction, signposted Aberfeldy, turn south-east (left) for an easy return to the padlocked gate, map ref 859514.

FACT FILE	
Map	OS map 52, Pitlochry & Crieff
Distance	10 miles
Height	750m
Terrain	forestry tracks and fire-breaks to heathery slopes and craggy summit
Start point	track off minor road east of Weem, signposted Cuil and Glassie, map ref 854498
Time	6 hours
Nearest town	Aberfeldy
Refreshment spot	Breadalbane Bakery & Tearoom, Dunkeld Road, Aberfeldy

67- Glen Devon to Castle Campbell and back

Elsewhere in this book, I describe a walk which partly follows an old right of way across the Ochils from Auchterarder to Dollar. En route to Glendevon, that walk traverses the 440m/1450ft high point known as the Cadgers' Yett, used by travelling packmen (cadgers) to transport goods and to walk livestock to market in Falkirk. Yett, as in nearby Yetts o' Muckhart, is an old Scots word for a gate. Muckhart, from the Gaelic muc airde, means pig height, a reference to the wild boars that roamed the area over 600 years ago.

Rhona and I met at Glendevon to traverse the southern section of the right of way, going as far as Castle Campbell and Dollar Glen before retracing our steps.

From the Tormaukin Hotel, walk back up the A823 to a green sign on the left (Path to Dollar 5 miles), from where steps lead to a metal bridge over the River Devon. Turn right on a grassy path to reach the Burnfoot road and turn right again to cross a burn, the outflow from Glenquey Reservoir. Then turn left to reach a signboard ('Welcome to Glen Devon') with a map showing the route through Glen Quey.

A zigzag grassy path then climbs to the right of way, now signposted Dollar 4½ miles. A lovely grassy track, passing the reservoir built in 1909, eases the way up the glen to the obvious gap on the skyline. The name Glenquey likely comes from the Gaelic *gleann coimich*, meaning the stranger's or foreigner's glen, presumably a reference to those travelling cadgers.

FACT FILE	
Map	OS map 58, Perth & Alloa
Distance	9 miles
Height	400m
Terrain	mostly track and path
Start point	Tormaukin Hotel, Glendevon, map ref 993044
Time	4 to 5 hours
Nearest town	Dollar
Refreshment spot	Tormaukin Hotel, Glendevon

With craggy slopes to the right, the path cuts through the narrow defile, then, still rising gently, reaches the high point of the walk at 325m/1100ft to give the first views south to the flood plain of the Forth.

The right of way goes through a forest on the left but, due to forest operations on our visit (clearly shown by neat lines of stacked timber), the path was closed, replaced by a temporary diversion following the right-hand side of the dyke that marks the forest boundary. After days of rain, not surprisingly, the boot-trodden temporary way was muddy in places.

The temporary 'path' descends to the Burn of Care, crosses the water and climbs to the other side to regain the dyke. The right of way is rejoined where it leaves the forest and the excellent track gives easy descent by the deepening ravine – and there below is Castle Campbell overlooking the rocky chasm that is Dollar Glen, where the Burn of Sorrow joins the Burn of Care.

On reaching a white house, turn right on a narrow tarmac road to descend to the ravine and so to the well-preserved castle ruins. Originally named Castle Gloom (from the Gaelic *glom*, meaning chasm), the fortress was built in the early 1400s and became the chief lowland stronghold of the Campbells of Argyll. The 8th

Glenquey Reservoir

Castle Campbell - R Fraser

Earl of Argyll sided with Cromwell's brutal invasion and occupation of Scotland. Rival clans, loyal to the Stuart monarchy, sacked the castle in 1654. The Earl was executed in 1661 by the restored King Charles II.

At the time of writing, admission to the castle was £5.50 for adults; check www.historic-scotland.gov.uk for opening times.

The east ravine path was marked unsafe on our visit so, on leaving the castle, we followed the signposted west glen path. The path briefly climbs to the top edge of the wooded ravine then, after passing a golf course on the right, cuts back and descends into the ravine to a wooden bridge leading to the east bank. Heading back uphill, another path goes past a stone-built viewing platform then climbs right to reach the tarmac road at the lower car park. Turn left on the road to the upper car park and so return to the right of way.

68 - Grandtully Hill and Two Lochs

One March I had a short though satisfying outing to Lady Mary's Walk and Laggan Hill by Crieff; it was a raw day when the original intention had been to go to the sheltered tracks of the extensive Griffin Forest, south-east of Aberfeldy, for a trip to two lochs and the seldom visited, forest surrounded, Grandtully Hill. However, although the A826 was clear at its 400m high point, recent significant snowfall meant that only extensive shovelling would have cleared access to the parking area. I promised to return another day.

Well, I did return – not once, but twice. On the first return, the forest tracks, despite a lengthy thaw, were still deeply snow-covered. I should have made prior investigations. I subsequently read that there are a multitude of tracks suitable for walking, biking and *cross-country skiing*. It was a deep-snow, tiring trudge past Loch Kennard to the base of Grandtully Hill, its tree-free summit ironically free of snow. By this point, I had had enough and trudged back to the car.

The third visit was two weeks later, with a delayed start to take advantage of forecast improving weather. It was a

FACT FILE

Map	OS map 52, Pitlochry & Crieff
Distance	8 miles
Height	300m
Terrain	track and heathery hillside
Start point	A826 car park, south end of Loch na Craige, map ref 887452
Time	4 to 5 hours
Nearest town	Aberfeldy
Refreshment spot	Howies Bistro, Atholl Street, Dunkeld

Loch Kennard

day of low cloud and gradually lifting mist, but no snow on the tracks!

The official large car park is at the south end of Loch na Craige, map ref 887452. An entrance signpost, with a map giving cycle routes, makes it clear that the mapped cycle routes are not rights of way and may be subject to temporarily closures for forestry operations. The forest consists mostly of Sitka spruce, a mono-culture that suggests a dull blanket with few breaks. It is in fact surprisingly open.

Follow the broad track that ascends north-easterly through the open strip beneath power lines and round the northern shoulder of a 500m hill to a junction. (The right branch gives access to the wind farm.) Follow the left branch with a gentle descent to the half-mile long, though seemingly larger Loch Kennard (lovely, tranquil and partially ice-covered on my day). Continue by its northern shore, ignoring a side track, to reach the eastern end; here the not-immediately-obvious outflow goes east then south-east to become the Ballinloan Burn which then joins the Braan and so continues to the Tay at Dunkeld.

Continue on the track as it curves to the north. On my Sunday outing, there was a warning notice regarding timber operations ('Do not proceed beyond this point until advised by machine operator'), though none were

underway. In any case, stay well clear of any trackside-stacked timber.

After almost one mile, keep an anxious lookout to the left for the open slopes that give access to Grandtully Hill. In fact, that point is quite obvious and is just before the track descends to Loch Scoly. Climb some 100m WNW, keeping to the right of the mapped crags. Initially, it is a steep climb through deep heather, made more difficult on my day by snow patches. However, the summit dome gives easier walking to the 532m high point. The summit is reminiscent of Kindrogan Forest in that it just struggles to be free of the encroaching Sitka spruce. The 500m northern spur gives excellent views towards the Tay and the namesake village.

Having made careful note on ascent of the break in the trees, return to the track for the short walk to Loch Scoly (a miniature when compared with Kennard but an enchanting spot). From the north end of the loch, continue to the large track junction; then retrace your steps.

69 - Two routes to Kindrogan Hill

The first route

For Jimbo, John and me, following the eastern mapped path to Kindrogan Hill in the centre of Kindrogan Wood, it was yet another example of the best-laid schemes o' mice and hillwalkers going aft agley. As we discovered, that is not now the way to the 495m/1624ft high Kindrogan Hill. Indeed, Ordnance Survey should delete this path from their maps.

All went well until crossing the track at map ref 054625. The just-discernible mapped path continues south-west through clearfell – a slow traverse to the edge of the forest by which time the path had disappeared. However, as explorers, we were keen to see if the path would re-appear. It did not. A good hour was spent trying to find a way through the dense coniferous forest. At one time, judging by my altimeter, we got agonisingly close to the tree-free dome of the hill, before sensibly deciding to retreat to the track.

Drive up Strath Ardle to Enochdhu and the bridge spanning the Allt Dubhagan, then take the second turn on the left to the signposted A924 roadside car park, a point where the Cateran Trail crosses the road.

Head south-east on a track parallel to the road, pass by a line of cottages, and then turn right towards the River Ardle, crossing by the old triple-arched stone bridge rather than the modern functional one. Turn right on the broad track leading to Kindrogan Field Centre but, on reaching East Lodge, head south (left) on another track. A few yards later, follow the mapped path that slants

FACT FILE	
Map	OS map 43, Braemar & Blair Atholl
Distance	4 miles
Height	250m
Terrain	mixture of path, track and forest 'paths'
Start point	signposted car park by the A924 at Enochdhu, Strath Ardle
Time	3 hours
Nearest village	Kirkmichael
Refreshment spot	The Strathardle Inn, Kirkmichael

off to the right – a rough mossy way of old that climbs through an area of clearfell.

At map ref 054625, rejoin the track from East Lodge. Do make the short detour to the west (right) to the old stone-walled Laird's Graveyard on an elevated position overlooking Strath Ardle. Once owned by the Balfour family, Kindrogan Estate was sold to the Forestry Commission in 1960.

The following route is the way to the summit. Head south-east on the track for some 200 yards to a break in the new plantation from where a path goes in a straight line south-west beside an old stone dyke. Ignoring a few side paths, continue gently ascending in a straight line, passing a commanding 18ft-high wooden watchtower.

Later, the by now more defined grassy path winds its way through steepening ground to enter the forest. One section requires a detour to avoid fallen trees blocking the way. The path curves to the right to reach the old dyke. Cross by a large break in the dyke, turn left for a few yards, and then head north-west into the reasonably open forest by way of a vague path.

18ft high wooden watchtower

Kindrogan Hill summit trig point

Fairly soon reach a small heathery tree-free flattish area. No, this is not the summit; that lies further north-west. From the west side of this area, continue north-west to a narrow grassy firebreak to reach an impressive line of mature trees.

Follow the west side of those trees and, all of a sudden, the large tree-free heathery summit dome appears. (At this stage, it is important to take a careful note of where to re-enter the forest on your return. Do have a compass with you.) The prominent trig point eventually comes into view.

The hill, equidistant between Mount Blair to the east and Ben Vrackie to the west, gives glorious views to the northern hills, snow-capped on our day. Near the trig point is a concrete post and, at the northern end of the dome, we could see another one, presumably indicative of a pathed way. Whether it refers to another mapped path that descends NNW or to our lost path, we know not. We will need to return another day by the NNW path to find out!

The second route

A fortnight after that first visit, Rhona, en route to nearby 641m Blath Bhalg, had a look but reported that the path disappeared into a jumbled area of fallen timber. With more time at our disposal, John and I returned to see if the path was viable and, if so, to explore the missing eastern path, this time starting from the summit. At the end of a fascinating outing, we achieved both objectives!

Leave the A924 at either Enochdhu or West Lodge, with a broad gravel track leading to the Kindrogan Field Centre's large car park. The Centre is situated in its own grounds on the banks of the River Ardle; the main building is a converted Victorian country house.

Head north-west on the track and, just before Davan, a forestry track zigzags south-westwards to a junction. Follow the left-hand (eastern) track a short distance to reach the mapped path at map ref 041632. (The path to the north, crossing a stream, gives a rougher approach.) The path of old, by a drystane dyke and a line of fence posts, is quite obvious at first and promises well –

until reaching the fallen timber area that Rhona had discovered.

However, make a sweeping detour, curving right then left through easier wooded terrain, to return to the dyke. The wall continues in a straight line south-east with enough space between it and the trees to give mostly easy progress. Stay wherever possible on the right-hand (south) side of the dyke.

At map ref 045627, leave the dyke, which continues south-east, and head south following the line of fence posts, with odd sections clearly showing the mapped path of old. Once there is an open area on the left, leave the fence posts, continue southwards to a small wooded strip, and continue to the large tree-free heathery summit dome. The 495m/1624ft prominent trig point eventually comes into view.

Delighted at the ascent success, we lingered on top, noting a well-worn path going due north on the line of the mapped path we had failed on before. Such a trodden way indicated that others had succeeded where we had failed. How so?

The path entered the wood and, by now a narrow strip, muddy in places, weaved its way north, east then south-east, following the line of the mapped way. Then we heard the sound of children and suddenly came across pupils and teachers from Kirknewton Primary School, led by a staff member from Kindrogan. Obviously enjoying themselves, it was clear that there had to be an easy way down. There was!

At map ref 051623 we suddenly cleared the densely mapped forest to reach the newly planted area, a few hundred yards from our first battle with the trees. One theory for the large area of fallen timber is that the felling of a wide expanse of trees that had adapted to taking the brunt of the wind had then exposed the higher previously-sheltered forest. The shallow-rooted Lodgepole pine and Sitka spruce are particularly susceptible to wind.

Ignore the line of the mapped 'path' on the north side of the plantation. Instead, immediately follow the grassy plantation track that slants south-east to the commanding 18ft-high wooden watchtower visited before; then gently descend in a straight line north-east to a forest track. Head south-east, then north, on the track to reach East Lodge and so back to the Centre.

70 - Little Glenshee to the Craig Gibbon obelisk

Glen Shee is associated with skiing. However, in Perthshire is another Glen Shee, smaller and less known. Drained by the Shochie Burn, the glen, though little more than three miles long, is still typically Scottish in being enclosed by steep craggy slopes. Not surprisingly, the farm building at the end of the glen is mapped as Little Glenshee.

There are few public road fords these days

FACT FILE	
Map	OS map 52, Pitlochry & Crieff
Distance	8-9 miles
Height	250m
Terrain	mostly track all the way
Start point	car park on south side of ford, map ref 989339
Time	4 hours
Nearest village	Bankfoot
Refreshment spot	Gloagburn Farm Coffee Shop, Tibbermore

On a dry though raw day I went with a small group from the Edinburgh Glenmore Club for a track walk organised by Alison Wilson. The track goes by the eastern slopes of 456m Creag na Criche and over the Moine Folaich to an obelisk on Craig Gibbon. Unless snow-covered, the track gives an easy stroll and even on a misty day it would be difficult to get lost.

We met at the car park, map ref 989339, on the south side of the Shochie Burn, adjacent to a ford and south of the sharp bend on the minor road from Bankfoot or Luncarty. (There is limited parking at the bend but this may inhibit cars making what is a very tight turn.) There are few public road fords these days. This one, a broad concrete strip, gives an easy drive over – unless of course the burn is in spate. A white height marker post is placed in the water. The walk was heading north, we were on the south bank and the ford water was too deep for walking over dry-shod. Problems at the start of the day? No. There is a wooden footbridge a few yards downstream, from where a short path leads to the north-side road and the start of the track.

The broad track goes past an old slate quarry and then climbs northwards. (Ignore the road, mapped as

Creag na Criche

a path, coming in from Loch Tullybelton.) Continue to a gate where the track passes through a barbed-wire fence. At this point, a few of us set out to climb Creag na Criche. The hill is more frequented nowadays following a re-survey in 2009 when it was promoted to Marilyn status (a hill of any height with a drop of at least 150m all round). Level ground, then a short grassy rake, leads to the deep heathery, craggy slopes. The high point, a small cairn on a rocky slab, may not be obvious on a misty day. Our watery-sun day posed no problems and the cairn is an impressive viewpoint.

The Craig Gibbon obelisk

Rejoining the track, it is then a pleasantly easy northwards traverse over rolling heathery moorland, the Moine Folaich. On the way we made a slight detour to a cairn marking a large stone circle of some antiquity. The track turns to the east; then, at a junction (map ref 001371), take the left-hand way that gently climbs to a 384m spot height, from where a short descent leads to a wooded knoll, Craig Gibbon. At first, the mapped obelisk is hidden in the clump of trees and only becomes visible at close quarters.

The tall, tapering four-sided stone pillar has small window-like openings on three sides and a doorway giving access to the small space within. I was forwarded the following information about the obelisk by Isobel Morrison, who gleaned it from a neighbour: it is recorded in the Statistical Account 1838, Parish of Auchtergaven (Bankfoot), that the landowner, Col. Mercer, had the obelisk built so that he could distinguish his own hill from his residence at Meikleour in a neighbouring parish. The obelisk is perched on the eastern face of the crag with a steep 200m drop. At the half-way stage, and with superb views over Bankfoot and the fertile Perthshire farmland, it is the obvious place for a lunch stop.

Retrace your steps from here. On the way back, I was told by those with binoculars that the large birds overhead were red kites.

However, it is possible to go south from the junction (map ref 001371), following the track to a high fence that encloses a very large pheasant-rearing area. Cross the stile and continue to another junction and turn right, with a small green signpost pointing the way to Little Glenshee.

71 - Loch Skiach and Craig Lochie

FACT FILE	
Map	OS map 52, Pitlochry & Crieff
Distance	10 miles
Height	500m
Terrain	track to loch, then heathery slopes
Start point	Logierait
Time	5 hours
Nearest village	Ballinluig
Refreshment spot	Ballinluig Motor Grill

In the midst of typical April weather – showers, hailstones and the return of snow – I remembered the high moorland area, south-west of Ballinluig, that I had been saving for winter or inclement weather. Nowadays much afforested, the tree-free craggy centre holds three lochs. The largest and highest at 430m is the irregularly shaped Loch Skiach, surrounded by low, rounded heather-clad hills, of which 518m/1700ft Craig Lochie is the nearest.

I also wanted to inspect the old railway bridge across the Tay at Logierait. The Tay Viaduct, opened in 1865

The old railway bridge across the Tay at Logierait

by the Inverness and Perth Junction Railway (later part of the Highland Railway), passed into the hands of Kinnaird Estate after the last train had crossed on 1st May 1964. In 1994, the estate gifted the bridge to the local community. During 2000 and 2001, it was comprehensively restored at a cost of around £400,000 and re-opened as a community-owned road bridge, used by local traffic and cyclists.

The Logierait–Loch Skiach–Craig Lochie walk luckily gave Jimbo and me a dry outing, apart from one short, sudden hailstorm. Further south there had been torrential rain.

From Logierait, walk across the bridge, all users doing so at their own risk. Admire the structure, turn left on a tarmac road, then left again on the B898. Head south for some 500 yards to a sharp bend (map ref 972512), from where a gate gives access to a track that curves south-west to meet a mapped path (in fact, now a track). Continue to a junction where the main track curves east, but follow the smaller rougher track, the mapped path, heading south. Clear the open mixed woodland to reach a major track at the north end of a small un-named loch (the point of return later in the day).

Continue south to the east-side boathouse and follow the track to a junction (map ref 977487). Then turn south-west for the surprisingly long approach to Loch Skiach. You will notice some unobtrusive wind turbines, only the tops showing, part of the 68-turbine Griffin Wind Farm. Once over the watershed, there it is – the secretive Loch Skiach and a small house, variously described as a boathouse, fishing hut or bothy, the property of Kinnaird Estate. Please leave the unlocked bothy tidy. A lovely snug place with a bench outside, this is the sensible resting spot.

The Bathymetrical Survey of the Fresh-Water Lochs of Scotland, 1897-1909, gives the loch a maximum depth of 55ft, a maximum breadth of nearly ½ mile and a length of over ¾ mile – and plenty of brown trout.

(If Craig Lochie is a climb too far, return along the track to map ref 959475, where a post marks the start of the mapped path/vehicle track, overgrown in places, that leads to the north end of the loch.)

Craig Lochie trig point and a slightly higher cairn

A pretty, clockwise perimeter walk, eased by strips of clean shingle and a vague path in places, leads to a grassy rake on the west side of Craig Lochie. Later, a struggle through high heather is required to reach the summit's trig point and a slightly higher cairn, an impressive viewpoint north-westwards to Schiehallion. The map gives a choice of height, 518 or 520m; a heathery traverse leads to the northern 518m cairn-less bump, then an easterly descent.

At the northern end of the loch, cross a fence by the water's edge and head north-east to join the mapped path, the vehicle track from map ref 959475. A bit overgrown at first, though the line of the old pathway is still clear, the track improves then meets the mapped path/broad gravely track at map ref 957486. Follow that track on its undulating descent west of Creag Martach and so back to the small loch.

72 - Meall Dearg and the Arthurs

One book I suggested for my Christmas stocking one year was Caleb's List by Kellan MacInnes, in which the author intertwines his own personal struggle with HIV with the life story of Caleb George Cash, a Victorian mountaineer. Cash's long-forgotten list of 20 mountains visible to the north from Arthur's Seat was published in The Cairngorm Club Journal of 1899. As 'the Cashs' or 'the Calebs' didn't sound right, the author has called those hills the Arthurs.

I realised I had climbed them all bar one – 690m/2264ft Meall Dearg, which lies five miles south of Aberfeldy,

overlooking Glen Cochill. Hey ho, another target and another Graham (Scottish hills with a height of between 2000 and 2499ft and with a drop of at least 150m on all sides).

Starting from the car park at the south end of Loch na Craige on a Sunday in early January, Rhona and I had in mind an approach to the hill from the north-west, blissfully unaware of the 14-turbine Calliachar Wind Farm then being constructed beyond Loch Hoil. The forestry track, now a broad expanded way, was temporarily closed to the public during the construction

An easily missed small bridge

FACT FILE

Map	OS map 52, Pitlochry & Crieff
Distance	5 miles
Height	400m
Terrain	line of old military road, rough and oft wet, then new track leading to heathery hillside
Start point	A826 car park, south end of Loch na Craige, map ref 887452
Time	4 hours
Nearest towns	Aberfeldy and Dunkeld
Refreshment spot	Howies Bistro, Atholl Street, Dunkeld

period. From Loch Hoil, we had intended to go south by track to the high ground north-west of Loch Fender, then over Creag an Loch.

Not to be deterred, we had a quick change of plan. From the car park (map ref 887452), walk a short distance south to join part of General Wade's Military Road, accessed by a stile at the bend of the A826 (map ref 887445) or by crossing a fence further south (map ref 890444) by a side stream. We chose the latter, with a gap in the trees leading to a lovely cleared strip. Both routes lead to map ref 888441, where there are some small ruins.

Built by Hanoverian soldiers in the 1730s, much of the Crieff to Aberfeldy section of the military road can still be walked. However, in upper Glen Cochill, passing through the forestry plantation, most of the road, if not its line, has been lost. The way gradually opens and leads by the side of a wide fire break. Around the Cochill Burn (there is now no bridge), the tussocky ground can be extremely boggy. The route is only recommended during a dry spell!

Later, walk over an easily-missed small bridge and so to another stile on the left-hand side of the perimeter fence to leave the plantation.

Continue a short distance on the by now obvious road to meet a new track which cuts uphill, easing the effort to reach the corner of the plantation, map ref 888426. Leave the track and continue to Meall Dearg and its prominent trig point.

As an extension to the walk, we continued south-west by Loch Fender to Creag an Loch. Noting that the hill has a spot height of 663m, we wondered if there might once have been a trig point there. We found no trig point base,

but I did discover a penny coin well-hidden in the depths of the cairn. Dated 1919 and in much poorer and thinner condition than another 1919 coin I have at home, I can only speculate as to why and when it had been secreted there. It must have been a long time ago, possibly over 90 years, and the date may be significant.

Once back at the military road, you may prefer to (carefully) return by the A826.

Meall Dearg and its prominent trig point

73 - Meall Reamhar

After bacon butties and coffee at the House of Bruar, Rhona and I headed the short distance west for Meall Reamhar, a hill that even those within the hillwalking fraternity would have problems in identifying. Situated between Glen Errochty and Loch Tummel, Meall Reamhar is the central bulge amid the Tummel Forest. (Reamhar is Gaelic for fat or plump.) The immediate area around the bulging dome is free of trees. Elsewhere my map shows a heavily forested area, albeit in recent times there has been extensive felling.

At 493m/1617ft, Meall Reamhar is not quite the highest point (that honour belongs to a tree-swathed 512m bulge to the north-west). However, its summit boasts a trig point, indicating that there are good views all round. Two mapped communication masts at a slightly lower level reinforce that prospect.

The following anti-clockwise walk on forest tracks approaches the summit from the south and then returns to a northern track via a grassy clearing: a circular walk which, apart from one small detour, retraces not one step. On our day of drizzle and strong winds, unsurprisingly, we met not a soul.

Drive along the B847 to the bridge over the Errochty Water, map ref 766636, half a mile west of Kinaldy. Park

Mapped communication mast, but now just the stump remains

just over the bridge, but no further than the 'Authorised vehicles only' sign. Head westwards for one mile, then turn left (south-east) at the first junction on a steady rise past a large felled area on the right (fenced off on our day, presumably ready for new planting).

Turn right (south-west) at the next junction and then, before the main track curves east and starts to descend, make the short detour on a narrower grassy track to a communication mast with the promise of good views. Mapped it may be, but now just the stump of the mast remains beside a locked stone-built hut – and the views are not outstanding.

The main track winds its way through more mature trees, descending past another cleared area on the right to give good views of Schiehallion, mist-shrouded on our day. At the next junction, map ref 765604, curve left (east) to reach the second communications mast, this time a 100ft-high metal pylon.

There are superb views down to the Tummel Bridge power station and the lines of electricity pylons, with the conical peak of Farragon instantly recognisable to the south-east. From the mast, immediately climb over heathery ground interspersed with silver birches to meet an unmapped and much smaller mast. Then follow a vague all-terrain vehicle 'track' up the hill by the edge of the forest to reach 477m Creag nan Caisean. The combination of low-clipped heathery terrain and the 'track' makes for an easier traverse to Meall Reamhar.

FACT FILE	
Map	OS map 42, Glen Garry & Loch Rannoch
Distance	9 miles
Height	400m
Terrain	forestry track and heathery slopes
Start point	Off the B847, south side of bridge over Errochty Water, map ref 766636
Time	4 to 5 hours
Nearest town	Blair Atholl
Refreshment spot	The House of Bruar, by Blair Atholl

Meall Reamhar

74 - Pitmedden Forest

The hill's trig point is enclosed by an unusual and charming turf circle that gives grand shelter.

The descent is over rough wet moorland (sensible boots advised), heading for the hidden-at-first burn to the north, map ref 778625. I advise taking a 330 bearing. Cross to the west bank and over a line of old fence posts and follow them into a narrow clearing, with the burn gradually forming a small gorge on the right. A grassy way through the tall trees leads to a track; follow this west back to the start.

On a lovely crisp day but very cold in the shade, especially when catching the breeze, the high wind-chill factor made us glad we were not on the high tops. In seeking out a low-level walk, it was Jimbo's suggestion to go to Pitmedden Forest, most surprisingly a new area for him but one of some familiarity to me from my time living in Auchterhouse near Dundee. Joe and the Mountain Hare were more than happy to come along though, much to the latter's disappointment, Jimbo decided not to bring his two Springer Spaniels, being concerned that in chasing deer in the forest the dogs might get lost.

Covering its modest hills in patchwork fashion, the mostly coniferous Pitmedden Forest lies between Abernethy and Auchtermuchty. Once a royal hunting forest (Falkland Palace is nearby), it straddles the border between Perthshire and Fife, though the following walk stays on the Perthshire side. Passing close to its 282m summit, the walk completes a circuit of Pitcairlie Hill to the north-east. If new to the area, it would be prudent to take Ordnance Survey map 58, Perth to Alloa. There are a few potentially confusing track junctions as well as miles of undulating track.

Part of the Kingdom of Fife Millennium Cycleways, the forest is a popular venue for mountain bikers. Despite the initial limited views, the main attractions for walkers are two subsequent magnificent vantage points: to the south over the Howe of Fife and, later, a northern panoramic view over the Carse of Gowrie.

FACT FILE	
Map	Ordnance Survey map 58, Perth to Alloa
Distance	7½ miles
Height	200m
Terrain	forest track
Start point	Abernethy Glen car park, map ref 188141
Time	3 to 4 hours
Nearest village	Abernethy
Refreshment spot	Dobbies Garden Centre, Turfhills, Kinross

A mile west of Abernethy, the minor Glenfoot road leads to a car park in Abernethy Glen, map ref 188141. Turning right from the car park, follow the track that climbs southwards. Ignore the first junction, the Turflundie track, then turn left (north) at the second junction. On our visit, the hard snow-covered track with ice underneath gave very slow walking with many a skid. In places, it was safer to walk on firm snow by the track edge. We met no other walker!

A mile later, by now heading north-east, reach the narrow width of the forest, circa map ref 204152, and the

Hard snow-covered track with ice underneath

gradually curves to the east. Just before reaching the double line of electricity pylons is the second viewpoint, overlooking the broadening Tay with the much smaller River Earn meandering in from the west – a watery area of reed beds and islands. The whitewashed 18th century cottages in the picturesque village of Swanston beneath the Pentlands are the only group in Lowland Scotland to be thatched with reed from the Firth of Tay. The stunning views gradually open to the east as far as distant Dundee.

With many a crossing under the pylons, complete the loop round Pitcairlie Hill. Once back at the green metal barrier, it was quite a surprise, considering the slippery conditions, to meet a solitary and intrepid lady cyclist. On our then return to the car park we could see her bike's many slithery skid marks on the icy sections. On her return she planned to dismount on the down slopes.

first vantage point, with superb views to the south. The twin-peaked Lomonds show up well and, further to the left, the distant Largo Law can be identified. Further left still are the less attractive electricity pylons that dominate the summit of Pitcairlie Hill.

We were out for three-and-a-half hours though, with a clear track, we would have expected a time of less than three hours. However, on a lovely clear-track day, more time is likely to be spent admiring views and identifying distant hills.

Continue to a multiple track junction, map ref 210154. Ignoring the immediate track on the left to Stewartshill, go past the large green metal barrier, then turn left (north). This track gently descends northwards, then

After the walk, we drove south through Abernethy Glen, an interesting icy traverse.

The River Earn meandering in to meet the Tay

75 - The Cateran Trail

FACT FILE	
Map	OS map 43, Braemar & Blair Atholl
Distance	6 miles
Height	400m
Terrain	signposted track and path
Start point	car park by the A924, Enochdhu, Strath Ardle, map ref 062628
Time	2 to 3 hours
Nearest village	Kirkmichael
Refreshment spot	Kirkmichael Community Shop and Cafe

Named after the ruthless cattle-rustlers of the 15th to 17th centuries, the Cateran Trail is a circular 64-mile route through glens, hills and farmland that starts and finishes at Blairgowrie. Very well waymarked, it should be well-nigh impossible to get lost! I recommend the excellent book, Explore the Cateran Trail, by Chic Leven and Ken Roberts (phone Perth & Kinross Countryside Trust, 01738 475239).

Local councillor and Chairman of the Perth & Kinross Countryside Trust, Bob Ellis, one of the founders of the Trail and a fount of information, very kindly agreed to accompany Jimbo and me on part of the trail, the very modest six-mile Enochdhu to Spittal of Glenshee section. This old road, connecting the communities of Strathardle and Glen Shee, is shown on General Roy's Military Survey of the 1750s.

Last visited by me in January 1984, the high point of the traverse is the 648m An Lairig which overlooks Spittal. The hamlet lies at 350m; it is a steep 300m climb to the pass. Enochdhu is lower, at 250m, but the 400m climb has an easier gradient over nearly five miles. The direction chosen is up to you!

Drive up Strath Ardle to Enochdhu and the bridge spanning the Allt Doire nan Eun, from which the name Dirnanean is derived, and take the second turn on the left to the car park where the Trail crosses the A924.

Cross the road to the broad gravel track and a green sign (Public footpath to Spittal of Glenshee), also signposted The Cateran Trail. Pass on the right Dirnanean Highland Garden and Burn Walk. The broad track ends at the farm buildings. Turn left as signposted and continue uphill, now on a narrower track which continues to climb to open country.

At a junction of tracks, map ref 073644, take the signposted left one, also marked with a white sign. A gate and stile give entrance to the Calamanach Wood, bisected by a lovely grassy track through the broad firebreak. A slight descent leads to the normally fordable Allt Dubhagan, but there is a footbridge a few yards downstream with a sign (Footpath to Enochdhu 45 minutes).

Clear the wood by a stile and gate (Greengate). The track undulates through open moorland fringed by the hills ahead, mist-enshrouded on our day. Pass another track coming in from the right and then, just round the corner, suddenly come across the Upper Lunch Hut, kindly provided by the estate, where footpath walkers are welcome to take shelter. This was much appreciated on our cold misty and wet day. The hut was visited by Queen Victoria in 1865, arriving on horseback rather than by shanks' pony.

Allt Dubhagan footbridge

The Upper Lunch Hut

At a split in the track, follow the right branch as signposted. A narrower path leads to the Allt Doire nan Eun (no footbridge this time) for the start of the final climb. At An Lairig is a sign giving optimistic times: Enochdhu 1hr 40mins, Glenshee 20 minutes.

A track descends steeply into Coire Lairige, then becomes lost in a boggy area. However, once over a stile, a delightful grassy path by the burn gives a fitting end to the walk to Spittal of Glenshee, which means refuge for strangers in the glen of peace. No Caterans then?

76- The Deil's Caldron

The need to be out and about during a wet October week was such that Jimbo and I met on a drizzly, dreich day. With a wet spell likely to make a waterfall even more attractive, Jimbo had suggested The Deil's Caldron, part of a circular route, mostly signposted Glen Lednock Circular Path. Despite needing to be dressed in full waterproof gear from the start, it was an inspired choice – an enjoyable three-hour stroll to admire the waterfall and the views from Lord Melville's Monument.

Back in Comrie, dry-clothed and sipping coffee, we concluded that we had made the best of the day.

The Deil's Caldron and the Wee Caldron are a series of waterfalls where the River Lednock, the outflow from Loch Lednock Reservoir, cuts through a dramatic tree-lined gorge in its 300m drop and six-mile dash to join the River Earn in Comrie. (Lednock, from the Gaelic *Leathad Cnoc*, means the wooded knoll.) Dammed in 1957, the reservoir supplies water via a tunnel to St Fillans

River Lednock

FACT FILE

Map	OS map 52, Pitlochry & Crieff
Distance	4½ miles
Height	250m
Terrain	path, possibly slippery in places, and minor road
Start point	car park by start of Glen Lednock Road, map ref 770223
Time	3 hours
Nearest town	Comrie
Refreshment spot	Stuart Crystal Visitor Centre, Crieff

power station on Loch Earn and, being situated near the Highland Boundary Fault, is a rare example of a dam designed to cope with earthquake hazards.

Start from a small car park 100 yards up the minor Glen Lednock road, well-known to hillwalkers for giving access to Ben Chonzie. A lovely track – leaf-strewn on our day – heads north-east through mixed open woodland, gradually curves northwards, and then crosses a small burn by a wooden bridge to meet the Lednock.

On our visit, after days of rain, the water was in full spate – a noisy promise of the delight in store. A broad path goes high above the gorge, followed by a short detour to the Wee Caldron, reached by a series of wooden steps (very slippery on our day). Further on, more steps lead to the Deil's Caldron, its watery cascades and deep pools well-viewed from wooden balconies.

More steps lead back to the path adjacent to the Lednock road. Carry on for 100 yards, then cross the road at the 'Lord Melville's Monument' sign. A steep 150m climb, at first through a conifer-lined dark clearing, leads to 256m Dunmore Hill and a 72ft-high granite obelisk, in memory of Henry Dundas, Viscount Melville. The obelisk was erected in 1812 by "his personal friends in the County of Perth in grateful recollection of his public services and of his private virtues." Odd, then, that

he was the last person to be impeached by the House of Lords, albeit he was later acquitted. Nearby is a Millennium Indicator, erected by Strathearn Ramblers.

Descend north-west on a broad, tree-lined grassy path to a gravel track, the well-named and signposted Maam Road that traverses high ground between Strathearn and Glen Lednock. Now into open country, the track easily zigzags down to the Lednock road which is followed downhill (to the right) to meet a signpost. Positioned for the benefit of those coming up the road, check that it reads 'Laggan Wood.'

Descend left to the Lednock and a high wooden bridge, the far end built through a sycamore tree. The riverside path heads for Laggan Wood. Further on, at a signpost, turn right and later descend by wooden steps to a broad new path, replacing the path of old just below. The new path zigzags down to the water's edge and a weir built in the late 1700s. Water from a small lade once powered a sawmill and corn mill and a small hydro-electric station, built in 1911, that gave Comrie House the first electricity in the village.

Turn right and cross the River Lednock by the pedestrian bridge that has replaced the railway bridge of the Perth to Lochearnhead line, closed in 1964. A long narrow path by houses then goes past Comrie Primary School and so back to the A85.

The Deil`s Caldron

77 - The Fungarth Walk by Dunkeld

In appreciation of their participation in the outings featured in my 100 Scotsman Walks book, I had invited friends to a Sunday evening meal in Dunkeld. With a few hours to spare that afternoon, it was unthinkable not to take advantage of the good weather. It was a crisp day with touches of frost on the ground, but warmed by the sun and with scarcely a puff of wind.

I drove Margaret to Loch of the Lowes, the wildlife reserve managed by the Scottish Wildlife Trust. I then set off on the well-signposted Fungarth Walk, a five-mile almost circular route of some charm, covered in less than two hours. However, a more relaxed two to three hours would give time in Dunkeld for mid-route refreshment.

From the north end of Dunkeld, follow the A923, the road to Blairgowrie, for one mile then turn right as signposted on the minor road leading to the car park at the south-west end of the loch. Before starting the walk, do stroll down to the visitor centre (check www. scottishwildlifetrust.org.uk for opening times). Visitors are encouraged to make use of the observation hide, open at all times.

At the far end of the car park are two green signs, Cally car park 2 miles and Loch of the Lowes path to Dunkeld 1½ miles; a common path runs towards both destinations until you reach a junction, map ref 041429, above Fungarth – hence the name of the walk. An 85-year old local resident who lived there as a child remembered going to wash clothes in Loch of the Lowes, though she was not aware of the meaning of Fungarth (pronounced 'Foonart').

A lovely path goes south-east through the strip of woodland between loch and road. Then, very close to the loch edge, cross the minor road (take care, traffic ahead) to more signs and a narrow track that steadily rises above a golf course on the right. On reaching the junction, take the track slanting to the left. On descent, join a broader track going south-west to reach a tarmac road (½ mile to Dunkeld), where a right turn leads to the 30mph sign, followed by a steep descent on Brae Street and so to the town. Turn right along Atholl Street, the old A9, but using the pavement.

Two walkers along the way

Turn right on the A923 but take care as there is no roadside path. Go past the first turning on the left, Cally Industrial Estate, then left at the second, a broad track, signposted ¼ mile to Cally car park.

By the car park is a five-direction signpost. Take the route on the right, Loch of the Lowes 2¼ miles, a broad grassy forestry track. After a gentle rise, look out for the sign on the right and after some 20 yards again turn to the right, this time on a smaller grassy track. This curves its way downhill towards the sharp bends on the A923.

FACT FILE	
Map	OS map 52, Pitlochry & Crieff
Distance	5 miles
Height	150m
Terrain	path, track and minor road
Start point	Loch of the Lowes wildlife reserve car park, map ref 041436
Time	2 to 3 hours
Nearest town	Dunkeld
Refreshment spot	Howies Bistro, Atholl Street, Dunkeld

A steep descent on Brae Street and so to the town

However, look out for a sign on the left, from where a lovely path cuts through the beech wood, parallel to the twisting road below.

The path reaches the road, to be crossed with care. Briefly turn right on the far side path to the entrance to Dunkeld and Birnam Golf Club (founded 1892, visitors welcome). The golf road climbs and traverses one fairway. Walkers should be mindful of golfers. Continue to the far right of the car park and a green sign (1¼ miles back to the loch). Pass through a gate to open fields bisected by a rough grassy track. Please keep dogs on the lead. Then it is on to the Fungarth farm track, a short re-ascent and so back to Loch of the Lowes.

A present from Jimbo - J Seath

78 - The Loch Leven Heritage Trail, Vane Farm to Kinross

The Loch Leven Heritage Trail, a 13-mile path round the loch, was completed in May 2014 with the opening of the final section between the RSPB's Vane Farm (now called the Loch Leven nature reserve) and Kinross. The Trail cost £3 million, £800,000 of which was required for the final four-mile section. The principal funder of this final section was the Heritage Lottery Fund. Further contributions included a bequest from the late Jean Lindsay, a member of the congregation at Cleish Church, who gifted £83,600. She had greatly enjoyed the existing Trail and wanted it to be completed. Furthermore, the final section was made possible by the generosity and willing co-operation of the landowners.

The first phase of the Trail, a three-mile stretch on the northern side of the loch from Kinross to Burleigh Sands, was started in 2006. The second phase extended the Trail to Vane Farm at which time I wrote "Plans still remain to complete the final phase round the south-west end of the loch, albeit that may take a couple of years. I look forward to that. The pleasure of both these sections has convinced me that the complete 13-mile circuit path will quickly become a favourite Central Scotland low-level walk."

FACT FILE	
Map	OS map 58, Perth &Alloa
Distance	4 miles
Height	negligible
Terrain	superb path
Start point	Vane Farm car park, off the B9097, map ref 160990
Time	2 to 3 hours
Nearest town	Kinross
Refreshment spot	Loch Leven nature reserve visitor centre cafe

And so it has proved to be. The final section, at times surprisingly distant from the loch side, is not as attractive or wooded as the earlier sections, though doubtless time will change that.

The Tour de France is next

Loch Leven, Scotland's largest lowland loch and famous for its brown trout, is home to thousands of breeding and wintering birds. Dogs must be kept under proper control at all times. With access points for walkers, cyclists and wheelchair users, the Trail provides a low-level, partly sheltered outing – ideal for Jimbo and me on our grey winter's day.

Loch Leven is on Ordnance Survey map 58 (Explorer map 369 gives more detail), but neither is really needed. Just stay with the path.

From the Vane Farm car park, map ref 160990 (by the B9097 on the south side of the loch, two miles east of the M90), go past the RSPB buildings to reach the pedestrian subway under the road. Once through that, turn sharp left as signposted, Lochleven Mills 6km (3.7 miles). The perimeter path goes westwards, parallel to the road and on the south side of the reserve, and then curves right by the south-west corner of the reserve to a hillock; at 125m, this is the highest point on the Trail.

Dedicated to the memory of Jean Lindsay, this is the East Brackley viewpoint, the Trail's best open panoramic view of the distant loch and surrounding area. Another sign shows Lochleven Mills 4¼km (2.6 miles).

A short zigzag descent from the viewpoint leads by the west side of the reserve. Eventually, the path turns to reach the Gairney Water, later crossed by a new footbridge. The loch side is now close-by.

Later, slanting in from the left is the grassy overgrown track bed of a dismantled railway. (To contrive a shorter Edinburgh-Perth route, via the Forth Bridge, the North British Company in 1890 doubled their existing lines from Kelty to Kinross and Milnathort and undertook new construction including two tunnels through Glenfarg.) The path goes parallel to, but surprisingly does not use, the track bed (by now with traces of ballast). On reaching the Todd & Duncan building, turn right as signposted (Kinross Pier ½km). (To the left is Lochleven Mills car park.) Continue by the loch side and a bridge over the Killoch Burn to reach the pier on the south side of Kinross – and perhaps a pre-placed car.

Having mostly cycled to the pier, Jimbo and I continued by bike for a most enjoyable circuit of the loch.

The East Brackley viewpoint on a dreich day

79 - The Water of May, Forteviot

On a day when Rhona, Jimbo and I had but the afternoon free (the Springer Spaniels were free all day), a six-mile stroll round the wooded glen of the Water of May gave us a sheltered escape from stormy weather. The Water of May rises in the western Ochil Hills and runs north past Invermay, described as one of the most romantic and pleasant spots in this part of Perthshire, to join the River Earn close to the village of Forteviot.

Once the ancient capital of the Pictish kingdom of Fortrenn, and a favourite residence of Kenneth MacAlpin and Malcolm Canmore, Forteviot was rebuilt in the 1920s by the 1st Lord Forteviot in the style of an English garden city. Its admittedly attractive lawns and white painted cottages may seem at odds with the surrounding area.

The walk passes through the Invermay estate; the plethora of paths and tracks in the estate, not all mapped, may cause some confusion. I would suggest printing the appropriate section of Ordnance Survey map 58, Perth & Alloa, but on a larger scale.

A beautiful expanse of snowdrops

FACT FILE	
Map	OS map 58, Perth & Alloa
Distance	6 miles
Height	100m
Terrain	tracks and minor roads
Start point	Forteviot Bowling Club, map ref 053175
Time	2½ to 3 hours
Nearest village	Forteviot
Refreshment spot	Gloagburn Farm Coffee Shop, Tibbermore

From Forteviot Bowling Club, walk past the charming village hall, opened by no less a person than Sir Harry Lauder. On reaching Forteviot Church, which dates from 1778, immediately turn left (south) on the broad lane adjacent to the graveyard. The lane, muddy on our day after heavy rainfall, leads by the east bank of the Water of May, then becomes a grassy broom-fringed way between fields. Cut left, avoiding the immediate environments of a house, to reach a minor road. Turn right and cross the Water of May, then immediately left to enter the Invermay estate with a tarmac drive leading through an attractive wooded strip which, on our day, had a beautiful expanse of snowdrops by the river bank.

Pass by the mandatory rhododendrons and some very old trees to approach two bridges across the burn. The upstream bridge has been badly eroded and is barricaded; the lower one is used on return. At the junction of tracks by the bridges, straight on leads to Invermay House which dates from the late 18th century. However, take the right branch, signposted Hill of Invermay and Home Farm, with the tarmac road passing by beautiful parkland to the right. The road crosses a large pond and continues uphill to the massive mansion that is Hill of Invermay. At this point, turn left (east) on a track. Cross the small burn and branch left, passing by an impressive high tree hut, and through another stretch of lovely open woodland to reach the edge of the very large wooded gorge, albeit with the Water of May hidden from view.

Pass on the left the remains of Muckersie Chapel, roofless but quietly evocative, sited on a bluff overlooking the Water of May. It continued to be used for worship until circa 1638. It was then refurbished in the mid 19th century to provide a mausoleum and chapel for the Belsches who had acquired Invermay in 1717.

Turn left on reaching the minor road and pass Ardargie Cottage; then turn left at a junction, signposted Forteviot 2 miles. Pass on the left the road giving access to the Ardargie new homes development. Turn left by Ardargie North Lodge, signposted Forteviot 3 miles! Have these signs been switched? A long gentle descent then leads to a track on the left to return to the lower of the two bridges, from where retrace your steps to Forteviot. On the day of our visit, the track was muddy due to excessive rain and the ground had been churned up by timber operations. Thinking of the mess his two dogs were likely to get into, Jimbo continued by the minor road.

The remains of Muckersie Chapel

Angus and Aberdeenshire

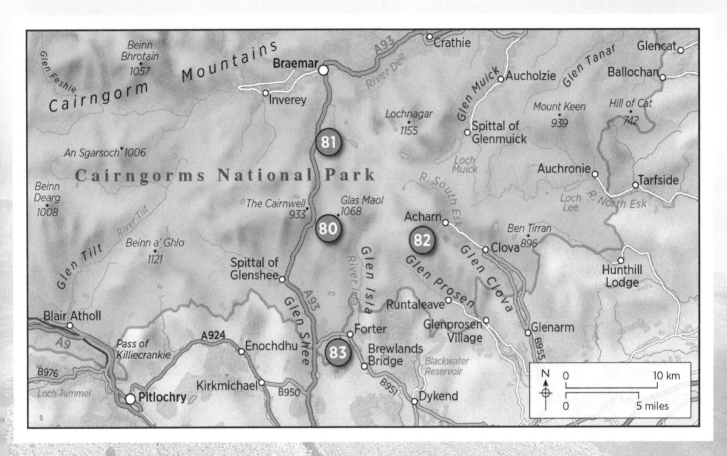

80 - Creag Leacach

81 - Creag nan Gabhar

82 - Mayar and Driesh

83 - Mount Blair

80 - Creag Leacach

There is nothing like a sudden, hard cold spell to give warning of the first intimations of winter. On a day when Jimbo, Lindsay and I were free to go to the hills, the weather forecast was distinctly unpromising: wind 20 to 30mph, with gusts of 40mph; periodic showers; only a 50% chance of cloud-free summits; and only +4C at 3000ft, before adjusting for wind chill. A short day was called for and where better than 987m/3238ft Creag Leacach, the southernmost of the line of four Munros on the east side of the A93, close to the Glen Shee ski area. Thanks to the ski area, the road is well cared for with regard to snow clearance.

Glen Shee – in Gaelic, *Gleann Sith* – means glen of peace or reconciliation, perhaps a reference to the former hospice, Spittal of Glenshee, so it is ironic to pass the still-mapped site of the Devil's Elbow. My sister, Frances, can recall driving there on a scooter. With both driver and passenger laden with rucksacks, and the scooter unable to cope with the steep bends of the old road, the passenger had to dismount and walk.

Given the weather forecast, we unashamedly opted for the easiest route, from the ski area with its starting height advantage of 665m. The six-mile walk takes only some four hours, of importance bearing in mind the short daylight hours.

(Other routes start further south from the A93, at map ref 139757: a path, then track, climbs north over Leacann Dubh for a circuitous route; a steep approach goes direct to the top; a southerly loop goes by Meall Gorm and a

FACT FILE	
Map	OS map 43, Braemar & Blair Atholl
Distance	6 miles
Height	500m
Terrain	track and worn path to stony ridge
Start point	track, map ref 142775, just north of the 665m high point of the A93
Time	4 hours
Nearest village	Braemar
Refreshment spot	Glen Shee Ski Centre café

subsidiary Top, the uninspiringly-named 943m South-west Top.)

From the A93 high ground, map ref 142775, follow the ski track, climbing north-east to reach the less than attractive ski workings. The track turns south-eastwards and passes on the right the track from Leacann Dubh. After some ups and downs, eventually reach 922m Meall Odhar, a subsidiary Top of Glas Maol, just an undistinguished bump along the way. A minor dip then leads to the base of the summit dome of Glas Maol.

Lindsay and I took the obvious side path that slants round the west side of Glas Maol to reach a flatter area just north of the mapped cairn at map ref 160759. Jimbo, to his credit, climbed Glas Maol and joined us later. In many ways, Creag Leacach is little more than an extension of Glas Maol, part of that hill's long south-west ridge. Indeed the re-ascent from Glas Maol is a mere 68m.

Follow the undulating dry-stane dyke that goes all the way south over very stony quartzite ground. Creag Leacach, after all, does mean *hill of slabby rock* or *large flat stones*. Very firm snow makes it easier. At one dip on the

The undulating dry-stane dyke

ridge, look out for a small easy-to-miss stone shelter on the east side of the dyke. Well constructed and with a narrow entrance, it is a snug shelter that can hold three to four people at a pinch. It is a bit too claustrophobic for my liking and the best way in is to slide feet first.

The small bouldery areas can be avoided, or carefully walked over, and you can make up your own mind as to which side of the dyke you prefer. At the highest point, the wall and the summit cairn are much the same thing.

On our day it certainly was breezy and cold, hence winter gear on, but we did have clear summits and there were no showers. It had been wet during the drive there and was again on returning home. Happiness indeed!

Happiness is not something you experience; it is something you remember – such as an earlier day out on Creag Leacach. It was summer 1999 and my daughter, Louise, had come up from England for a short holiday. "Dad, I want to go hillwalking … something not too demanding and not too far away, just to see what it is like."

An easy-to-miss stone shelter - J Wyllie

So we went to Creag Leacach and had a wonderful time, on what turned out to be possibly too short a day for her liking. In the evening, back home, she simply said that it had been marvellous – and so it had been.

81 - Creag nan Gabhar

The A93 traverses the area between Spittal of Glenshee and Braemar. Overlooking the road on the east side is a long line of undulating hills of which 1019m/3343ft Carn an Tuirc is the most northerly of four Munros. Further north is the Corbett, Creag nan Gabhar, situated in a wedge of land between Glen Clunie and Glen Callater that narrows where the glens meet at Auchallater.

A Corbett is a Scottish hill between 762m/2500ft and 914m/2999ft high with a drop of at least 152.4m/500ft all round. With a height of 834m/2736ft and a drop of 178m, Creag nan Gabhar (more properly Gobhar), *hill of the goats*, comfortably qualifies on both counts.

Jimbo, John, Alan and I were bound first for the hill and then for the high-level slowly descending northern ridge that leads to Sron Dubh, the dark nose overlooking Auchallater. We opted for a south–north traverse on a superb day of much sunshine and little breeze. Heather burning, to promote the growth of green shoots for young birds, was in progress but the smoke came from fires on distant hills.

Park by the west side of the A93, map ref 141835, on a grassy area once the site of a phone box, just north of the bridge over the burn to be followed. (A parking spot further south, by the track to Baddoch, can be a congested area and is rather close to two bad bends on

the A93.) Cross the road with care. Head east over a grassy area on the south side of the nameless burn to enter the nameless glen and its small but impressive ravine.

FACT FILE	
Map	OS map 43, Braemar & Blair Atholl
Distance	6 miles
Height	450m
Terrain	paths and tracks
Start point	west side of A93, map ref 141835, just north of bridge over burn to be followed
Time	3 hours
Nearest town	Braemar
Refreshment spot	Taste Coffee Shop & Deli, Braemar

The stony summit

The excellent path gives an easy gradual ascent then, after one mile, dips down to cross the burn. (This was my third visit and the crossing has never posed problems.) The mapped path then takes a straight line slanting ENE through heather, although in places it is easier to follow a worn path on the right.

Creag nan Gabhar can be tackled directly from this point but the more attractive and scenic way is to continue for another mile to the top of the glen and a small cairn where a track comes in from Glen Callater. This viewpoint gives the first sight of Loch Callater nestling below the Lochnagar group of hills.

Turn left on the All-Terrain Vehicle (ATV) track to reach a rounded dome, the south-east shoulder of Creag nan Gabhar. A path descends north-west, passing to the left of a tiny lochan; this is an oft-wet and peaty moorland traverse, albeit fairly dry on our day. The obvious path then climbs north-west to the summit area, then westwards to the first of two cairns. The second cairn is marginally lower.

Although it had taken us less than one-and-a-half hours to reach the summit, more time was required for the mandatory photo stops, mostly with the dramatic snow-clad Cairngorms as the backdrop. Nevertheless, as befits a Corbett, the summit is a superb viewpoint in all directions. Next is the broad north ridge gentle descent – 500m over almost three miles to the Glen Callater track.

Briefly heading north-east and then north, traversing dry ground with clipped heather, the obvious stony path leads to Sron nan Gabhar, the approximate mid-point. A worn ATV way gradually develops and this leads to the zigzag track descent to Glen Callater. The glen track gives an easy stroll to the Auchallater car park and a pre-placed car or bicycle.

At the time of writing, the Invercauld estate were requesting a voluntary contribution of £2.50 per day for parking (all proceeds going towards the upkeep of the car park) but I was unable to oblige. Perhaps the meter was full, but it would not accept my £1 coins.

82 - Mayar and Driesh

Hemmed in between Glen Doll and upper Glen Prosen, and somewhat adrift from neighbouring Munros, the easy pair of Angus hills, Mayar and Driesh (it sounds better and is arguably best approached in that order) lie just two miles apart. The midway 800m dip between the hills leaves a gentle ascent of less than 150m in either direction. A line of fence posts and a worn path for most of the traverse make for easy navigation even on a misty day. Consequently, unless in the event of sudden adverse weather, they are invariably climbed on the same day. With both hills just making the 3000ft mark, there are no subsidiary Tops.

The popular route, as described below, starts from Glen Doll, but there are other approaches from Glen Prosen. The Shank of Driesh path gives direct easy access to that hill. To the west, the Kilbo path, a right of way by the Shank of Drumwhallo, leads to the mid-point of the plateau. Further west, the White Glen gives a circuitous approach to Mayar via the 835m spot height by South Craig.

FACT FILE	
Map	OS map 44, Ballater & Glen Clova
Distance	9 miles
Height	850m
Terrain	good paths and grassy plateau
Start point	Glen Doll car park, map ref 284761
Time	5 hours
Nearest town	Kirriemuir
Refreshment spot	The Glen Clova Hotel

Rainbow in Glen Doll - B Lobodzinski

Looking tired at the summit cairn of Driesh

At 250m, the Forestry Commission Glen Doll car park by Acharn was as busy as ever on my visit with Jimbo and Lindsay. (The parking fee was £2 per day at the time of writing.) Head west on the Glen Doll track and cross the White Water by a concrete bridge at map ref 267758. Continue south-west to the track-end, then by path to emerge from the forest to the sudden exhilarating sight of Corrie Fee, one of nine National Nature Reserves within the Cairngorms and accurately depicted as "...a wild amphitheatre of rocky landscape sculpted by the power of ice and water." The corrie crags give winter climbing.

Somewhat poor visibility might prompt doubts as to this being a sensible route via the corrie rim to the plateau but, on the south side of the Fee Burn, there is a superb path, stepped where required, which leads to a gully and so through the crags. Once clear of the crags, head south over easy ground to the 928m/3045ft summit. Mayar's name possibly comes from *magh ard*, meaning high plain, an accurate description. Some older sources call it The Mayar.

The two-mile stroll from Mayar, on a more-than-ever eroded path, boggy at times, easily leads to the 800m dip just below a prominent boulder. We encountered many other hillwalkers, and their dogs, on the traverse, enjoying the warm, breezy day.

On the easy climb to the 947m/3107ft summit of Driesh, we had one shower and, looking north over the Burn of Kilbo to the Glendoll Forest, the brief sight of a rainbow, albeit not so dramatic as the one so expertly photographed by Brian Lobodzinski on a previous visit.

Driesh's name comes from *dris*, meaning bramble – not that there are any at the summit. However, on the cairn surrounding the trig point was something I had not seen before – a small swarm of wasps.

How best to return? The long undulating south-east ridge that extends above Glen Clova leads via Hill of Strone to a 550m dip between Cairn Inks and Cairn of Barns. From there, an easy descent leads to the front door of the Glen Clova Hotel – but this is some three miles distant from the car park. A descent by The Scorrie, with good views of Winter Corrie, is steep and stony.

The popular and safest way is to return to the prominent boulder then continue by the Shank of Drumfollow path (albeit sometimes awkward if iced up). Many, however, prefer to lope down the high ground of the Shank, an airy route with spectacular views into Corrie Sharroch and Corrie Fee. Despite the ever-present tree roots, the path through the Glendoll Forest is much improved. The path cuts across a bend in the forestry track, later followed east and north to another White Water bridge, map ref 278762.

83 - Mount Blair

Bisected by the counties of Angus and Perth & Kinross and surrounded by minor roads, Mount Blair is the highest point of a small area between Glen Shee and Glen Isla. At 744m/2441ft and with an all-round drop of some 400m, it comfortably qualifies as a Graham – hills from 610m to 761m high (2000 to 2499ft), with a drop of at least 150m on all sides.

Its situation, height and drop make Mount Blair, *hill of the plain*, an obvious landmark and explain why the summit 'boasts' a 50ft-high, ugly steel communications tower (useful no doubt, though hardly enhancing the beauty of the hill). A solo hill maybe – and a short climb to the summit – but the outing can be extended by a north–south traverse, then a return by the western minor road.

From the A93, turn east on the B951, passing Cray and the entrance to Castle Dalnaglar, and continue to the road signs showing the transition from Perth & Kinross to Angus. There is a parking space by trees on the north side of the road, map ref 154643. The section of road from the castle entrance to the parking spot covers part of the

Cateran Trail. On a raw grey day, only +3C and with a cool breeze, it was a surprise to meet a happy female camping in the trees by the roadside.

Walk along the road to the eastern end of the forest and head SSE on grassy slopes by the edge of the trees. Continue to the end of the forest, by now at nearly 500m, and soon meet a fence which is then followed all the way to the summit. The fence swings south-east, following the shire boundary line, with heather replacing tussocky grass.

At 600m, cross to the other side of the fence and follow a narrow path then a broad worn vehicle strip through the heather. The top of the communication tower slowly appears, disclosing its massive height.

The small summit plateau, bisected by the shire boundary fence line, is a crowded place. On the Angus side is a trig point and a circular stone viewpoint with a memorial plaque to those who loved this place. Sadly, parts of the viewpoint indicator are now missing. The views include the remarkable prospect of no less than 37 Munros. Not on my day! The northern snow-capped hills were indistinct and Kindrogan Hill was but a grey blur on the horizon, identified only by a compass bearing. On the Perthshire side is a massive cairn whose base perhaps denotes the highest point.

From the summit, continue to follow the shire boundary, marked by fence and drystane dyke, that goes south-east then southwards to Over Craig. There is also a worn path on the eastern side, perhaps indicating the popularity of that route.

FACT FILE	
Map	OS map 43, Braemar & Blair Atholl
Distance	7 miles
Height	450m
Terrain	grassy slopes, track and minor road
Start point	car park on the B951, map ref 154643
Time	4 hours
Nearest village	Bridge of Cally
Refreshment spot	The Bridge of Cally Hotel

The less than attractive communications tower

A slight rise leads to Over Craig's 551m summit, marked by just a scattering of stones.

Continue the short distance to where the dyke forks eastwards, then head west over heathery ground, using cleared strips to descend to the mapped path, in fact a small track of old. Descending south-west, the 'path' becomes a farm track that may be wet and muddy in places. The track makes its way to a small clump of trees where it curves left through a gate. Now with stone walls on either side, the track passes by Coldrach Cottage, then a small pond, and crosses a stream, beside which is the old mill cottage, the mill-wheel still extant.

Reach the minor road coming in from Glen Isla and turn right. Later, where there is a telephone box and a sign (Old Alyth Road), turn right again for the minor road on the east bank of the Shee Water. It is a charming three-mile undulating return past Mount Blair Lodge to the car, though younger family members might prefer to have had bikes pre-placed at the cross roads.

Highlands

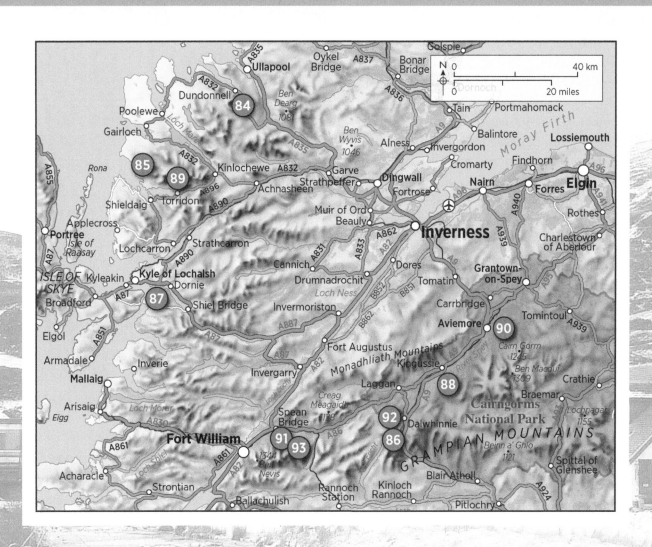

84 - Corrie Hallie to Loch a'Bhraoin

With a mixture of track and path, a horse-shoe route from Corrie Hallie to Loch a'Bhraoin offers an alternative outing when the high tops may not be appealing. Mind you, the overall climb is still some 600m and the distance 15 miles. Over the years I have covered all sections of this route, but not in a single day; however, Jimbo has.

We all set off together but, once in Strath na Sealga, John and I headed for the deleted Munro, Beinn a'Chlaidheimh, leaving Jimbo to continue on his own. His route goes past Lochivraon bothy, last visited by Jimbo, John, Rhona, Peter and me on a late November day of dreadful weather. The name means *place of rain showers* and, yes, we experienced torrential rain and wind! Previous dates had all been aborted for various reasons but we were desperate to complete our target of one bothy meet per year.

Gathering at the Loch a'Bhraoin track end, the plan to walk in, do a hill the next day, then walk out, was quickly amended to no hillwalking. Even so, what with full waterproof gear, heavy packs and the certainty of side streams in spate to cross, it was a masochistic two-hour struggle. However, on reaching the charming bothy our spirits were revived; the fire was quickly lit and we had a most convivial evening. Although worried about the overnight storm and the thought of the red corrugated-iron roof being blown away, we slept reasonably well. The walk out, with lighter packs and the wind behind us, was an easier affair.

From the Corrie Hallie car park, map ref 114850, follow the track climbing southwards through the lovely

FACT FILE	
Maps	OS maps 19, Gairloch & Ullapool, and 20, Beinn Dearg & Loch Broom
Distance	15 miles
Height	600m
Terrain	mixture of mostly good track and path
Start point	Corrie Hallie car park by the A832, map ref 114850
Time	7 to 8 hours
Nearest hamlet	Dundonnell
Refreshment spot	The Dundonnell Hotel

wooded Gleann Chaorachain and so into open country. On reaching the ford used to cross the river, note the new footbridge just upstream, possibly useful in times of spate! Ignore the path to Shenavall and continue on the track, descending gently over the next mile to 350m, map ref 093807. (I prefer to reach this point from the A832 at Fain Bridge; it is a higher starting height than Corrie Hallie and a shorter distance, albeit it does mean traversing the oft-wet, lochan-studded moorland. A dry spell and a non-misty day ease the traverse.)

It is a steep descent of 200m to Strath na Sealga and the Abhainn Loch an Nid, which meanders round Beinn a'Chlaidheimh like a castle moat. Leave the track and cut over past a ruin to the path by the Abhainn Loch an Nid. The way south, by river and loch, has a mixture of track and path which fade away in grassy places though the route direction is always obvious. From the north end of the loch, the path gently rises, turns ESE and goes through a gap in a dyke to reach a ruin by the 340m watershed. Continuing east by a meandering stream, the

Heading to Lochivraon bothy - R Fraser

path deteriorates, then joins a track half a mile before Lochivraon at the west end of Loch a'Bhraoin.

Lochivraon has two buildings, of which the main one, a lovely white-walled cottage, is used by the estate. The other is the bothy open to the public. Once but a dismal shelter, it has been renovated by the estate. In excellent condition, it now has an internal toilet and running water. Do not abuse it.

Nowadays, a roughish track follows the loch side, obliterating much of the mapped path, albeit at times it is pleasurable to stay with shingly sections by the water's edge. Before reaching the Loch a'Bhraoin boathouse, the track curves away from the loch to join the broad track that climbs gently to the A832, map ref 163761 – and a pre-placed car.

Lochivraon bothy - R Fraser

85 - A wet day at Craig Bothy

On a day most decidedly not for the high tops, it seemed a good idea to opt for a short lower-level Torridon walk to Craig bothy, the remote west coast two-storey former SYHA hostel now maintained by the Mountain Bothies Association. Fully waterproof clad, Jimbo, John and I set off on what turned out to be the wettest day of that year, with torrential rain brought in by the tail-end of Hurricane Bertha.

Two Ordnance Survey maps cover the area – 19, Gairloch & Ullapool, and 24, Raasay & Loch Torridon. In terms of the nearest road end, the former serves better if approaching from Redpoint to the north; the latter is better if approaching from Torridon and Diabaig. Staying at Achnasheen, a regular haunt of ours, we took the (arguably) shorter road journey to Diabaig and a shorter walk – two-and-a-half miles compared with the five miles from Redpoint.

The narrow twisting road to Diabaig always requires a slow drive. This time there were some very watery sections, the worst being by the 140m high shores of Loch a'Mhullaich, the aptly named *loch of the summit*. Anyhow, we continued to the Diabaig road end, map ref 790606, a parking spot that may be difficult to locate at first.

The generally good path traverses broken terrain before the 90m descent to the bothy. I had been on this path the previous year, on a warm dry day when one takes little, if any, notice of the three mapped streams to be crossed. This time, more streams had materialised. The crunch came at the third mapped stream, map ref 776623.

Large boulders, high stepping stones, were now a foot under the torrent of water. I managed to cross higher up, wading thigh high then leaping. Jimbo and John, rightly concerned that the two Springer Spaniels could be swept away, returned to the car. I continued to the bothy.

FACT FILE	
Map	OS map 19, Gairloch & Ullapool, or 24, Raasay & Loch Torridon
Distance	5 miles
Height	150m
Terrain	undulating path, stony in places, with stream crossings
Start point	Diabaig road-end, map ref 790606
Time	3 hours
Nearest village	Torridon
Refreshment spot	Torridon Stores & Café

Bridge over the River Craig - S Smith

Given its large catchment area, and after two days of almost non-stop rain, it was no surprise that the Craig River was a muddy brown and impassable spate, bursting its banks to from a large delta. The bridge over the Craig spans a very deep gorge but the water level had risen to the walkway. It looked decidedly unsafe to cross, leaving no escape route back to Redpoint.

Stranded in the snug bothy were two brothers-in-law, Stuart Smith and Alan Walker, their young children Samantha and Mark, and Max, and one dog. They had walked in from Redpoint on the Saturday, a glorious day, and had planned to return on the Monday, the day of my visit. Nevertheless, with sufficient food for two days and a multi-fuel bothy stove, they could afford to make the sensible decision to wait until the spates had passed.

Stuart gave me his wife's phone number – for reassurance that they were safe but would be delayed. I managed to contact her that evening and suggested that she phoned Mountain Rescue.

The sudden, unexpected but gratefully welcomed helicopter rescue on the Tuesday has given the children something to boast about with their friends and a reminder of an unforgettable week end.

On return, I waded the 'stream' again and so re-joined the kindly waiting Jimbo and John. Our drive back to Torridon was interesting! Water levels had continued to rise, leaving the Loch a'Mhullaich side road well submerged but with just enough verge and a passing place sign to indicate the way. The road leaving Torridon was a river bed, giving the impression that my never cleaner four-wheel drive diesel car was being driven through a shallow canal.

We had all been lucky to escape.

Samantha, Mark and Max

86 - Geal-charn

FACT FILE	
Map	OS map 42, Glen Garry & Loch Rannoch
Distance	6 miles
Height	500m
Terrain	track to northern shoulder of hill
Start point	car park by Balsporran Cottages, map ref 628792
Time	4 hours
Nearest village	Dalwhinnie
Refreshment spot	The Tollhouse Restaurant, Station Road, Dalwhinnie

A railway line to be crossed

In his book *The Highlands and Islands, A Nineteenth-Century Tour*, J E Bowman wrote that in approaching Dalwhinnie from the north it was difficult to conceive of anything more cheerless and forbidding:

"In the middle of this inhospitable region stands the solitary inn of Dalwhinnie.... It is near the north eastern, or upper, extremity of Loch Ericht, whose waters stagnate among bogs and morasses, that in this lovely season of summer scarcely put on a shade of green."

In Bowman's time, 1825, Loch Ericht had its outflow towards Dalwhinnie. Since then, an aqueduct has diverted the upper River Truim past Dalwhinnie to the loch and the outflow has been reversed to the south-west. The ground may be less boggy but the area can still be bleak.

It was like a scene from a film set. Four men stood on the otherwise empty Dalwhinnie station platform, patiently awaiting the arrival of the Inverness train. Bang on time, the train slowly pulled into the station, then went on its way. Just one passenger had alighted. Thank goodness it was Rhona. Jimbo, Brian and I had arrived by car, as had Steve, who was having a week's winter break in Speyside.

It was then a short drive to the car park by Balsporran Cottages; our target was Geal-charn.

I had last been at Dalwhinnie station five years previously. With my car in the garage and hillwalking friends committed to other exploits, I had to come up with a last-minute plan to make the most of the forecast good weather. I established that a train could get me to Dalwhinnie by lunchtime, with a return that evening – just enough time to climb Geal-charn. My route that day was perforce a longer one: six miles there and back, from the northern end of Loch Ericht, then south to reach Creagan Mor and the long undulating NNE ridge.

This time it would be a shorter day. A modest hill at 917m/3008ft, Geal-charn is rather too close to road and railway; nevertheless, with a 425m start, it was ideal for our January outing.

This Geal-charn (there is quite a cluster of them nearby, albeit with slightly different spellings) is sandwiched between the A9 and the more formidable barrier of Loch Ericht to the west. Consequently, the popular route starts from Balsporran. With flavours of Brigadoon, that name is likely a corruption of Beul an Sporain. For a circular route, Rhona, Steve and I decided on a circuit of upper Coire Beul an Sporain, *corrie of the mouth of the purse*, then a return by the more direct popular route; the latter was used by Jimbo, Brian and two dogs for both ascent and descent.

There is a sign at the bridge over the Allt Coire Fhar: Geal-charn 3.15 miles, A'Mharconaich 3.5 miles. Pass by the former railway cottages then take full precautions – Stop, Look, Listen – at the level crossing gates of the railway line. The mapped path, in fact a track, soon has a junction on the right with a newish track heading west on the north bank of the Allt Beul an Sporain, the start of the circular route. (The second junction on the right, a rough track for a bit, leads to the popular route. Straight on is the track into Coire Fhar.)

Our track made light of the 300m ascent to the high ground of the NNE ridge south-west of Creagan Mor. Continue round upper Coire Beul an Sporain, then leave the track and head south for the summit. On our day, there were lots of white hares in the corrie and a dozen dazzlingly white ptarmigans that scarcely moved away from the summit plateau. With most of the hill snow-free

that day, their white camouflage was premature. So much for Geal-charn meaning *white hill*.

On the small, stony summit area are two cairns. It is best to visit both. On our disappointingly raw and misty day (the forecast had been for a 60% chance of clear summits), we were not tempted to wait for views, nor to continue to neighbouring A'Mharconaich.

Careful navigation may be needed on descent, north-east then east. It is all too easy to drift too much ENE towards steep, best-avoided eastern slopes. On reaching the lower eastern slopes, the horribly eroded path betrays the popularity of the route.

Rhona had over one hour to wait for her next train so the obvious place to wait was at the open-all-year Tollhouse Restaurant, in Station Road. After the arrival of the train, we went our separate ways, delighted to have climbed our first Munro of the New Year.

87 - Glas Bheinn

James Hogg, on his highland tours in the early 1800s, commented on the Glen Shiel district: "The mountains are very high and steep, especially those of them most contiguous to the sea. The snow never continues long … the frosts are seldom intense, but the winds and rains are frequent and terrible." With regard to the latter, that weather pattern remains true today. Nevertheless, even on a poor weather day, the district offers a choice of lower-level walks.

Rhona was particularly interested in climbing 394m Glas Bheinn, classified as a Marilyn (hills of any height but with a drop of at least 150m all round).

The hill lies amid a 10-mile clockwise route – a beautiful coastal walk to Ardintoul then by track to Bealach Luachrach, and on to the hill, followed by a track descent to Glenelg Bay. I was more interested in the coastal walk but was happy to accompany Rhona on the short detour to the hill.

Drive over Mam Ratagain to reach the Glenelg ferry crossing to Skye at Kylerhea. The ferry car park is the start of the partially-waymarked Lochalsh Trail (a green circle with a white boot), identified by the roadside green sign Ceum Path (*ceum* is the Gaelic for footpath), Ardintoul Bay 5.7km (3½ miles).

Follow the lovely grassy track which later descends to go parallel to and overlooking Kyle Rhea, known for its

swirling tide-race, and pass by the Kylerhea Otter Haven on the far shore. Then, at a signposted junction, turn left and go under one very high electricity pylon, at odds with the wild landscape. The track becomes a narrow scenic path overlooking the shore line, crossing side streams and passing by silver birches; it is surely one of the best coastal walks in the country.

The path descends to the shingly shore by Loch Alsh, later continuing on the landward side of a drystane dyke through the pasture area before Ardintoul Point. Then turn right on the mapped path, in fact a grassy track. In the distance to the left are earth banks and a perimeter

Resting on top of Glas Bheinn - R Fraser

FACT FILE

Map	OS map 33, Loch Alsh, Glen Shiel & Loch Hourn
Distance	10 miles
Height	450m
Terrain	track and path, then tussocky climb to hill
Start point	Glenelg Ferry car park, Kyle Rhea, map ref 795213
Time	5 hours
Nearest village	Glenelg
Refreshment spot	Kintail Lodge Hotel, Glenshiel Bridge

fence, all that remains of the Second World War Royal Navy oil fuel depot.

The grassy track leads to a broad gravel track. Turn left and pass by the remains of Ardintoul House, completely destroyed by fire in August 2012. The remote estate house was built in the 1700s for the MacRae family at about the time of the destruction of their hereditary stronghold, Eilean Donan Castle.

Continue to Ardintoul Bay, turn right on the shore then head inland (south) to pass more ruins, evidence of a once bigger township. The partly tarmac track (perhaps surfaced for the construction of the fuel depot?) climbs steeply uphill. Later, the track, a mixture of gravel and tarmac, easily leads to 238m Bealach Luachrach. Time for the hill!

It is rough going by the edge of the felled area, following the line of an old dyke and metal fence posts, to reach the tussocky south-east ridge. As with other hills, the summit trig point adds an air of authority – unjustified in this case. We enjoyed a pleasant rest until the heavens opened and any thought of visiting a bump to the north was quickly abandoned. Oh dear! It was only on getting home that Rhona realised that the 'bump' is 3m higher than the trig point and is hence the Marilyn point. She can go back on her own!

It is a zigzagging but quick track descent into Glen Bernera, where most of the lower slopes have been felled, and then a pleasing one-mile road return to the car park. Not surprisingly, given the weather, we met not a soul all day.

88 - Glen Tromie

Some years ago, Bert Mackenzie from Bo'ness wrote to me about a walk which, being so good, he and his fellow walkers thought should be a Robin Howie Walk of the Week – a relatively low-level, sheltered walk, ideal for their stormy day. Starting from the RSPB Insh Marshes National Nature Reserve, the walk involved a traverse to Glentromie Lodge, a walk up Glen Tromie, a return on the east side over 640m Croidh-la, and then a descent to Tromie Bridge.

I know Glen Tromie well. Using a bicycle, the glen is my favourite approach to Meall Chuaich and the Drumochter hills, to Meallach Mhor, the Corbett further up the glen, and to the Gaick Pass, an old right of way. What I had not covered was the traverse to Glentromie Lodge and the long ridge leading to Croidh-la. I have been unable to find the meaning of Croidh-la, though I have come across an alternative name, Cruaidhleac, possibly *stone stack*.

I did the Glen Tromie circuit with the Mountain Maid and Hare, on a day when the high tops had forecast winds of 45 to 60mph. The walk was thoroughly enjoyable and, thanks to Bert, here it is.

From the small car park by the B970, map ref 779996, at the head of the track to Invertromie (not the main car park further west), walk east along the road to a metal barrier on the right-hand side and the start of the mapped path (in fact, a grassy track) which heads south-east for the northern fringe of the Woods of Glentromie. The track gives a delightful stroll, albeit a bit muddy on our day, through the open birch woodland.

A gentle descent leads to the River Tromie. Head upstream to reach a gate and stile and the private drive to Glentromie Lodge. In the days before the bridge over the Tromie was built, this route had been the original cobbled carriageway to the lodge, where we heard the

Looking down to Glen Tromie

FACT FILE

Map	OS map 35, Kingussie
Distance	9 miles
Height	400m
Terrain	path and estate road then return by grassy ridge
Start point	small car park by the B970, map ref 779996, at head of track to Invertromie
Time	5 hours
Nearest village	Kingussie
Refreshment spot	Loch Insh Boathouse Restaurant, Kincraig

local ghost story of the general who did not arrive by coach for dinner.

Cross the bridge to reach the tarmac road of gentle gradient on the east side of the river and head south into the glen. Pass Lynaberack Lodge and continue to the southern end of the wooded area, map ref 767939, that fringes the steep slopes beneath Croidh-la.

Leave the road and follow a rough track to the immediate juniper-covered slopes. The mapped path, vague to non-existent at first, gradually becomes more defined. Slant towards the fence, then follow it uphill on heathery slopes. Pass a small cairn/shooting butt and, as the fence turns left, continue to a rocky outcrop with a small cairn at the southern end of the summit plateau. The fence reappears and runs parallel to the undulating summit ridge. Pass another bump, then on to the northern bump with a circular concrete trig point – an understandable point for map-makers. We had glorious views all round. However, with the blustery wind making walking difficult, we were glad to be only at some 2000ft.

It is a long gradual descent, parallel to the fence on the left, following the small meandering path through the short heather. The path then swings a bit to the right away from the plantation and fence. At map ref 789971, south-west of Maol a'Ghiubhais, head north on the path for the descent to Glen Tromie. (This path would be difficult to find if the route was tackled in reverse.)

A gentle one-mile stroll leads to Tromie Bridge and the spectacular gorge of the river. Walk carefully along the B970 to return to the start point.

89 - Round the back of Liathach

The Torridon area is renowned for its spectacular scenery and rugged hills, of which the best known – Beinn Eighe, Beinn Alligin and Liathach – lie in National Trust for Scotland land or in a National Nature Reserve and hence are not stalked commercially. With its multi-terraced, southern sandstone slopes rearing up from the Glen Torridon road like some enormous castle wall, Liathach (*the grey one*, from the quartzite that caps the reddish sandstone) is the most awesome.

Tucked away, the almost secretive northern side of Liathach could hardly be more different – wild, precipitous and spectacular, with 600m-high sheer cliffs above the rough Coire na Caime. Nestling beneath a line of spires and towers, this well-named *crooked corrie* holds two irregularly-shaped lochans. The rough grandeur of the northern side and its corries (west to east, Coireag Cham and Coire na Caime, then Coireag Dubh Mor and Coireag Dubh Beag) is well seen from the good path that links two glens, Coire Mhic Nobuil and Coire Dubh Mor (glens tend to be called corries in Torridon). This path offers an attractive west–east traverse on a poor day when cloud is low on the hill. Arguably, however, the best time to go to appreciate the rugged scenery is on a good day. Ignore the high tops for once!

FACT FILE	
Map	OS maps 24, Raasay & Loch Torridon, and 25, Glen Carron & Glen Affric
Distance	7½ miles
Height	400m
Terrain	mostly good path, though rougher in middle section
Start point	Beinn Alligin car park, map ref 868576
Time	3 to 4 hours
Nearest village	Torridon
Refreshment spot	Torridon Stores & Café

Liathach

How should Liathach be pronounced? There appears to be no definitive answer. Most hillwalkers are not exactly au fait with the Gaelic, and even native Gaels may disagree as to pronunciation. I usually say Leeatach, though this is unlikely to be correct. Leeagach is probably the most-used pronunciation, perhaps with justification, as an older form of spelling is Liaghach. Nevertheless, I am told locally that the 'g' is not pronounced, hence Leea-ach.

From the Beinn Alligin car park, map ref 868576, cross to the east side of the Abhainn Coire Mhic Nobuil (not to be confused with the direct path to Beinn Alligin) where there is a green signpost (Scottish Rights of Way Society

The Abhainn Coire Mhic Nobuil

Public footpath to Coire Dubh). The path goes parallel to the river's impressive ravine and the pleasantly noisy cascading water, at first through a lovely pinewood then by gate into open country. After one mile, at the confluence of the river with the Allt a'Bhealaich, reach and cross the high wooden footbridge (there is also a small wooden marker arrow). Follow the path that heads towards the Horns of Alligin but, after a short distance, leave this path at a big cairn and head eastwards.

The middle section of the path, though rougher, eases the way through bouldery, hummocky terrain, with a steady rise leading to the initially tucked away Loch Grobaig of magnificent isolation. It is a slow-going traverse, passing other lochans, some reed-studded and of still water, to eventually reach the indeterminate watershed by the junction where the Coire Mhic Fhearchair of Beinn Eighe comes in beneath the mass of Sail Mhor.

The by now well-improved path follows the north bank of the Allt a'Choire Dhuibh Mhoir, then crosses the stream, seldom a problem, at the ford stepping stones. The path then descends more steeply from Coire Dubh Mor to reach the large car park (map ref 958569) on the north side of the A896.

A pre-placed bicycle gives an easy and enjoyable return to the Alligin car park, albeit after a stop at Torridon. Recommended for its homemade food and baking, the Torridon Stores & Café is normally open 10.00am to 5.00pm, though seasonal opening times vary: phone 01445 791400 or e-mail **jo@torridonstoresandcafe.co.uk** to check.

90 - Ryvoan and Meall a'Bhuachaille

Keen to maintain the tradition of at least one Elite Bothy Club meet a year, Rhona, Peter and I opted for Ryvoan, one of the most accessible bothies. Amid a spell of gale-force winds, this was well-chosen. After refreshment in Aviemore, we walked in on a December Sunday afternoon, hoping on Monday morning to climb Meall a'Bhuachaille, the Corbett that overlooks the bothy, and then walk out.

Written by a Mrs A M Lawerence, who lived for a while as a young girl in Nethybridge, it is appropriate that a framed copy of her much-admired poem is affixed within the one-roomed bothy. The poem ends:

And again in the dusk of evening
I shall find once more alone
The dark water of the Green Loch,
And pass by Ryvoan.
For tonight I leave from Euston
And leave the world behind;
Who has the hills as lover
Will find them wondrous kind.

We had a convivial AGM around the fire before retiring early. However, we were woken at 2am on Monday morning by two members of the Cairngorms Mountain

Ryvoan bothy

Rescue Team involved in an extensive search to locate a male walker who had become lost while walking alone. That walker had not taken refuge in the bothy, though he was eventually located by an RAF rescue helicopter. The Mountain Rescue Team had also been involved on the Sunday when a woman walking in a group in the Glen Feshie area had to be rescued and taken to Raigmore hospital, Inverness, to be treated for a broken leg. In one of those amazing coincidences it later transpired that I knew the lady in question, a fellow Scottish country dancer. Alas Agnes, no dancing for six months!

Start from the small car park, map ref 990097, east of Glenmore Lodge, the National Outdoor Training Centre. If staying overnight at the bothy, all burning material for the fire has to be carried in. So, heavily laden, we set off. The track goes north-east, with the first stop being at the green lochan, the frozen-on-our-day Lochan Uaine. It is small, beautiful, hemmed in by scree slopes, and the water is more emerald than green – all in complete contrast to the wide-open area of Loch Morlich. And the colour? Why, fairies wash their clothes there. The track to the lochan has been improved such that disabled ramblers now have easy access.

A short distance beyond the lochan, take the left fork at a junction on a rougher track that leads to the bothy (the right-hand track leads towards Bynack More). Regardless of climbing Meall a'Bhuachaille, this is a popular stroll, even on a good day.

FACT FILE	
Map	OS map 36, Grantown & Aviemore
Distance	6 miles
Height	450m
Terrain	track and path
Start point	Car park, map ref 990097, east of Glenmore Lodge
Time	4 hours
Nearest village	Aviemore
Refreshment spot	The Mountain Café, Aviemore

Starting directly from the bothy, a much improved broad and waymarked path on the lower eastern flanks makes this *hill of the herdsman* easier to climb – appreciated on our early morning start on a poor day. Above around 500m, the path was obliterated by a covering of snow but underfoot we had a firm white pavement. Navigation was required later to ensure we were heading for the massive cairn at the 810m/2657ft summit. It took us one hour for the ascent. I had last climbed the hill 30 years before and the cairn is more tumbled down these days. Meall a'Bhuachaille is renowned as a superb viewpoint, especially south to the Cairngorms, but not on our day. Visibility was less than 100 yards and we did not linger.

The quickest way back to the car park is to head west then descend SSW by the mapped path. However, we had to return to the bothy. It took little time to fill the backpacks and clean the bothy and then head back to the road-end to conclude a successful and eventful bothy trip and hill.

A cold, cold Meall a`Bhuachaille with visibility less than 100 yards

91 - A Spean Bridge woodland walk

Despite the oft-wet weather (the locals get rust-coloured, not tanned), I really like the Fort William area. On good days, there are umpteen high tops to climb; on other days, there are alternatives such as a trip to the Aonach Mor gondola, a swim at the leisure centre, a cycle on the many tracks in Leanachan Forest – or a choice of several easy short walks. One such walk, the signposted Spean Bridge Woodland Walk, I had often noticed when heading from Corriechoille to the Grey Corries – yet somehow had never done. It turned out to be a lovely six-mile stroll of negligible ascent and with the option of some exploring.

I did the walk on my own (the Mountain Maid and Hare were cycling elsewhere) and the only person I met was a lightly-clad runner. From Spean Bridge, head east for two miles on the minor road on the south side of the River Spean to the start point, a small parking area on the west side of the bridge over The Cour, map ref 247811.

Cross the bridge and walk to the road end, then turn right (south) on the broad gravel track that climbs to

FACT FILE

Map	OS map 41, Ben Nevis
Distance	6 miles
Height	100m
Terrain	woodland track and path
Start point	west side of bridge over The Cour, map ref 247811
Time	2 to 3 hours
Nearest village	Spean Bridge
Refreshment spot	Spean Bridge Hotel

Path amid a beautiful stand of silver birches

Corriechoille Lodge Guesthouse, once an 18th century fishing lodge. However, if you fancy a bit of exploring, the lodge can also be reached by following the mapped path from the bridge. The path has gone in the early stages, but do persevere. Briefly follow The Cour, keeping on the east side of an old metal fence, and a path gradually emerges through the wood. Later, the path develops into an obvious grassy track cut into the hillside.

From the lodge, head south on the track with good views of the Grey Corries. Reach a junction, map ref 253794, and a three-pointed wooden sign: Spean Bridge, back the way; The Lairig straight on, passing the Wee Minister; Spean Bridge via Woodland to the right (west). A horse-rider-friendly side gate gives access to the eastern end of the vast Leanachan Forest, Killiechonate Woodlands, to be enjoyed by walkers, cyclists and horse-riders. (The use of motor bikes is prohibited.) As a result of felling, the wooded area is surprisingly open. It is almost two miles heading south-west on the forest track (ignoring an unmapped track on the right) to a T-junction with a Spean Bridge sign pointing right (north).

Half a mile later, look out for a possibly easy-to-miss Spean Bridge sign on the left, map ref 238784. A path leads to a high narrow wooden footbridge, supported by girders between concrete piers, that spans the Allt Coire an Eoin. This *stream of the corrie of the birds* has as its

source the rocky amphitheatre beneath Aonach Beag. The footbridge is just downstream from a concrete bridge, presumably for forestry purposes, under construction at the time of my visit.

Cross the footbridge, turn right and follow the charming mapped path by the stream. Another footbridge then leads to the west bank of the confluence of two rivers, now mapped as The Cour. Continue northwards on the narrow heather-lined path amid a beautiful stand of silver birches. The path, leading into more dense forest, then gradually develops into a grassy track.

At a junction, turn right over a small wooden bridge to reach a white house. With Cour House on the right, turn left then immediately right down a grassy track, passing Courdale to reach the road. The walk can be extended by ignoring that grassy track and continuing west by Killiechonate Lodge on the tarmac road. Either way it is a pleasant stroll back along the road to the start point.

A high narrow wooden footbridge
that spans the Allt Coire an Eoin

92 - The Fara

At long last a good day arrived, with a forecast of blue skies and a gentle breeze, that coincided with convenient travel arrangements. I met Rhona at Dalwhinnie; our target was a trip to The Fara that overlooks the northern end of Loch Ericht. The name, referring to the long, high ridge and not to the actual highest point, may be derived from the Gaelic *faradh* meaning ladder (the long summit ridge being like a recumbent ladder) or, perhaps, more aptly, from *faire* meaning horizon or skyline. At the south-west end is 897m Meall Cruaidh. Further northwards is a 901m bump, beyond which the ridge, now mapped as The Fara, gently rises to a nameless 911m/2989ft rocky outcrop, the (just) highest point of the ridge, overlooking Dalwhinnie.

The hill's qualification for Corbett status (Scottish hills between 2500ft and 2999ft and with a drop of at least 500ft all round) is easily met and the ridge offers an undulating high-level viewing platform. We enjoyed tremendous views over Loch Ericht and Dalwhinnie to the A9 Munros, with the more distant snow-covered Feshie hills and the Cairngorms as a backdrop.

I first climbed The Fara by the popular route, using the railway level crossing at Dalwhinnie, then the Loch Ericht side track, to reach just beyond An Tochailt. From there, following a firebreak, then fence posts and a drystane dyke, gives you a direct line all the way to the summit. This time Rhona and I were keen to explore the north-east end of the ridge, so we started just north of Dalwhinnie at map ref 636858, from where a track leaves the A889 at a welcoming height of 360m.

FACT FILE	
Map	OS map 42, Glen Garry & Loch Rannoch
Distance	7 miles
Height	550m
Terrain	tracks and grassy slopes
Start point	A889, just north of Dalwhinnie, map ref 636858
Time	4 hours
Nearest village	Dalwhinnie
Refreshment spot	The Pottery Coffee-Shop, Laggan Bridge (check www. potterybunkhouse.co.uk for opening times)

The broad track bridges the Allt an t-Sluic then reaches a padlocked fence. However, a stile on the left-hand side gives access to Caochan Wood. A post with a small map shows a choice of woodland walks. Continue on the gradually rising track through the broad firebreak. The end of the mapped track is at 500m, but a narrower and more recent track continues to slant upwards, then more steeply, to clear the trees by a padlocked gate, by now at some 600m.

Climb the high gate then zigzag easily up the grassy slopes. Slant leftwards to the line of sporadic fence posts and follow them to meet the drystane dyke. This leads over steepening ground to merge with the rocky outcrop on which is built the massive summit cairn. The snow level contour lines eased identification of the surrounding hills so we lingered awhile.

Descend NNE on clipped heather and grassy slopes, then curve north-east well above the Allt a'Ghiubhais to reach the top end of an obvious track, circa 680m. The track easily loops its way downhill and crosses that stream. A short distance downstream from the mapped

Looking down to Loch Ericht

from the southern end of the Corrieyairack Pass to Drumochter. Nowadays seldom frequented (now that's an idea for a traversing walk), it is no longer apparent as a visible line over the whole of its length. Navigational skills required!

Carefully return on the short stretch of the A889 to the start point, taking heed of traffic hidden on the road's steep rise from Dalwhinnie.

The summit of Fara

estate house and buildings, the track crosses the Allt an t-Sluic, map ref 629863, by way of a hidden-at-first ford. The brick-lined ford looked very new and, unless the stream is in full spate, I cannot imagine any difficulty in crossing.

The estate track then leads back to the A889 opposite a quarry. This latter stretch is part of an old drovers' route from Feagour on the A86, the Laggan Road, that gave a shortcut, likely used by soldiers in the 18th century,

The rocky outcrop on which is built the massive summit cairn.

93 - The Wee Minister

Despite the area's high annual rainfall, Fort William is an excellent base for hillwalking, and also has a number of local low-level walks suitable for those damp days. One such walk served well during a wet April week that Margaret and I partly shared with the Mountain Maid and Hare.

Although I had known of him before, we had never met – and now, thanks to Jimbo, I knew where to go to meet the Wee Minister. Jimbo's information had come from the June 2010 edition of the local community newspaper, *The Braes of Lochaber*. And that is how we spent a few hours on an interesting umbrella walk on a very wet day.

From Spean Bridge, go east on the minor road on the south side of the River Spean heading towards Corriechoille. It is possible to drive (or cycle) to the road end at Corriechoille; however, with no parking spot at that point, go only as far as the large metal bridge at map ref 248810. A parking area is on the east side. In any case, it is a delightful walk, first by road, and then turning right along the track to Corriechoille.

FACT FILE	
Map	OS map 41, Ben Nevis, Fort William & Glen Coe
Distance	4½ miles
Height	150m
Terrain	quiet minor road and track
Start point	east side of bridge before Corriechoille, map ref 248810
Time	2 hours
Nearest village	Spean Bridge
Refreshment spot	The Moorings Hotel, Banavie

Allt Leachdach gorge, still partly spanned by the old railway bridge

It is possible to continue driving to Corriechoille and, indeed, beyond but – even on a wet day – some exercise is called for. It is a walk of just over one mile on the roughish track, heading south to reach the line of a dismantled narrow-gauge railway just before the start of the forest, at map ref 256788. The railway was built by the British Aluminium Company to assist in the construction of the tunnel from Loch Treig to Fort William. For a minor and recommended detour of just a few yards, follow the line east to the Allt Leachdach gorge, still partly spanned by a bridge that enabled the line to continue to Loch Treig. The remains of the bridge may be reminiscent of an old Wild West film, but it would be folly to ignore the obvious danger sign – keep out.

Using the gate, enter the forest track which gently climbs through a felled area. After some 300 yards, suddenly there he is on the right-hand side – the minister, patiently waiting to greet you.

A plaque affixed to the flat base of a tree stump states:

"A stone statue of the Wee Minister dating from the 1900s once stood on a site near here and was said to bring good luck to climbers and walkers. The statue, believed to be of the Rev John McIntosh, was destroyed in the 1970s. However, in May 2010 the local tourism group decided to resurrect him and replace him with this replica crafted in cedar wood by Peter Bowsher, champion wood carver. Good fortune to all who pass this way. Erected by the Glen Spean & the Great Glen Tourism Marketing Group with special thanks to Mr Rik Eppens."

However, it would appear that the original statue was not of the Rev John McIntosh, who died in 1910. The Rev Donald MacQuarrie of Fort William is convinced that it is of Dr Thomas Chalmers, first moderator of the newly established Free Church in Scotland. It was gifted in 1886 to Fort William where it was erected in the manse garden of the Moderator, John McIntosh – hence the confusion. The statue stayed at the manse; later, when the then current minister was away during the First World War, his wife had it removed because she found the figure to be somewhat eerie. In 1968, it was taken via the Puggy Line (the narrow-gauge railway) to near the present site. He became an icon among walkers and visitors, many of whom put money in his outstretched hands, believing it would bring good fortune. However, the statue vanished in the 1970s, allegedly because the then landowner was tired of people crossing his land to see it.

Nowadays, a box for contributions to the local mountain rescue group is built into the tree stump and, judging by the sound of falling coins, that tradition is continuing.

Keeping the Minister dry

Islands

94 - Canna

FACT FILE	
Map	OS map 39, Rhum & Eigg
Distance	6 miles
Height	300m
Terrain	track to grassy but craggy terraced hillside
Start point	Canna pier, map ref 278051
Time	3 to 4 hours
Nearest town	Mallaig
Refreshment spot	Café Canna (check www.cafecanna.co.uk for opening times)

The Caledonian MacBrayne (CalMac) ferry from Mallaig goes to the Small Isles – Canna, Rum, Eigg and Muck. Another ferry goes to Skye. In August 2015, Margaret, Rhona, Eilidh and I went to Canna. (Check www.calmac.co.uk for sailing times.) Not long into the voyage, a lady realised that the ferry was not going to Skye. To our amazement, and solely for her benefit, the captain returned to Mallaig.

Many go to Canna on an eight-hour Saturday visit. Despite Canna's modest size (five miles long and one-and-a-half miles wide), even our three-day stay at the very comfortable Tighard Guest House was insufficient to explore the whole of the island.

Lime-rich basalt lava flows have given the island not only its distinctive terraced topography but also unusually fertile soil and abundant plant life, and Canna's cliffs make the perfect home for seabirds and birds of prey.

In 1821, 436 people lived on Canna and Sanday but, within 40 years, following emigration (voluntary or forced) to the New World, that number had declined to 127. John Lorne Campbell, an eminent Gaelic scholar, bought Canna in 1938. He managed it as a working farm and nature reserve, then gifted the island to the National

Trust for Scotland (NTS) in 1981. During our visit, following the departure of the last children, the number of residents had fallen to 19. Whether the best way forward is for the NTS to continue its ownership, running the estate in partnership with the tenants/islanders, is the subject of much debate.

Intrigued by the island with an unlocked community shop and an honesty box, the looting in 2015 became a newsworthy story for the world's press. The appalling abuse of the honesty system resulted in many messages of support, and donations large and small, from all over the world.

Rhona in a souterrain

A walk to a souterrain, then to the highest point, 210/689ft Carn a'Ghaill, is best done in a clockwise direction on a clear day – otherwise, the souterrain will be hard to find. In thick mist, a straight-line compass approach will not cope with the many rocky undulations.

Follow the 'road' from the pier, pass the shop and café, then branch right as signposted (a pink circle with a black arrow) to the camp site, rather than crossing onto Sanday. The 'road', by now close beneath the impressive columnar basalt cliffs, gives a superb coastal stroll. On our clear day, we could see the five-mile distant white lighthouse on Oigh-sgeir.

A rise then a short dip leads to a hairpin bend. Turn right (north) to leave the 'road' (as signposted on a wooden block) and follow a rough then grassy way with periodic signs. Later, turn right as signposted to cross a drystane dyke. A few yards beyond is a grassy

Carn a`Ghaill - R Fraser

mound and the almost hidden souterrain, an enigmatic 2000-year-old underground chamber with two narrow entrances; an adult can enter the first, but perhaps not the second.

Head eastwards to 180m Beinn Tighe, which gives good views west to the Uists. Descend north-east (left) to a line of fence posts above the dramatic north coast cliffs, then east to the circular concrete trig point on Carn a'Ghaill, *rocky hill of the storm* (a Marilyn – hills of any height but with a drop of at least 150m all round).

Descend east to another line of fence posts, netted and barbed, and follow them southwards to a gate. (A short detour to Compass Hill, named because the large amount of iron in it affects compasses, may be of interest. The compass needle really does move!) Go south-west by the edge of the mapped wood to reach a metal gate by Tighard, from where a charming zigzag path leads back to the shop.

Sanday from compass hill - R Fraser

95 - The Raasay Iron Mine and Dun Caan

On a visit to Skye one May, the weather deteriorated. With a raw north wind bringing snow on the hills, a lower-level walk was deemed preferable.

One of our group was a Liberal-Democrat local councillor so, in tune with the then political times, a compromise was reached – to climb Dun Caan, at 443m, the distinctive highest point on Raasay, and to visit the remains of the iron-ore mine opened just before the First World War. *The Raasay Iron Mine, where enemies became friends,* by Laurence and Pamela Draper, is recommended reading. (German prisoners of war were used.) Some 200,000 tons of raw ore were extracted during that war. The only iron yielded in the Second World War was scrap from the dismantled installation.

The Sconser–Raasay ferry service is approximately hourly. However, the detailed timetable is somewhat essential and there is only a limited Sunday service (see www.calmac.co.uk, phone 0800 066 5000 or e-mail enquiries@calmac.co.uk). It is expensive to take a car on this 20-minute crossing, but pedal cycles are free. At the time of writing, the adult pedestrian fare was £3.50 single.

The Raasay ferry

The shortest route to Dun Caan, on a lovely well-graded path of old with the summit hidden until the last moment, starts from Balmeanach, map ref 561406. However, unless taking bike or car, that means a longer walk, which also bypasses the old mine workings. Accordingly, the following walk starts and finishes at the old pier and slipway at Suisnish and not at the new ferry terminal at Clachan.

From the pier (signposted 2.5k to Iron Mine and 7k to Dun Caan), climb by the left-hand side of the old processing plant to reach the long straight line of the dismantled narrow-gauge railway used to transport iron ore from the mines. The first mile is over grassy moorland; the next section is through delightful woodland, albeit with an extra climb. Tall concrete pillars once supported the railway across a ravine. The railway is no more so it is necessary to descend by path to a stream and climb back to the line.

Cross Fearns Road and continue north by the remains of No 1 Mine Building to a forestry track. (The building to the north-east is the gated, padlocked entrance to the mine's ventilation shaft. Further uphill is the site of opencast mine workings – danger, keep out.) The track continues north, curves north-east, and then crosses the Inverarish Burn by bridge to reach a large clearing at map ref 566370. An obvious sign points the way to Dun Caan.

The path goes by the lovely wooded ravine edge of the burn, reaching open country by a gate at 135m.

FACT FILE	
Map	OS map 32, South Skye, or 24, Raasay & Loch Torridon
Distance	9 miles
Height	500m
Terrain	path of variable quality all the way
Start point	Raasay pier, map ref 554342
Time	4 to 6 hours, allowing for diversions
Nearest village	Sconser
Refreshment spot	Raasay House café bar

Thereafter the path, following the west bank of the burn to Loch na Mna, is dry in places but boggy elsewhere and sometimes indistinct. On approaching the loch, Dun Caan appears not to have a flat summit area, seemingly tilting more to the right.

The summit, an old volcanic plug, is deceptively close but there is a surprise. The path leads, with a short climb, to the edge of an escarpment, with a long defile between escarpment and summit holding Loch na Mna and Loch na Meilich, the latter a public water supply. A scree path leads down to that lochan from where there is another 100m to climb, albeit a well-made zigzag path eases the gradient and avoids rocky sections.

The small and flat summit gives glorious views over to Skye and we were fortunate on arrival to have a break in the weather. The more immediate view of Raasay discloses a gloriously rough lochan-studded terrain of gullies, rocky slopes and grassy moorland. The eastern side drops 1400ft to the coast, from where we heard a cuckoo as we lunched awhile. The summit trig point is not quite the highest point – there is a slightly higher bump a few yards to the south.

Return to Loch na Meilich, then stay in the defile, passing below the escarpment on a short bouldery path. The weather changed on our return to a mixture of snow, sleet and rain – but that is how it goes!

96 - Loch Coruisk to Sligachan

Traversing the area between the Black and Red Cuillin, a walk from Loch Coruisk to Sligachan via upper Srath na Creitheach and Glen Sligachan offers a panoramic view, superior to that from Glen Brittle, of the east-facing horseshoe curve of the Black Cuillin.

Margaret, Rhona, Jimbo (plus two Springer Spaniels) and I reached Loch Coruisk on the Bella-Jane from Elgol – a four-mile boat trip on Loch Scavaig to the atmospheric, rock-enclosed Loch na Cuilce. (Being pedantic, boats do not sail to Loch Coruisk.) Check www.bellajane.co.uk for sailing times. Booking is advisable (phone 0800 731 3089 from 7.30am). The journey from Broadford to Elgol car park, opposite the village store above the pier, may take 45 minutes. There is also a bus service.

With its accessibility by boat, Loch Coruisk was one of those must-visit spots for Victorian tourists and artists. *Loch Coruisq near Loch Scavig*, by William Daniell, is one of the best-known paintings. On the way, our boat passed close by The Bad Step, a narrow ledge across a sloping slab above the sea, and a tricky spot for those walking in from Camasunary. Almost as if pre-arranged, two walkers were traversing the step – an easy dry-day scramble for those with no heavy backpacks.

Now for the walk, starting with an immediate climb. The tide was out when we reached the landing stage, hence a long climb up the metal ladder. The dogs had to be part lifted, part cajoled, over the grating steps. To applause from those waiting to go aboard, the dogs, with tails a-wagging, scampered ashore. Nearby is Coruisk Memorial Hut, built in memory of two climbers who died on Ben Nevis. I had last stayed there 30 years before

FACT FILE	
Map	OS map 32, South Skye
Distance	8 miles
Height	400m
Terrain	mostly good paths
Start point	Elgol
Time	4 to 5 hours depending on photo stops
Nearest town	Broadford
Refreshment spot	Broadford Hotel, Torrin Road, Broadford

A bracing dip in Loch Coruisk

Jimbo, dogs and the mighty Cuillin

(a Highland Hillwalking Club weekend of glorious weather).

Margaret spent a while in the area before returning by boat. For those who walk to the hut, and with no escape by boat, there is always the possibility of becoming marooned. To the west is the Allt a'Chaoich, known as the Mad Burn, and to the east is the short outflow from Loch Coruisk, the Scavaig River. Both are frequently in spate. However, with the Scavaig but a gentle flow, we crossed the famous stepping stones dry-shod.

We saw a rare sight: four folk from a yacht moored in Loch na Cuilce bathing in Loch Coruisk (not that we actually saw them swimming). West of the loch, "carved from the naked gabbro in a rock basin without parallel in

**The dogs had to be part lifted,
part cajoled, over the grating steps**

Scotland" (Tom Weir), a prominent ridge leads over Sgurr Dubh Beag to Sgurr Dubh Mor. 'Doing the Dubhs' is one of the classic Cuillin scrambles.

Continue on a choice of paths to the burn that flows from Loch a'Choire Riabhaich. The rough gabbro path later eases to a grassier zigzag to reach the 320m bealach on the Druim Hain ridge. From a choice of cairns, admire the Cuillin peaks, whose seven-mile traverse in one day from Gars Bheinn to Sgurr nan Gillean is the classic long-distance mountaineering route in Britain. That brought back memories of doing the traverse years ago with Peter. To the east is the long SSW ridge of Bla Bheinn, my favourite way up.

The descent path, now of red granite, is steep and eroded in places, but then it is an easy stroll to join the path from Camasunary and the indistinct watershed by Lochan Dubha. Despite the superb path, the gradual descent to Sligachan took us a long time – a slow pace due to the heat and time spent chatting to the Swiss, Spanish and German tourists we met. On the left is Sgurr nan Gillean, very marginally the most northerly peak, and Pinnacle Ridge, a jagged series of four sharp rock towers, leading directly to the summit.

Our traverse ended at the new car park off the A850, east of the bridge over the River Sligachan, and my pre-placed car.

Two tiny figures on the Bad Step

97 - Raasay

Time may appear to move slower on Raasay (Ratharsair), *Isle of the Roe Deer*, but things do change. A £12m ferry terminal, with waiting room and toilets, at Clachan – some two miles to the north-west of the ageing pier and slipway at Suisnish, and more central to the main area of habitation – was officially opened in August 2010.

The Sconser–Raasay ferry service is approximately hourly. However, the detailed timetable is somewhat essential and there is only a limited Sunday service (see www.calmac.co.uk, phone 0800 066 5000 or e-mail enquiries@calmac.co.uk). It is expensive to take a car on this 20-minute crossing, but pedal cycles are free. At the time of writing, the adult pedestrian fare was £3.50 single.

I recommend *Exploring Raasay, Twenty Walking Routes*, by Nick Fairweather, published in 2015 by Thirsty Books, and the Forestry Commission Scotland booklet *Explore the forests and trails on the Isle of Raasay* (see www.scotland.forestry.gov.uk, phone 0300 067 6100 or e-mail invernessrossskye@forestry.gsi.gov.uk). The following walk, a clockwise route from Clachan via Inverarish, and

FACT FILE	
Map	OS map 32, South Skye, or 24, Raasay & Loch Torridon
Distance	4½ miles
Height	100m
Terrain	paths, tracks and minor roads
Start point	Clachan ferry terminal, map ref 545363
Time	3 to 4 hours
Nearest village	Inverarish
Refreshment spot	Raasay House café bar

Dun Bhorghadail Broch

The stone memorial to Kit

so back to the terminal, makes use of some of the latter's waymarked trails.

With clag on the high tops and swirling light mist at sea level adding a certain air of mystery and intrigue, it was a well-chosen atmospheric day for Margaret and I, plus the newly-engaged Sarah and Peter, to go to Raasay. The sun broke through from time to time before the heat of the day dissipated the mist.

From the ferry terminal, head west round Churchton Bay, on a grassy strip at first, then on the charming shoreline path which swings north, passes through an area of overgrown rhododendron bushes (escapees from Raasay House) and continues to North Bay – but alas no seals or otters. At the northern end of the bay, turn right to briefly join the coastal road, then leave it on the signposted Orchard Path. This leads to the northernmost and highest part of the walk.

Head south, passing by the stone-walled Raasay House orchard, now derelict, and so to the tarmac road that leads to the cemetery. However, at first traversing an area churned up by timber operations, a fine path

of old heads west on a detour to Temptation Hill and a grassy platform – a marvellous viewpoint overlooking Churchton Bay and beyond the Narrows of Raasay. The local story is of the quasi-mythical kelpie, tempted by the smell of a roasted sow, only to be slain by a blacksmith whose daughter had been devoured by the beast. There is a stone memorial to Kit who died aged 19 in 1917: not a soldier who fell in the First World War, but a woman who died of the fever. The stone was erected by her fiancé and refers to Raasay as "an earthly paradise because it's like heaven to me."

Return to the road and head downhill by road or path to the southern end of Loch na Muilneadh, *the mill loch*. From here, a path leads south-east to descend past Dun Bhorghadail Broch (Dun Borodale), the remains of an Iron Age fortified settlement site, well worth having a look at. Continue past the manse and church, then take the riverside path by the Inverarish Burn to reach Inverarish, the island's main village, built to house the iron ore miners. Turn right, pass the village hall, school and hotel (cue refreshment stop) and so return to the pier.

98 - Rubh' an Dunain and Loch na h-Airde

Well known to hillwalkers and climbers for its immediate access to many of the Cuillin peaks, Glen Brittle may be a disappointing place if on arrival those high tops are so mist-enshrouded that staying at or near sea-level is the only sensible option. But all is not lost. Stretching southwards from Glen Brittle is a peninsula that offers a low-level walk, terminating at Loch na h-Airde by Rubh' an Dunain, headland of the fort. A circuit of the loch goes past not only the fort but

also a 'Viking' canal and a chambered cairn. This ancient land, occupied continuously for more than 5000 years and steeped in history and mystery, is now the subject of a dedicated website (**www.macaskillsociety.org**), describing every aspect of the area including archaeology, history, flora and fauna.

Although there is a good rough vehicle track (mapped as a path) for most of the way, on nearing the headland, the way is almost pathless and boggy. Careful navigation

FACT FILE

Map	OS map 32, South Skye
Distance	8 miles
Height	200m
Terrain	rough vehicle track then vague path traverse
Start point	Glen Brittle road end car park, map ref 409207
Time	4 hours
Nearest villages	Carbost and Sligachan
Refreshment spot	Glen Brittle campsite café

Akroyd. Gerry, an MBE no less, is a former guide and still active as the Skye Mountain Rescue Team Leader. Having known them both for many a year, and with lots of news to catch up with, it was with some reluctance that I was dragged away by the others for our walk.

Head to the back of the camp site toilet block from where the very walkable track heads south. A number of streams are crossed but only one, the merged waters of the Allt na Buaile Duibhe and the Allt Coire Lagan, which you reach after one mile, may inhibit progress. However, there is a metal handrail-free bridge a short distance downstream.

The track heads towards the prominent 124m Creag Mhor. Ignore any side paths and continue on the track which goes high above the spectacular western headland, Rubha na Creige Moire. By now Rum and Canna seem very close to hand.

Continue to the track end, from where a short grassy area leads to a saddle, map ref 402174, the high point of a mostly intact impressive drystane dyke which traverses the peninsula. Cross the dyke through a large gap and follow the far side southwards on the mapped path. Later leave the dyke and slant south-west, gently descending by a vague path. Pass by the ruins of a large house once home of the Chief of Clan MacAskill, a sept of Clan

(take a compass) as well as good boots may be required. Rhona, John and I had not been to the loch so Jimbo was appointed our guide.

From the Glen Brittle road end car park, map ref 409207, we headed to the camp site café for pre-walk coffees. There to my delight I bumped into Joan and Gerry

A handrail-free bridge - R Fraser

Loch na h-Airde - R Fraser

McLeod; this area was occupied until the clearances of the 1860s.

With Loch na h-Airde now in sight, pass by a wetter area, roughly following the stream that flows to the east side of the loch. Seemingly bigger than mapped, the loch was an important site for maritime activity for many centuries, spanning the Viking and later periods of Scottish clan rule.

The shallow 'Viking' canal, constructed along the length of the outflow stream, allowed boats to exit at high tide. It was low tide when we were there so it was more difficult to envisage boats being pulled in or out.

Climb to the overlooking promontory and its Iron Age fort. All that remains of the fort now is an admittedly impressive 10ft-high wall near the cliff edge. Now for a clockwise walk round the loch. A collapsed edge, deliberate or otherwise, makes a crossing point of the canal. At the northern end of the loch is a Bronze Age chambered cairn from the 2nd or 3rd millennium BC. It is possible to squeeze through the original entrance to enter the now roofless inner chamber.

Complete the circuit, then retrace your steps by path and track.

The Viking Canal - R Fraser

99 - Sgurr Alasdair

At 992m/3255ft, the highest point on the Cuillin, Sgurr Alasdair would be beyond the abilities of non-scrambling hillwalkers were it not for the peak's most distinctive feature, the Great Stone Chute. This massive scree slope runs 300m from a steep gully just east of the summit all the way down to Coire Lagan.

The first recorded ascent of Sgurr Alasdair was made by Alexander Nicolson (Alasdair MacNeacail, in Gaelic) in 1873 and the peak now bears his name (a practice almost peculiar to Skye). Nicolson had modestly named it Scur a Laghain, and his wishes should have been adhered to. Admittedly, such a name, *peak of the little hollow*, does scant justice to the airy summit from where every Cuillin Munro can be seen, as can the outer isles.

East of the small stony saddle at the head of the stone chute, a short rampart leads to Sgurr Thearlaich, a subsidiary Top named after Charles Pilkington. South-east of the Top is the Thearlaich-Dubh Gap, a barrier for non-climbers. A south-east ridge extends over Sgurr Sgumain, another subsidiary Top, and on to Sron na Ciche overlooking Coire Lagan.

Easily missed when entering Coire Lagan is the Cioch, a rounded protrusion which resembles a breast on the cliff face of Sron na Ciche. Norman Collie noticed it in 1899 when its evening shadow was cast on the surrounding slabs. Collie and John Mackenzie were the first to climb it in 1906. The iconic picture of the Cioch is the one taken in late evening by Ben Humble, with W H Murray silhouetted on top – a picture Humble called the photograph of a lifetime.

Hillwalkers, even those with no intention of climbing Sgurr Alasdair, should still visit Coire Lagan with its charming lochan. On a previous visit, the corrie had a number of visitors sunbathing by the edge of the lochan, including one brave soul who went for a swim that lasted all of five seconds. The noise of their enjoyment contrasted with the silent sweaty slog as we climbed the scree.

The 1:50,000 Ordnance Survey map 32, South Skye, covers the area, though I prefer the larger scale 1:15,000 James Renny's map, The Black Cuillin. Many now use Harvey's 1:25,000 map, The Cuillin, on the back of which is an enlargement of the ridge at 1:12,500.

FACT FILE	
Map	OS map 32, South Skye
Distance	5 miles
Height	1000m
Terrain	good path to eroded scree slopes
Start point	Glen Brittle road end car park, map ref 409207
Time	5 to 6 hours
Nearest villages	Carbost and Sligachan
Refreshment spot	Glen Brittle campsite café

From the Glen Brittle campsite, cross the fence behind the toilet block and climb east on the superb renovated path. Gone are the days of a boggy, eroded way to the base of the hill. Keep east at a junction after half a mile. (The other path goes south-east towards Coir' a'Ghrunnda.) The path climbs ENE on the north side of the Allt Coire Lagan and into beautiful Coire Lagan and its lonely lochan dammed by large slabs.

The scree is not what it used to be, as thousands of

Looking down the Great Stone Chute

boots each year push the debris further downhill. It is a slog, a case of two steps forward, one step back – a non-scrambling approach that comes at a price! The bottom section, a light-coloured strip of small stones, is where the debris forms a fantail. The middle section is a mixture of boulders, bare patches and smaller stones. The top section is now bare and is to be treated with caution, though the slog is relieved by a bare zigzag path below the south wall of the now stone-chute gully.

From the stony saddle, a short and airy ridge goes west to the summit. Do not go near the edge of the sharp drop above the gully. Inadvertently kicking a stone into the chute will not be appreciated by other hillwalkers.

Return the same way with extreme caution – most accidents occur on descent – but perhaps this time enjoying the lower section of the scree.

100 - St Kilda

Now for something different – a visit to 'islands on the edge of the world,' the St Kilda archipelago, to climb the highest point, 430m / 1411ft Conachair. Marilyns are UK hills of any height, with a drop of at least 150m all round, and Conachair is the only one in the region that is relatively accessible.

There are no saintly connections; the name St Kilda possibly derives from the Norse *sunt kelda* meaning sweet well-water. The four main isles sit on the rim of a large submerged volcano, active some 60 million years ago. Glacial and climate erosion have sculpted their rugged shores; breathtaking stacks and cliffs rise sheer from the sea.

Scotland's first UNESCO World Heritage Site and home to the world's largest gannetry, plus huge colonies of puffins, fulmars and skuas, St Kilda was bequested to the National Trust for Scotland (NTS) in 1957. Nowadays, four organisations work in partnership to conserve the islands: NTS, the Ministry of Defence (MoD), Historic Scotland and Scottish Natural Heritage.

FACT FILE	
Map	leaflets available from NTS
Distance	3 miles
Height	450m
Terrain	concrete road and grassy slopes
Start point	Village Bay jetty
Time	3 hours
Nearest town	far, far away
Refreshment spot	none

For thousands of years, people lived on Hirta, the largest island, harvesting the seabirds (a hazardous operation), fishing and growing crops. In 1930, the last remaining 36 islanders left bringing to an end a unique culture and way of life.

Dr John McGregor, my railway historian friend, told me that one of his father's contemporaries in the Forestry Commission was evacuated from the island as a boy. Furthermore, John's principal 'railway source,' Fort William lawyer, Nigel MacKenzie, was born on St Kilda, although he moved to Appin at an early age.

NTS leaflets giving a wealth of background information, including a small map, can be downloaded from www.nts.org.uk.

Although climbing Conachair is very easy, getting to Hirta and being able to land may be anything but. At 40 miles WNW of North Uist, 110 miles from the

1411ft 430m Conachair

A stone cleit, built to store food and fuel

mainland and remote from rescue services and medical care, St Kilda faces the full blast of the open Atlantic in total isolation. Even in seemingly benign conditions, the prevailing Atlantic rollers can produce a swell in Village Bay which may bar any landing; in summer, low temperatures and cloud can prevail for days. Expensive full day sea-trips operate from Leverburgh, South Harris. Many a return may be required for success.

We had a day stop en route to Iceland. During an anxious wait, hoping the swell would reduce, NTS Ranger, Paul Sharman, came on board to give an interesting introduction to Hirta. March until late September is the bird nesting season, though the breeding of individual species varies and may also change from year to year. Do make contact with the Ranger for up-to-date information – for your own and the birds' protection.

Eventually we were able to land. We had only three hours on the island, but it was the holiday highlight.

From the landing jetty, a ramp leads to a concrete road which is followed round Village Bay. The road dips slightly in crossing the Abhainn Mhor, then turns right: an L-shaped bend avoided by taking a diagonal line over grassy terrain to the west end of Main Street. Note the numerous stone cleits, built to store food and fuel.

Cross the stream and re-join the road. With many a zigzag and viewpoint, the road eases the climb to a junction (left to a lower mast, right to the higher mast on 361m Mullach Mor and the MoD radar tracking station for the rocket range on South Uist).

A short descent then climb, by now on grassy slopes, leads to Conachair's well-built stone cairn, close by the highest sea cliff in Britain. A short detour south leads to the 376m mapped point overlooking the village. Be

Conachair`s well-built stone cairn, close by the highest sea cliff in Britain - Taken by a kind fellow walker

careful where you walk for ground-nesting skuas are not easy to spot. Move quickly away from any bird that is accidentally disturbed. Skua attacks, as I experienced, can be alarming affairs!

Once back at the village and the flocks of Soay sheep (a unique primitive breed going back to the Bronze Age), look out for the endemic St Kilda mouse and wren, both larger than their mainland relations.

Follow the grassy track that is Main Street, with its line of blackhouses and improved cottages. Six of these have been re-roofed and are used by NTS, one as a small museum. Take back to the boat photos, memories, litter and food scraps.

ABOUT THE AUTHOR

Robin Howie was born and educated in Edinburgh where he qualified as a Chartered Accountant. During his working life as a Finance Director hillwalking became a vital leisure activity. Now retired, that call to the outdoors is still a way of life. Robin has completed ten rounds of Munros (two of them since a hip replacement) plus four rounds of subsidiary tops and one round of Corbetts. He has experienced high altitude climbing in Antarctica, South America and East Africa and has also climbed in Borneo, the Philippines, Norway, Mongolia and Cuba.

Lightning Source UK Ltd.
Milton Keynes UK
UKOW07f0916200616

276632UK00002B/6/P